D0933927

Mommy Queerest

University of Massachusetts Press, Amherst & Boston

Julie M. Thompson

Contemporary Rhetorics of Lesbian Maternal Identity

Mommy Queerest

Copyright © 2002 by

University of Massachusetts Press

All rights reserved

Printed in the United States of America

LC 2001008664

ISBN 1-55849-355-7

Designed by Kristina Kachele

Set in Monotype Fournier with FF Din Light and Eureka Sans display by Graphic Composition, Inc.

Printed and bound by Maple-Vail Book Manufacturing Group

Library of Congress Cataloging-in Publication Data

Thompson, Julie M. (Julie Marie)

Mommy queerest : contemporary rhetorics of lesbian maternal identity / Julie M. Thompson.

p. cm.

Includes bibliographical references and index.

ISBN 1-55849-355-7 (cloth : alk. paper)

1. Lesbian mothers—United States—Psychology.   2. Lesbian mothers—Legal status,

laws, etc.—United States.   3. Lesbians—Identity—United States.   4. Children of gay

parents—United States—Social conditions.   5. Gays in popular culture.   6. Lesbians in

mass media.   I. Title.

HQ75.53 .T49 2002

306.874'3—dc21

2001008664

British Library Cataloging in Publication data are available.

Dedicated to the memory of my beloved grandmother
Mary Irene Thompson
1907–1996

to the wonderful spirit from whom I learned the joys
of self-confidence, perseverance, and laughter
Tillie Odell Osterdyk

to Michelle Marie Salmonson
confidante and treasured friend
thirty years and counting

and to Tricia Lynn Gallagher
with "all the love I've got"
for everything

Ashamed, people turned their faces away from

the woman ranting, asking: *Justice, stretch out your hand.*

Come down, glittering, from where you have hidden yourself away.

MINNIE BRUCE PRATT, *Crime against Nature*

Language constructs thought. . . .

It's a great way to do battle, dear sisters, with the pen.

ANONYMOUS, *Lesbian Connection*

Language is at the same time a living thing

and a museum of fossils of life and civilisations.

ANTONIO GRAMSCI, *Prison Notebooks*

Contents

Acknowledgments

Any critical endeavor approached from a feminist perspective values the craft of collaboration. While I take sole responsibility for the critical interpretations rendered here, I do wish to acknowledge collaborators. The National Center for Lesbian Rights assisted with the identification of lesbian child custody court cases, as did the Lavender Families Resource Network. Barbara Richards at the University of Wisconsin Memorial Library Special Collections, Ed Dusterhoeft of the University of Wisconsin Microform Services, and Keith Rabiola of the State Historical Society of Wisconsin Microforms Department facilitated my search for lesbian-feminist periodicals from the 1970s and 1980s. Mark Hammons and David Klassen from the University of Minnesota Social Welfare History Archives and R. Russell Maylone at the Charles Deering McCormick Special Collections at Northwestern University also assisted in this capacity. Kath Pennavaria of the Kinsey Institute Library provided back issues of *Lesbian Connection*. Desireé Vester of the Lesbian Herstory Archives/Educational Foundation supplied documents crucial to the completion of chapter 2. The Gay/Lesbian Historical Society of Northern California opened their archives during odd hours so that I could obtain background information for chapter 2, and I appreciate their support.

I extend my sincerest gratitude to my mentor and trusted friend John Louis Lucaites. Thanks also to colleagues Robert Ivie, Julia Lamber, Wen-Shu Lee, Phil Wander, Danae Clark, John Lyne, Lester Olson, Dennis Jaehne, Marquita Byrd, Carole Blair, Marouf Hasian, John Sloop, Ralph Smith, Tom Kane, and Ray Smith. Bruce Wilcox and the staff at the University of Massachusetts Press made the publication process as painless as possible. I am also thankful for the critical readings provided by Diane Helene Miller and the anonymous reviewer of the original manuscript.

To my friends, a heartfelt thanks, especially to Robert Stachowski, Jerel Blake, Rob Elliott, Courtney New, Michelle Salmonson, Karen Rader, Dana Cloud, Katie Feyh, Nicole Shoener, Brian Owens, Ilon Lauer, Robin Sease, Yung-Hsing Wu, Paula Gardner, Greg Elmer, Heather Radawski, Eric Fluharty, Christine Gaus, Barbara Honeycutt, Kelly Happe, Lisa Schwartz, Mike Tumolo, Carol Willis, Elliot Howard, and Arlene Dent. For our years of cooking and eating, learning and writing, and laughing and crying together, I am privileged to enjoy the dear friendship of Elizabeth Green Musselman and Jack Green Musselman.

This work has also benefited from the passionate discussions held with my students at San Jose State University, the University of Pittsburgh, and Southwestern University. I hope they know how much I appreciate their contributions. Robyn Crummer read a late version of the manuscript, and I benefited from her questions and revision suggestions. The Communication Department at Southwestern University was a welcoming new home in which to complete the final manuscript, and I am fortunate to be graced with such colleagues and friends as Christine Kiesinger, Bob Bednar, and David Olson.

My circle of jazz buddies in San Francisco—Berigan Taylor, Dave Jordan, fellow and sister fans at Yoshi's, Rasselas, Club Deluxe, and the Saint John Coltrane African Orthodox Church—provided endless hours of joyful entertainment. Although I am not a particularly devout individual, spiritual inspiration and salvation were also provided by the music of John Coltrane, Horace Silver, Lee Morgan, Hank Mobley, Dexter Gordon, Wayne Shorter, Ella Fitzgerald, Diana Krall, Etta James, Shirley Horn, Thelonius Monk,

Everything But the Girl, Prince, Sasha, Digweed, and Michael Franti and Spearhead.

I am honored by the camaraderie and collegiality of John Poulakos and Mark Harrison, both of whom possess the remarkable ability to challenge my arguments and make me laugh at the same time. Susan Barron's guidance and insight enabled me to have confidence in this project, and I appreciate our many visits. For singing, making sushi, and taste-testing my new Ethiopian recipes, Amos Tevelow won my permanent devotion and loving friendship. Among other things, Jody Baker helped me to develop a sharper critical voice, and the final revisions to this text are improved because of Jody's keen insight, willingness to engage in stubborn theoretical arguments, and patience in formatting the final version of the manuscript to specifications. Most important, Jody opened the door for me to learn the joys and responsibilities of a healthy loving relationship, and I am a better human being for it. Finally, I wish to acknowledge my grandmothers, Tillie Osterdyk and Mary Thompson, whose love sustains me.

J. M. T.

To establish a social identity is really to determine what one's "kind" is:
Who is one of us? Who is not? And to "be kind" is at once to express a gentle,
generous attitude and to treat someone as one's own "kind." One's kind deserves
kindness; one's kind is to be treated kindly. And obversely, to extend kindness,
to treat kindly, is to deal with another being as if that creature were one's own kind.

EDWIN BLACK, *Rhetorical Questions*

LESBIAN MOTHERHOOD IN AMERICAN CULTURE

My concern here is for the rhetorically contested terrain of lesbian motherhood. Who is a lesbian? Who is a mother? When the two identities intersect,
who is a lesbian mother? As Edwin Black might ask, what "kind" of identity
has been carved for lesbians? For mothers? To what kinds of treatment have
lesbians been subjected? Mothers? Lesbian mothers? What "kind" of status
do lesbian mothers have in American culture? Are they treated kindly by
non-lesbians? By lesbian non-mothers? How might examination of contemporary public argument about lesbian motherhood help us understand how
language and identity intertwine?

Adrienne Rich once wrote, "Any woman who believes that the institution
of motherhood has nothing to do with *her* is closing her eyes to crucial aspects
of her situation."[1] When I began this project, I had only the vaguest sense of
how motherhood affected me, since I had made the deliberate decision a

decade earlier to be child-free. Motherhood appeared too limiting—though I imagine now that the fear of losing the newly found freedom of early adulthood is common to many college-age women. As I observed my own mother and other mothers around me (including those my own age), the responsibilities and burdens of motherhood seemed to produce only depression, anxiety, and loss of self; I had tremendous difficulty even *imagining* the realms of possibility created through mothering.

I paid attention to motherhood only within the narrow framework of the reproductive rights debates that raged during the Reagan and Bush administrations and within the context of a burgeoning feminist consciousness. I had been persuaded by the rhetoric that polarized the "childless woman" and the "mother," which, as Rich points out, had "served the institutions both of motherhood and heterosexuality." She notes, however, that "a woman may have looked at the lives of women with children and felt that, given the circumstances of motherhood, she must remain childless if she is to pursue any hopes or aims."[2] As a young adult, I could not imagine living within the confining bounds of motherhood and marriage. It never occurred to me that a significant population of women were struggling to *become* mothers or to retain custody of their children.

Studying the discourses related to lesbian motherhood has taught me that rhetorics of gender and sexuality function, above all, to convince women that our "natural" duty is to reproduce—but *only* if we direct our emotional and erotic energy toward men within the context of legal marriage. The belief that "you can't be a mother if you're a lesbian," as well as the corollary "you're not really a lesbian if you have children," are particularly haunting within the framework of my own experience. I remember taking a feminist studies course in college; my friend Kylene also enrolled. We were both newly "out" as lesbians, and excited about the new worlds of promise open to us. We read everything we could obtain on lesbian identity and the feminist movement in the United States. For her term paper, Ky chose to write about lesbian motherhood. I distinctly remember thinking, "Why would a lesbian want to be a mother?" The word "lesbian," to my twenty-year-old mind, suggested total freedom from the apparent drudgery of a life revolving around mothering.

But that "total freedom" in which I believed naïvely had painful costs. The first words spoken to me by my father upon learning of my lesbian identity were, "Now you are never going to give us grandchildren"; he and my mother subsequently exiled me from the family. My father's own uncompromising faith in the impossibility of lesbian motherhood typified my research findings nearly a decade later, as various speakers and writers constructed lesbian motherhood as an oxymoron. He must have forgotten (or denied, or not believed) my own intractable claims, beginning at the age of fifteen or sixteen, that I had neither the intention nor the desire to bear and raise children.

I have repeated this claim to the point of nausea over the last twenty years, as various individuals have tried to encourage, persuade, or pressure me to reproduce. One person urged me in 1994, "You could have a baby while you're in the final year of graduate school—it wouldn't be so bad—you could stay home, write, and take care of the baby." This statement, of course, grossly oversimplified the labor involved both in raising a child and in completing a Ph.D. Two different girlfriends thought our relationship would be stronger if we raised a child: "What do you mean, you don't want children? I would take care of both of you." Both wanted me to become pregnant and stay home with the child; both eventually harassed me on a daily basis to "get over" my reluctance to raise children and thereby fulfill my feminine duties. The man with whom I fell in love during graduate school, who wished for us a conventional marriage, including children, was perhaps the most understanding, but he could not envision a marriage without children. My refusal to bear and raise children was one primary factor in our heartbreaking decision to abandon our hopes and plans for a fulfilling long-term commitment.

I tell these stories not as a form of pathos but to indicate the extent to which the ideological pressures for women to bear children exist on a day-to-day level, even in the life of one woman. Over the years I have heard many people respond to my reproductive choice in various ways. Some tried to convince me that I was a traitor to womanhood for not wanting children. Many who already were parents claimed I simply wasn't ready and would eventually change my mind, or that if I met the "right person," the desire for a child would materialize magically. Perhaps my "biological clock" simply hadn't started ticking—or, worse, had malfunctioned. At least two acquaintances argued that by writing about motherhood, I was expressing some secret wish for a child. Many others have responded with disdain, thinking that I must be a child-hater. This response has produced the most anguish, but also demonstrates quite clearly the notion that motherhood makes womanhood natural and complete. A rhetorical culture that rewards (white, middle-class) women primarily for reproduction manifests itself through the voices of parents, girlfriends, and boyfriends who doubt the veracity of any woman's claim that she has no wish to breed by casting her as some sort of traitor. Of course, my words here should not be interpreted as a denigration of other women's important decisions to mother. My point is that women should be able to choose, without private or state-sanctioned harassment, whether, when, and under what circumstances to become mothers.

The casting of a woman as a traitor is perhaps more complicated for the woman who may identify primarily as queer. Periodically the voices of some lesbians tell her that she is selling out and is not really queer if she chooses to mother. I found myself subject to such an attack from the lover of a graduate school friend. I was familiar with anti-lesbian and sexist questions from non-lesbians, but was patently unprepared for an attack from another lesbian. She told me over lunch that I was "selling out" simply by *writing* about lesbian motherhood. Her argument went something like this: lesbians who raise children are not "really" lesbian because they have either participated in heterosexual intercourse or have had access to the requisite sperm through artificial insemination. In her estimation, only a woman who has never been connected with a man "counts" as a lesbian. Her position, one will find, is not unique; many heterosexual and lesbian writers define lesbianism in this way. I was thus a traitor to the lesbian nation (in 1996!) by even considering lesbian motherhood as a topic for scholarship. Other segments of the lesbian community, however, embrace and celebrate motherhood. Lesbian culture is thus not monolithic in its response to lesbian motherhood. The availability of artificial reproduction technologies makes conception and motherhood more accessible to lesbians who wish to avoid heterosexual intercourse in their quest to become mothers. A veritable "baby boom" in various urban lesbian communities commenced in the 1980s and continues today, as evidenced by the popularity of lesbian mother groups and publications across the United States. Lesbian culture's response to queer motherhood is thus rather ambivalent, and it is this ambivalence, among others, that I explore and explain.

The personal experiences I have recounted, and others too unspeakable to disclose here, taught me two crucial lessons. First, sexism and anti-lesbian attitudes affect the lives of all women, whether or not we are mothers and whether or not we identify as lesbian. More important, since my topic appeared to threaten such a variety of people, I decided that I must really be on to something. Rather than taking others' discouragement and censure as signs that I should have chosen another topic, I persevered.

My experience gave new meaning to the concept of "speaking truth to power." Phil Wander observes that "those who ask the question[s] may be silenced, and those who see this happen may decide that they should not do it, because it is too dangerous."[3] I certainly could have chosen a different research topic, one that was less dangerous. In so doing, however, I would have risked two things: betraying myself, and affirming the enthymematic claim that examining the material conditions of women's lives—especially lesbian lives as they are constituted in and through rhetoric—is somehow off limits. In Audre Lorde's words, my silence would not protect me; it never could.[4]

My own experiences thus provided one motivation for initiating and completing this project, given the pressures exerted on me both to identify as exclusively heterosexual and to reproduce. Pressure from multiple directions produced a profound curiosity about maternal identity, and I set out to discover the various narratives through which motherhood is produced in contemporary American culture. As I will explain, I have other, less personal reasons for taking on this project, such as a fascination with the poststructural notion that there is little essential sense of identity; rather, individual and group identities are constituted in and through complex linguistic webs. I decided to focus that fascination on an area not yet addressed in contemporary rhetorical theory: maternal identity generally, and lesbian maternal identity specifically. Cultural debates about gender and sexuality have certainly shaped my own notions of what it has meant, what it means now, and what it might mean in the future to try and live outside the patriarchal stranglehold on womanhood. Both personal experience *and* the more traditional questions that scholars engage thus activated this project. What follows is a story about rhetoric, identity, and the way discourses of gender, sex, and sexuality influence the construction of individual and group identities in American culture today. I think it only fair to disclose the more personal, anecdotal motivations, so that one might understand more fully the very real passion for improving lesbian lives that drives my own research.

Conventional wisdom tells us that a mother is essentially heterosexual. Rarely does one think of a lesbian as a mother, for the two terms apparently contradict each other. Identification as a lesbian excludes one somehow from legitimate status as a mother. The phrase "lesbian mother" conveys a logical implausibility, an oxymoron, deriving from the "fact" that lesbians are presumptively non-procreative and that mothers are presumptively heterosexual. The ways in which the oxymoron functions in various public discourses reveals deeply rooted cultural anxieties about the meanings and practices of both lesbianism and mothering. While lesbians are excluded from legitimate maternity because of their ostensibly reprehensible erotic desires and practices, heterosexual mothers are excluded from the enactment of a non-procreative sexuality lest such activity be construed as immoral. Mothers are typically depicted as "selfless" and "nurturing," yet few characterizations draw attention to explicit sexuality. "Mother" reads awkwardly against "lesbian" because, in hegemonic usage, "lesbian" connotes little more than explicit and perverse sexuality.

Implicated within its explicitly sexualized renderings, the word "lesbian" has been invested in American public discourse with criminal and psychopathologic meanings. The dominant historical depiction of the American lesbian both as "sick" (beginning with the work of sexologists and continuing today with various psychoanalytic discourses) and as "criminal" (beginning in the colonial era with Puritan proscriptions against non-procreative sex and continuing today with sodomy statutes) anchors the "lesbian" in an inherently illicit rhetorical space. The lesbian mother would appear to be the strangest sort of mother, a "mommy queerest." The title of this book reflects the rhetorical baggage many Americans carry about lesbian identity and any form of eroticized maternal practice. In other words, "mommy queerest" highlights the oxymoronic cast of the phrase "lesbian mother." In its current discursive form, "lesbian motherhood" denies cultural authenticity to lesbians as mothers and to mothers as lesbians. Such a denial affects the estimated 1.5 to 5 million lesbian families in the United States, but also has the potential to affect other categories of mothers when it restricts their maternal and erotic practices. The current discursive boundaries of lesbian mother-hood hence point to significant sociopolitical problems for contemporary American society.

Broad public discussions of parenting and family issues thus tend to mea-sure and regulate these "new" or "alternative" family types against the model of the "traditional" nuclear family, even as various family types are simulta-neous recognized. Some discussions of lesbian motherhood, for instance, take for granted the existence of a female class labeled "lesbian" and ask how such an identity can be regulated by controlling the mechanisms that pre-sumptively produce lesbian identity. Such discussions are founded on the as-sumption of an essentialized erotic identity for the lesbian. It is indeed her chosen set of sexual practices that renders her a "lesbian." Subject to laws that prohibit sodomitical practices, the elastic potential of the term "lesbian" de-creases, because the "normalized" public has difficulty conceiving of a lesbian outside of any erotic practices in which they might imagine her engaged.

My purpose here is to examine the ways in which the words "lesbian" and "mother" have been articulated at the nexus of mass media, legal, and aca-demic discourses so as to constitute a dominant reading of "lesbian mother" that is oxymoronic and, in Louis Althusser's sense, "always already" illegiti-mate.[5] I show how multiple and competing voices negotiate and regulate the meaning of "lesbian mother" and also how these voices are constrained by a set of hegemonic assumptions that go deeper than we typically recognize. I maintain that there are three major public forums—the mass media, the law, and the academy—in which various advocates contest the meaning of lesbian motherhood. Although this book focuses on three specific domains of public argument, deliberation about identity occurs in other public spheres (reli-gion, for instance) and in the private realm of intimate relationships. Private contestation of identity, however, does not occur in a cultural vacuum, for it is influenced by larger public debates. One could trace the interplay *between* the publicized and privatized spheres of debate, but that is not my focus here. Rather, this project traces the trajectory of rhetorical influences among and between the three specified domains of public argumentation. I explore the rhetorical consequences of such characterizations for our understanding of how rhetoric constitutes identity through sustained public contestation. The task of legitimating "lesbian motherhood" is extremely problematic. Doing so necessitates unraveling each strand of argument that functions ultimately to create the oxymoron.

I argue that a rhetorical ambivalence pervades public discussions of lesbian motherhood. This ambivalence is an effect of the argumentative interactions among and between spheres. The ambivalence typically is not generated from a particular speech act, though single speech acts may recirculate or reproduce prior constructions. Rather, it is produced through discursive confrontation and collusion within particular spheres of debate or rhetorical struggle. The discourse of individual speakers tends not to be particularly ambivalent about lesbian maternity. Instead, the ambivalence becomes manifest in such a way that competing and sometimes contradictory characterizations of lesbianism and motherhood trap lesbian mothers in a web of illegitimate subject positions. Vilified in the courts as a criminal sodomite or potential pedophile, lambasted by journalists as a threat to the family, and sometimes rejected by other lesbians as a traitor, the lesbian mother is isolated by the rhetorical ambivalence, which inhibits the development of a culturally and rhetorically legitimate space for her existence. The ambivalence affirms, however, the material existence of lesbian mothers, as evidenced by lesbian advocates who characterize lesbian mothers as feminist revolutionaries, by judges who affirm two-mother lesbian families, and by lesbian mothers themselves.

The rhetorical ambivalence operates through two specific features, which I treat in more detail in subsequent chapters. At root, it represents the rhetorical contest between hegemonic and oppositional characterizations concerning the legitimate bounds of lesbian and maternal identity categories. A series of binary oppositions constructs the ambivalence: moral/immoral, not criminal/criminal, mother/not mother, not lesbian/lesbian, good/bad, and so forth. The particular binary characterizations employed by advocates tend to differ depending on the site at which the characterizations occur, but the characterizations work simultaneously to create a pattern of illegitimacy that transcends any specific boundaries marking the locus of debate. The existence of the binaries, however, disciplines public argumentation in such a way as to patrol the legitimate borders of lesbian maternal identity.

The rhetorical ambivalence thus includes an authorizing function such that each cultural site of argument (which Althusser refers to as ideological state apparatuses, treated in more detail later) regulates who may speak with power and authenticity in the debates themselves. Lesbian periodical literature, for example, tends to valorize the voices of lesbian mothers (but not in all instances, because the ambivalence is prevalent here too), but lesbian mothers typically do not have much authority in the straight press. Straight journalistic rhetoric might focus primarily on constituting the lesbian mother as a threat to the family, while judicial rhetoric draws on such claims to cast the lesbian as a criminal, and therefore inimical to the family. Characterizations of identity become rigidified or reified through repetitive articulation at these multiple sites, which work together to create a material sense of who "is" and who "is not" a member (or who may become so) of any particular identity category. This ambivalence structures competing and contradictory ideological commitments as advocates struggle to advance potentially hegemonic notions of identity.

A related feature of the rhetorical ambivalence is that it functions as the symbolic ground on which identity boundaries can be debated, negotiated, and produced. Although the rhetoric is not entirely open (in the sense that "anything" could count in the debate), because the binary oppositions themselves limit and structure the terms of the debate, the bounds of identity are not so rigid as to foreclose, once and for all, the possibility of their being revised. In this sense my treatment of ambivalence bears some resemblance to conceptualizations in postcolonial literary theory, most notably in the work of Homi K. Bhabha.[6] Both conceptualizations concern themselves with problems of domination and emancipation as such processes are tied to language usage itself.

I am concerned here with how public argument is structured over time to produce ambivalence about particular identities. "Ambivalence" in my formulation is thus an effect-structure of discourse, and represents the simultaneous cultural attraction to and repulsion from lesbian mothers and others inhabiting nonnormative identities. Bhabha writes that enactments of colonial authority require the "production of differentiations, individuations, identity effects through which discriminatory practices can map out subject populations that are tarred with the visible and transparent mark of power."[7] It is my contention that the structures identified by Bhabha also operate *within* specific societies.

Public discourses mark citizens within a particular society as "different," "other," or "nonnormative" and subject them to specific ideological controls.

The relationship between lesbian mothers and heteronormative citizens, however, is not *always* or *only* conflictual or oppositional. Lesbian mothers may sometimes be interpreted as revolutionizing the territories of lesbianism and motherhood, but they are also often criticized for mimicking, copying, or selling out to straight culture. The relationship between the heteronormative colonizer and the colonized lesbian, then, contains and produces the grounds of its own demise, whereby hegemonic characterizations of lesbians as sinful, criminal, or neurotic are, in the long run, ill-fated attempts to produce conformity.

Lesbian performances of motherhood never simply reproduce heterosexual or bisexual enactments. Rather, such performances draw attention to the utter superficiality of normativity, and lesbian maternal identity may in this sense be considered a hybrid identity. Hybridity calls into question the boundaries between self and other, between insider and outsider.[8] Bhabha claims that the "display of hybridity—its peculiar 'replication'—terrorizes authority with the *ruse* of recognition, its mimicry, its mockery."[9] Lesbian motherhood might thus be construed as an exemplar of ambivalent discourse, and as a site of "spectacular resistance."[10]

Rhetorical ambivalence, then, has two essential features relevant to the construction and negotiation of identity. First, the rhetoric represents the multitude of competing voices that struggle for the hegemonic right to patrol identity borders. The ambivalence is structured on a set of binary oppositions featured at various sites of public debate; the sphere-specific constructions collude to (re)produce the oxymoronic status of lesbian motherhood. Second, the ambivalence functions as the rhetorical space in which debates about identity occur and are negotiated. It thus authorizes and de-authorizes various voices as legitimate or relevant to the debates themselves.

My specific concern for how journalistic media, legal institutions, and the academy regulate lesbian maternal identities is significant for a number of reasons. First, state and cultural regulation and punishment of lesbian maternal identity, to the extent that such regulation impinges on the family planning choices of private citizens, pose a potential threat to individual procreative and associational freedoms protected by the state, regardless of sexual orientation. Such regulations, existing in multiple and invasive forms, limit women's maternal and sexual practices. Few categories of mothers are able to have a voice in, to control, or to escape such regulatory practices. For instance, mothers receiving public assistance have been subject to proposals that would either limit the number of children they could bear or, alternately, prevent the possibility of pregnancy through forced sterilization or contraception. Other groups, such as lesbians and single heterosexual women, are denied access to artificial insemination technology by fertility clinics that open their doors to married women only.[11] How legal practitioners and public cultures define "lesbian" and "mother" (and, by extension, who counts as "family") affects the whole of American society. Indeed, close examination of debates about lesbian motherhood will be instructive for understanding the contemporary politics of "The Family" that mobilize and deploy competing narratives of gender and sexuality.

I draw on critical rhetorical principles to explain how "lesbians" and "mothers" are invested with particular identities. This goal is central to a materialist conception of discourse that treats rhetoric as a powerful sociopolitical practice. The critical goal of materialist understandings of rhetoric is to look outward from discursive practice to the social functions of rhetoric.[12] For example, scholars interested in the relationships between rhetoric and ideology may attempt to explain how particular ideological commitments are constructed and distributed through rhetoric. Rhetoric constitutes such commitments in particular social domains, such as law, and exerts material influence on human lives. I direct attention primarily to the hegemonic functions of rhetoric that contribute to an uneven distribution of cultural resources. An examination of material practices such as journalistic discussions and legal contests illustrates the problem of cultural hegemony that, as Althusser notes, casts "concrete individuals as subjects."[13] An ideological commitment to the patriarchal nuclear family, for example, becomes manifest through public discussions of how single-parent households deprive their children, in some a priori fashion, of adequate parenting. I thus examine how the "lesbian mother" oxymoron, which simultaneously posits and reflects cultural anxieties about lesbianism and motherhood, is negotiated in various forums. The rhetoric of lesbian motherhood illustrates both the ideological conflicts concerning gender and sexuality and the rhetorical problem of identity. Many public discourses constrain lesbians' maternal and erotic agency. The work of Althusser on ideology is instructive here.

In his famous essay "Ideology and Ideological State Apparatuses," Althusser supposes that every "social formation" (such as the media, religious institutions, educational systems, and so on) is useful to the state only insofar as it perpetuates the capitalist system.[14] State power, according to Althusser, is constituted through two distinct types of apparatuses: repressive and ideological. Repressive State Apparatuses (RSA) include the police arm of the state, the government, and the legal system.[15] In essence, these state apparatus makes possible "the political conditions for the action of the Ideological State Apparatuses" (ISA) through "repressive measures such as violence, force (or threat thereof)," or "administrative commands."[16] ISAs socialize mass complicity with the ruling ideology, and Althusser argues that the educational ISA plays a particularly pernicious role in such socialization.[17] At the center of his formation is a materialist conception of ideology. Ideology presents itself as natural and transhistorical; moreover, ideology has a material existence because it is enacted through particular institutional practices. The premier function of ideology from this perspective is the constitution of individual subject identity.

ISAs may offer competing versions of truth or reality, so to speak, and may demand contradictory ideological commitments from individual subjects and communities. They are therefore not necessarily seamless in enforcing and representing the RSAs, but rather the two work together to foster compliance with prevailing norms. Domains such as the law, religion, media, and educational institutions in particular function as Ideological State Apparatuses. One could investigate effectively the rhetorical problem of identity by examining specific discourses within one or more of these ideological domains. In chapters 2, 3, and 4, I investigate three of Althusser's discursive domains—journalistic, legal, and academic—in order to theorize the processes through which identities are constituted, negotiated, and regulated by way of of public deliberation.

Critical Perspective, Identity, and Agency

Lisa Duggan contends that "stories of identity are never static, monolithic, or politically innocent. By situating people within shifting structures of social power and inequality, they become contested sources of authority and legitimation."[18] A critical rhetorical approach to discourse makes possible a meaningful analysis of oxymoronic identity formations in contemporary American culture. Lesbian identity functions as a lens through which to view motherhood; likewise, rhetorical constructions of motherhood function as a lens through which to study lesbian identity. I explain how ideological commitments to heteronormativity and patriarchal control of motherhood contribute to the contestation of lesbian maternal identity. Kimberlé Crenshaw reminds us that we need to consider "the way in which power has clustered around certain categories and is exercised against others."[19] Interrogation of this "clustering" can be accomplished by considering how ideological discourses relate to the production and enactment of categories of human identity. I argue that rhetorical conceptions of identity occur along five interdependent trajectories: constitution, negotiation, representation and reification, regulation, and performance / enactment.

First, ideological discourses *constitute* identities. Identity is an effect-structure of discourse, which is to say that discursive formations craft identities as an effect. The conceptualization of identity as an effect, as Judith Butler argues, "that is, as *produced* or *generated,* opens up possibilities of 'agency' that are insidiously foreclosed by positions that take identity categories as foundational and fixed."[20] Identities are thus not extrarhetorical but are instead constituted in and through ideological discourses. In particular, identities are constructed through what Michael Calvin McGee calls "ideographs."[21] Ideographic analysis attempts to articulate the complex relationship between rhetoric and ideological systems. McGee argues that scholars can learn about a community's consciousness by examining its political language. He explains that ideographs are common-language words that constitute the normative commitments of a particular community.[22] As the basic units of ideology, ideographs establish and warrant a historically situated community's ideological commitments. Ideographic analysis assesses the dominant ideographs' range of meanings in a particular discourse to understand *how* the ideology functions. In addition, such analysis assumes a view of public argumentation whereby various advocates compete to influence public opinion and policy in contingent matters. The ideographic perspective offers a detailed, complex mode for understanding the relationship between rhetoric and ideological systems operating in a particular culture or community. Ideographic analysis is a beneficial critical practice here for understanding normative and oppositional constructions of "lesbian mother" in contemporary American rhetorical culture, since the phrase "lesbian mother" is a condensed claim about the nature of lesbianism and motherhood.

An ideographic approach accounts for the varied usages of particular ideographs to explicate the development of a society's normative collective commitments.[23] Such diachronic analysis is crucial for understanding the constitution and maintenance of asymmetrical power relations in a particular rhetorical culture. Additionally, the critic accounts for the highly contextual and relational aspects of ideographs by explaining how particular ideographs are crafted in relation to one another within specific historical contexts.[24] Identifying and accounting for these synchronic ideographic structures is integral to a critical rhetoric because they illuminate the possibilities for successful oppositional rhetorics. Synchronic analysis also signifies context-specific rhetorical attempts to alter or oppose hegemonic norms. Taken together, diachronic and synchronic analyses can yield significant insights about how ideologies influence public behavior and belief through particular rhetorical formations. Advocates' deployment of specific ideographic characterizations illustrates the multivocal or heteroglossic nature of public argument. As Mikhail Bakhtin put: "At any given time, in any given place, there will be a set of conditions—social, historical, meteorological, physiological—that will ensure that a word uttered in that place and at that time will have a meaning different than it would have under any other condition; all utterances are heteroglot in that they are functions of a matrix of forces practically impossible to recoup, and therefore impossible to resolve."[25] The patterns of rhetorical struggle—indeed, the ambivalence of public discourse itself—are not monolithic but instead will feature different ideographs in different contexts and at different times. The rhetorical ambivalence about lesbian motherhood is not always between "good" and "bad," for instance, but sometimes between which negative characterization will prevail in deciding what lesbian motherhood is: Neurosis? Criminality? In other words, the rhetorical ambivalence, and the multiplicity of ideographic relationships that constitute, regulate, and reproduce it, is not particularly stable but will mutate from context to context.

Of course, one cannot neglect the effect that asymmetrical power relations have on identity formation, for not all identities are created equal. Anthony Giddens maintains that hegemonic groups "mobilize" various "structures of signification" in order to legitimate their "sectional interests."[26] Advocates thus deploy language to establish hegemony by constructing their particularized interests as *not* particular but universal. For instance, sexologists and psychoanalysts around the turn of the twentieth century developed a discourse of lesbian identity as an abnormal "inversion." Hegemonic religious discourses constructed lesbian desire as a "sin" and an "abomination" beginning in the seventeenth century. Legal practitioners built a discourse of lesbian identity around criminal ideographs, whereby sexual practices became conflated with the whole of one's identity—a legal variation, perhaps, on "love the sinner, hate the sin." The three discursive realms (law, psychiatry, and religion) advanced their own definitions of lesbianism; the realms have worked in concert to constitute the contemporary lesbian as a neurotic, sinful criminal in dire need of therapy, salvation, and punishment.

Second, ideological discourses *negotiate* identities. Once an identity category has been called into existence through rhetoric, the legitimate boundaries of identity substance and performance may be negotiated. The overlapping journalistic, legal, and academic discourses examined in subsequent chapters exemplify this negotiation process. Advocates contest the "true" substance of lesbian identity when they struggle to determine which key term best characterizes the lesbian: the recruiter or child molester, the nonprocreative woman (or, conversely, the mother), or the threat to the basic unit of society, the family. Each term highlights perceived dimensions of lesbian identity, but note how all three have as their primary concern the relationship of lesbians to children. By characterizing children as lesbians' desired choice of sexual object, recruitment metaphors negotiate lesbian identity as explicitly perverse and criminal. Such characterizations collude with other depictions, such as when anti-lesbian advocates worry that since lesbians are nonprocreative (at least in any "traditional" sense), they must recruit children into the "homosexual lifestyle."

Third, ideological discourses *represent* and *reify* identities. The rhetorical processes of reification complicate the constitution and negotiation of identity. Georg Lukács defines reification as the material symbolic means through which a state legitimates the economic and political order to its subjects.

Rhetoric is an integral part of this process. Reification occurs when a hegemonic order attempts to legitimate domination by presenting institutions, events, and structures as independent, permanent, and "the timeless model of human relations in general."[27] The family, for instance, has been characterized as the basic unit or building block of civilization, to the point that many citizens take such characterizations for granted. As a critical rhetorician, I am interested in discovering (and perhaps disrupting) the rhetorical, historical, and social conditions that make this "taken-for-grantedness" possible. Such an approach assumes a "doxastic" view of rhetoric, whereby prevalent ideological commitments and normative beliefs within specific historical and cultural domains function as implied argumentative premises and yet themselves are produced through public rhetorical struggle. My stance as a rhetorical critic, then, is less as a distanced observer and more as a person interested in intervening with language to see what possibilities for social change might emerge.

Lesbian bodies are constituted ideologically as a space in which only certain forms of energy, labor, and desire might be carried out; the current heteronormative formation typically discourages maternal practices. Mothers' bodies are regulated by ideological discourses that proscribe the enactment of "perverse" or nonnormative erotic desires. Non-biological lesbian mothers, for instance, are often denied custody on the assumption that biological, bodily connections to children "make" the mother.

Fourth, ideological discourses *regulate* identities. Identities, as particular subject positions within discursive relational webs, are constrained by their symbolic environs. Reification is one key constituent of such regulation. Lesbian motherhood is also regulated by the "secrecy requirement," whereby women are sometimes obliged to deny or mask their lesbian identity in order to obtain or retain custody and visitation rights. A lesbian mother may attempt to engage in the negotiation and regulation of her identity performances. As Butler points out, however, there exists "no subject who is 'free' to stand outside these norms or to negotiate them at a distance; on the contrary, the subject is retroactively produced by these norms in their repetition, precisely as their effect."[28] Lesbians, as Eve Sedgwick writes, are "physically and mentally terrorized through the institutions of law, religion, psychotherapy, mass culture, medicine . . . and brute violence."[29] The terms of identity negotiation are thus also regulated through ideology.

Finally, identities are *performed* or *enacted*. The range of socially acceptable and/or rhetorically legitimate identity-related performances is constrained by the symbolic contexts of which they are part. The performative is not sheerly aesthetic but is central to identity constitution, negotiation, representation, and reification. Concrete practices such as preparing a meal for one's children or naming oneself as a mother exemplify the performative dimensions of motherhood. The principle of performance leads to the next problem that must be accounted for in any critical rhetorical theory of identity: the problem of agency. "What we might call 'agency' or 'freedom' or 'possibility,'" Butler writes, "is always a specific political prerogative that is produced by the gaps opened up in regulatory norms, in the interpellating work of such norms, in the process of their self-repetition." Moreover, "freedom, possibility, agency do not have an abstract or pre-social status, but are always negotiated within a matrix of power."[30] The current normatively oxymoronic status of lesbian maternal identity constrains both lesbian agency and maternal agency in multiple ways. When lawyers advise their lesbian clients to "closet" themselves for the sake of obtaining custody, they constrain lesbian agency. When courts prohibit a lesbian from entering into or continuing a romantic involvement, they regulate her agency. When courts reject second-parent adoption petitions filed by the partner of the biological mother, maternal agency is constrained.

I am not proposing a linear or chronological progression of identity from constitution to negotiation to representation to performance. Such a conception would be naïve. The process of identity constitution and performance is complex, multilayered, and nonlinear. For instance, one's identity is constituted, negotiated, regulated, and performed simultaneously. Identity performances thus are subject to regulation and negotiation within specific temporal and symbolic contexts. Butler tells us that "where there is an 'I' who utters or speaks and thereby produces an effect in discourse, there is first a discourse which precedes and enables that 'I' and forms in language the constraining trajectory of its will."[31] In this way the bounds of legitimate identity construction and performance become constituted through ideology and are subject to constant public rhetorical struggle. The roots of today's struggles over lesbian maternal identity can be traced back to the turn of the twentieth century, with the initial construction of "lesbian" identity in scientific-medical discourses.

I turn now to a historical account of the introduction of the word "lesbian" into American vocabulary prior to the inception of the modern gay/lesbian rights movement in 1969. Such an overview places contemporary discussion and debate about lesbian identity within a particular historical context and reminds us that subject identity, although operating through various ideologies as transhistorical and individuated, is simultaneously specific within cultures and times. In particular, I contextualize the rhetorical development of contemporary lesbian identities in American culture within ideological narratives about sexuality, family, and womanhood that both compete and collude to define lesbianism in particular ways.

This discussion is not intended to provide an exhaustive historical account of the development of the lesbian community. Rather, my goal is to demarcate the broadest contours of the historical and rhetorical circumstances that made it possible for lesbian motherhood to become a topic of public debate over the last several decades. What rhetorical and historical circumstances made it possible for lesbian identity to be constituted as such? What rhetorical and historical circumstances made it possible for an empancipatory consciousness to arise among a "community" of gay men and lesbians? As Judith Halberstam observes so astutely, identities "do not suddenly emerge from some protean slime at the appropriate time; the possibility of a sexual identity or category is in fact years in the making and depends on all kinds of other factors in the community at large."[32]

I first describe the characterization of female same-sex relationships prior to the genesis of the word "lesbian," then explain the initial constitution of the lesbian mother oxymoron, with a particular focus on the criminal and neurotic ideographic characterizations whose legacy persists in contemporary psychologically based theories of homosexuality and lesbianism. The construction and negotiation of lesbian identity, of course, occurs outside of the psychological profession. For instance, the contemporary gay/lesbian liberation movement has played a primary role in critiquing heteronormative characterizations by arguing for the normality of lesbian/gay identity.

Public argumentation concerning lesbian *maternal* identity is also contained within narratives about motherhood. I will show how rhetorical ambivalence functions in the initial construction of the lesbian mother oxymoron through two competing yet complementary narratives of identity. Lesbianism as a medical/psychological pathology constitutes the primary construction, whereby lesbians are characterized as abnormal and in dire need of a cure or solution to their illness or problem. Undergirding yet distinct from the narrative of pathology is a criminal narrative in which lesbians are characterized as participants in a sodomitical culture that renders them outside the realm of respectable womanhood.

Sodomitical Creatures, Intimate Friends, but Not Lesbians

American women who directed their emotional, spiritual, and erotic energies toward other women prior to the last decade of the nineteenth century were not identified as lesbian. Such women instead fell into one of two primary categories: sinful sodomites or romantic friends. It was not until the 1890s that "lesbian" status as such became medicalized, as the work of sexologists such as Havelock Ellis and Richard von Krafft-Ebing contributed to the construction of lesbianism as a psychopathology.

Given the Puritan emphasis on procreative sexuality during the early American era, explicitly sexual relations between women were considered sodomitical and thus sinful. Sodomy laws including specific prohibitions against female same-sex relations appeared in colonial records as early as the mid-seventeenth century. In 1636, for instance, the Reverend John Cotton proposed a set of laws to the General Court of Massachusetts which defined "sodomy" as a "carnal fellowship of man with man, or woman with woman," and thereby an "unnatural filthiness" punishable by death.[33] The New Haven Colony in 1655 described female same-sex erotic relations as "against nature," as a "kinde of unnaturall and shamefull filthiness," also punishable by death.[34] Moreau de St. Mery, a French lawyer who visited the colonies between 1793 and 1798, condemned women who, "without real love and without passions," were "not at all strangers to being willing to seek unnatural pleasures with persons of their own sex."[35] Descriptions of female same-sex relations continued to be characterized as "unnatural" and "sinful" well into the eighteenth, nineteenth, and twentieth centuries.

Whereas colonial Puritans warned women against such sins, others later accepted the formation of romantic friendships between women. Lillian Faderman and Carroll Smith-Rosenberg have demonstrated that such friendships were an integral feature of nineteenth-century American culture[36] and were characterized by "closeness, freedom of emotional expression, and uninhibited physical contact."[37] Prior to the 1890s, the tendency was to characterize female same-sex desire and relationships either as "sinful" and "unnatural," or as intimate, romantic friendships.

The Medicalization of Homosocial Identity

The "homosexual" was not invoked into being until the late nineteenth century.[38] The word "lesbian" existed prior to this time, as the *Oxford English Dictionary* notes, referring to the Greek island of Lesbos, home of the seventh-century B.C.E. poet Sappho; it also described a carpenter's tool referred to as a "lesbian rule."[39] It was not until the 1890s, however, that "lesbian" signified any other meaning. That decade marked a turning point in public notions of female same-sex erotic relationships. Jeffrey Weeks argues that this was a "crucial period in the conceptualization of homosexuality as the distinguishing characteristic of a particular type of person, the 'invert' or the 'homosexual,' and the corresponding development of a new awareness of self amongst some 'homosexuals.'"[40] Women who engaged in same-sex erotic practices were no longer labeled primarily sinners but "inverts."[41]

During this period, sexologists such as Richard von Krafft-Ebing, Havelock Ellis, and August Forel medicalized same-sex erotic attachments, conceiving such attachments as congenital abnormalities or inversions. Krafft-Ebing, a professor of psychiatry at the University of Vienna, characterized homosexuality and lesbianism (in his classic *Psychopathia Sexualis*) as a matter of "antipathic sexual instinct" that was typically innate rather than acquired.[42] He described homosexuality as an "affliction" that "taints" the individual and could therefore be "treated."[43] Each instance of "genuine homosexuality has its etiology," he argued, "and must be reduced to an abnormal sexual instinct which is diametrically opposed to the physical sex of the affected individual."[44] The "majority of female homosexuals," however, "do not act in obedience to an innate impulse, but they are developed under conditions analogous to those which produce the homosexuality by cultivation."[45]

Havelock Ellis characterized homosexuality and lesbianism as a "congenital abnormality" that was in most cases biologically inevitable, claiming that some people were genetically predisposed to "becoming" homosexual.[46] Ellis spoke primarily of male homosexuals, for "we know comparatively little of sexual inversion in woman . . . [for] the chief monographs on the subject devote but little space to women."[47] Female homosexuals had not been the subject of much scholarly study, he hypothesized, because men tend to take an indifferent attitude toward lesbianism. Moreover, Ellis found, sexual inversion "is less easy to detect in women." He described lesbian alliances as "passionate friendships" rather than romantic sexual unions.[48] In those relatively rare instances when a lesbian would be identifiable, it was because she exhibited "a certain degree of masculinity."[49]

Ellis rejected explicitly the notion that homosexuality and lesbianism could occur without a genetic predisposition. He noted the hypocritical attitude of many scholars toward the formation of homosexual identity: "It must also be pointed out that the argument for acquired or suggested inversion logically involves the assertion that normal sexuality is also acquired or suggested. If a man becomes attracted to his own sex simply because the fact or the image of such attraction is brought before him, then we are bound to believe that a man becomes attracted to the opposite sex only because the fact or the image of such attraction is brought before him. This theory is wholly unworkable. . . . We must, therefore, put aside entirely the notion that the direction of the sexual impulse is merely a suggested phenomenon."[50] Given Ellis's notion that homosexuality was "natural" in a sense, he argued against the implementation of legal punishment of homosexuality and lesbianism, for "legislation against homosexuality has no clear effect either in diminishing or increasing its prevalence."[51] Ellis thus encouraged tolerance of homosexuality, given its apparent biological inevitability.

August Forel, also a psychiatry professor, drew upon Krafft-Ebing's typology to argue that "homosexual love is pathological in nature."[52] Moreover, he held, "nearly all inverts are in a more or less marked degree psychopaths or neurotics, whose sexual appetite is not only abnormal but usually also exalted."[53] A normal sexual appetite, Forel contended, could be characterized by the "fundamental axiom of the sexual question": *"With man, as with all living beings, the constant object of all sexual function, and consequently of sexual love, is the reproduction of the species.*"[54] Any non-procreative sexual activity was pathological and therefore subject to scientific control and treatment. As for the female homosexual, she "likes to dress as a man and feels like a man toward other women. She goes in for manly games, wears her hair short, and takes to men's occupations in general."[55] On the question whether a biological predisposition existed for homosexuality and lesbianism, Forel answered that such pathologies could be either congenital or acquired by "suggestion."[56] The latter characterization made it possible for later advocates to advance proselytical characterizations in arguments regarding lesbian/gay schoolteachers and parents.

Early sexologists developed elaborate taxonomies to describe a vast array of erotic desires and practices that were not or could not immediately be marked as distinctly procreative in purpose or outcome. As Michel Foucault notes, sexological rhetoric itself was part of a "transformation of sex into discourse" that was "governed by the endeavor to expel from reality the forms of sexuality that were not amenable to the strict economy of reproduction: to say no to unproductive activities, to banish casual pleasure, to reduce or exclude practices whose object was not procreation."[57] The development of multiple taxonomies of same-sex eroticism eventually produced the grounds on which an identity-based discourse could emerge—out of acts came identity, or what Foucault called a "new *specification of individuals.*" Whereas "the sodomite had been a temporary aberration; the homosexual was now a species."[58]

Sexological research has been critiqued on a number of fronts, with contemporary researchers noting the class, gender, and other biases troubling the work.[59] Wayne R. Dynes and Stephen Donaldson, for example, write that "for most of the twentieth century, writers considered lesbianism to be the female version of a sexual orientation called 'homosexuality.'"[60] Lesbianism, like homosexuality, was treated as a medical problem.[61] Such gender-blind treatment tended to neglect the asymmetrical subject positioning of women and men in American culture, to say nothing of the sexism inherent in the study of women as an afterthought. The taxonomies themselves, however, depended on the development and maintenance of binary systems of gender and sexual identity. Moreover, women were punished for being too explicit about their relationships. And lesbianism was associated with feminism as early as the turn of the century, when sexologists feared that feminism "turned" women into sexual inverts. Ellis, for instance, noted that the "modern movement of emancipation," which included women's demands for equality, could be linked to "an increase in [female] homosexuality, which has always been regarded as belonging to an allied, if not the same, group of phenomena." Although feminism did not *cause* lesbianism, in Ellis's view it certainly could encourage it.[62] Sexologists nurtured another legacy as well: the confusion of gender and sexuality, evidenced in their arguments that lesbians tended more often than not to be "masculine" in appearance and demeanor, perhaps even men trapped in women's bodies.

The legacy of the early sexologists' work lingered well into the twentieth century as the profession of psychoanalysis flourished. At least through the 1950s, the 1960s, and into the 1970s, homosexuality (and its female corollary, lesbianism) was characterized predominantly as a psychopathology, an "arrested development," and a congenital medical condition. A newly created class of individuals, simultaneously described as "sexual inverts," "homosexuals," and "lesbians," thus became subject to psychoanalytic and medical "treatment," including electroshock, aversion, hysterectomy, and lobotomy therapies employed from the 1940s through the 1960s.[63]

In sum, the conception of a distinct typology of homosexual and lesbian desire at the turn of the twentieth century created the grounds on which new subject identities could be regulated through public institutions such as medicine, law, and education. Prior to the 1880s and 1890s, individuals who engaged in same-sex erotic practices were conceived as engaging in aberrant criminal (or sinful) relations. From the turn of the century until the recent past, lesbianism was construed as a medical aberration that caused women to abandon traditional gender norms governing appearance and behavior and to seduce their feminine counterparts. The psychological profession did not constitute a solitary voice in the construction and negotiation of lesbian/gay identity, however. It is to another central group, lesbians and gay men, and their specific development of an oppositional rhetoric, that our attention now turns.

Stonewall: 1969 and Beyond

Lesbians and gay men began to develop a nascent political identity during the mid-twentieth century with the organization of groups such as the

Mattachine Society in New York for men and the Daughters of Bilitis in San Francisco for women. It was not until the Stonewall Riots in Greenwich Village that a distinctly emancipatory consciousness emerged among larger groups of gay men and lesbians. During the 1950s and 1960s, police raids on gay/lesbian bars were frequent and often resulted in police brutality.[64] Over one hundred patrons of San Francisco's Tay-Bush Inn, for instance, suffered a police raid on the bar in August 1961. The charges were later dropped, yet the mayor continued to support the police sweeps and encouraged revocation of many of the city's gay/lesbian bars' liquor licenses.[65]

On the evening of June 27, 1969, however, New York City police officers encountered unusual resistance to what was expected to be a standard raid on Greenwich Village's Stonewall Inn on Christopher Street.[66] As the detectives rounded up patrons for the paddy wagon, one lesbian's resistance to arrest quickly touched off rioting that lasted until the early morning hours and resulted ultimately in the torching of the Stonewall Inn.[67] The next evening violence erupted once again on Christopher Street as four hundred police officers tried to contain a crowd of over two thousand, who, between throwing beer bottles and stones, chanted "Gay Power!"[68]

The cultural significance of the Stonewall Inn riot should not be underestimated, for it represents the dawn of a new era of gay male and lesbian community pride. Historian Martin Duberman notes that "'Stonewall' is *the* emblematic event in modern lesbian and gay history. . . . The 1969 riots are now generally taken to mark the birth of the modern gay and lesbian political movement—that moment in time when gays and lesbians recognized all at once their mistreatment and their solidarity."[69] The gay liberation movement of the 1970s represented the "new militancy" of activism, whereby gay men and lesbians regarded themselves as "revolutionaries" in the struggle to escape a "fundamentally unequal and corrupt power establishment" that enforced compulsory heterosexuality.[70]

Of course, various historical conditions had to be in place before an event like Stonewall could occur, since revolts and rebellions do not materialize out of thin air. Massive organized resistance to hegemonic heterosexuality was made possible by a host of previous conditions. The seeds of queer emancipatory consciousness were planted decades before the 1970s Gay Liberation Front, 1980s ACT-UP and Queer Nation, or the 1990s Lesbian Avengers organized. Such seeds were sown by medical and scientific discourses (such as that offered by sexology) which contained the grounds of their own critique. Individuals throughout U.S. history often resisted the mandates of normative heterosexuality—even if "lesbian" or "gay" identity as such did not exist—as in the case of sex radicals, free love advocates, passing men, passing women, and butch-femme couples. The fact that such people probably did not enjoy a distinctly identitarian discourse tied consciously to a political group consciousness is not particularly problematic for my purposes, since those acts of resistance performed on an individual basis or on a small scale in the nineteenth and early twentieth centuries contributed to the possibility of a politicized *group* identity in the second half of the twentieth century.

The early 1970s were a particularly exciting time as the community emerged from the repressive silence of the previous decades and expressed pride publicly in its sexual orientation. While patrons of gay/lesbian bars were still subject to police harassment and brutality, members of queer culture busied themselves in grassroots efforts to obtain civil rights, in establishing new gay-owned businesses, and in publishing newspapers and periodicals targeted to a lesbian/gay audience. "After the apocalyptic Stonewall impulse," historian Rodger Streitmatter notes, a queer-identified press "erupted in so many directions that it is impossible to document when each publication was founded, how long it existed, or who edited it."[71]

Then, in December 1973, the American Psychiatric Association voted to remove homosexuality from its compendium of mental disorders published in the *Diagnostic and Statistical Manual*.[72] This did not mean, however, that homosexuality would no longer be characterized as pathology in public discourse. Like the sexologists who dominated public debate about homosexuality and lesbianism during the late nineteenth century and the first decades of the twentieth, psychoanalytic professionals have tended to dominate public discussions of lesbian and gay identity. Psychologists who devote their professional lives to the study of human sexuality are granted expert status by journalists, attorneys, and judges, and they enjoy great legitimacy in cultural debates about the meaning of lesbianism and homosexuality.[73]

Several discourse communities thus compete for hegemonic control over the construction of contemporary homosexuality and lesbianism; these include the professions of religion, law, and psychiatry, as well as gay men and lesbians themselves. Religious groups vacillate between vows of support and periodic pronouncements of lesbianism as a sin and an abomination.[74] Legislators draft—and sometimes repeal—sex-phobic laws that criminalize any activity beyond "vanilla" sex within the context of heterosexual marriage, but enforce such laws in an asymmetrical fashion.[75] Two well-known U.S. Supreme Court cases have excluded gay men and lesbians from the right to sexual privacy: in 1976 the Court upheld a Virginia statute criminalizing homosexual sex, then ten years later held constitutional a Georgia statute outlawing homosexual sodomy.[76]

The mental health industry exerts an influence on public attitudes toward lesbianism which evidences itself on a variety of fronts. In an attempt in the early 1970s to offer an expert opinion of lesbianism, Lawrence J. Hatterer, M.D., for instance, constructed homosexual identity as malleable: "Homosexuals, according to the best evidence so far, are made, not born, and a complex of life situations and influences throughout infancy, childhood, adolescence, and early adulthood are involved in the making."[77] Hatterer later told *Harper's Bazaar* readers "How to Spot Homosexuality in Children" by advising them to "consider the aggregate of signs, or the cumulative pattern of behavior." Little girls who did not play with dolls and little boys who did both stood on the edge of the slippery slope toward homosexual behavior.[78] Other psychiatric studies obsessed about whether children of lesbians or gay men would themselves be homosexual.[79] Implicit in such questions are assumptions about the nature and role of mothers in the family.

Twentieth-Century Motherhood

Specialized and authoritative discourses about homosexuality and lesbianism exist within a broader rhetorical culture determined to delineate the bounds of legitimate gender and sexuality. This preoccupation often emerges in public discussions about motherhood and the family. The idea of motherhood prior to the twentieth century in American culture focused on the moral guidance and character-shaping function of women's parenting, especially after the Industrial Revolution. Steven Mintz and Susan Kellogg note that mothers' primary responsibility in the early nineteenth century was to "shape the character of the children, make the home a haven of peace and order, and ex-

ert a moral and uplifting influence on men."[80] Motherhood was sentimental-
ized, yet mothers bore most of the responsibility for children's health and
character. It was also during this period that middle-class women were encouraged to devote full-time energy to mothering.[81] As the nation moved into
the twentieth century and the era of progressive reform, cultural notions of
motherhood altered in meaning. The emphasis on molding character gave
way to the new idea of "scientific mothering," whereby a mother's primary
function was to create and maintain a domestic environment "that would encourage proper growth and orderly development" of her children. The goal
of such an approach was to inculcate good moral behavior through specific
regimented schedules.[82] By the mid-1920s, "the family was undergoing a profound transformation, but few had any idea about the direction of change."[83]
In addition, the legal sphere took an increased interest in the family, insofar
as courts increasingly declared that they had a cultural obligation or duty
(rather than a right) to promote and protect families.[84] Judicial intervention
in family life encouraged citizens to envision judges, welfare workers, and the
like as sitting in loco parentis to the nation's children.

By mid-century, other changes in American culture were again contribut-
ing to shifting notions of motherhood and family. Arlene Skolnick argues that
structural changes such as the conversion from an industrial economy to
an economy oriented toward service and information, as well extended
longevity, changed American definitions of the family. The standard characterizations of the family so romanticized in the postwar era (breadwinning father, stay-at-home mother, and one or more children) had been reconceptu-
alized by the 1990s so that, according to Mintz and Kellogg, "the term 'family'
is no longer attached exclusively to conjugal or nuclear families comprising
a husband, wife, and their dependent children. It is applied to almost any
grouping of two or more people domiciled together."[85]

Such structural changes do not occur without cultural resistance, however.
While private citizens may describe their affective relationships under the
rubric of "family," legal institutions systematically fail to legitimate such
choices (through bans on same-sex marriage, strict adoption laws, and so on).
Mintz and Kellogg note that citizens of the postwar era retained a profound
faith in the institution of marriage, and associated marriage with personal
happiness and fulfillment. Moreover, a decision *not* to marry was typically

construed as a personal failure or sign of homosexuality.[86] There was thus strong social pressure to adhere to the conventional expectation of heterosexual marriage and parenthood lest one be tarnished with a reputation as a social failure or deviant. The ideological commitment to the nuclear family ideal has evolved into at least private acknowledgment of multiple kinds of domestic or family relations. Citizens continue to search "for a new paradigm of American family life, but in the meantime a profound sense of confusion and ambivalence reigns."[87] As Arlene Skolnick argues, this tension and ambivalence can be negotiated by considering "new social arrangements" that embrace these structural changes, but such consideration requires both "political will" and "social creativity."[88] It is within the overlapping contexts of contemporary family ideology, gay/lesbian liberation movements, the legal sphere, and feminism (among others) that debates over the meaning and legitimacy of lesbian motherhood occur.

Prior to the twentieth century, then, sexual orientation was not an identity marker, in the sense that there were no "lesbians" or "homosexual" men as such but only the existence and expression of same-sex desire. The earliest formation of the rhetorical ambivalence thus positioned ideological commitments to lesbian identity between the poles of criminality and neurosis. These commitments were not isolated or innocent; rather, they produced powerful narratives structured on the notion that good citizens should procreate (but only within the context of traditional marriage) and should also eliminate (or at the very least sublimate) any same-sex desire. Motherhood became constituted within narratives of the family, and lesbian identity lacked a distinctly visible presence within this rhetorical formation.

The following chapters trace a thirty-year period of public argumentation over the meaning(s) of "lesbian mother" as those debates emerged at the intersection of journalistic, judicial, and academic discourses. I will argue that for lesbian families to achieve civil rights and legitimacy in various public spheres, the meanings of "mother" and "lesbian" must be open to radical redefinition. Such a reconstruction can be effected by engaging critically the rhetorical ambivalence in each of these three areas of discourse, which play an integral role in the construction and maintenance of the lesbian mother oxymoron.

Chapter 2 examines journalistic discourse as an ideological apparatus instrumental to the circulation and maintenance of the oxymoron. I analyze representations of lesbian identity in several mainstream newspapers and periodicals from 1970 to March 2000, as well as in queer periodicals over the same period of time,[89] to show how the rhetorical ambivalence manifests itself in both kinds of journalistic accounts.

Chapter 3 focuses on the law as it subjects lesbian mothers to certain ideological controls. I examine the regulation of lesbian maternal identity in child custody disputes between heterosexual fathers and lesbian mothers from 1970 to 2000. (Lesbians and gay men face this type of custody battle more often than any other type of litigation.)[90] We will see how judicial discourse implicates the lesbian mother oxymoron in husband-wife custody disputes by invoking criminal, psychopathologic, and proselytic ideographic characterizations of lesbian identity to demonstrate a lack of maternal "fitness." I also examine rhetoric in custody disputes involving two lesbian mothers and in cases where one partner in a lesbian couple petitions to adopt her partner's child.

Chapter 4 analyzes academic rhetoric as it contributes to the problem of rhetorical legitimacy for lesbian mothers, with a particular focus on contemporary psychological studies. I examine several typical studies within this field, and argue that while such research is laudable for its attempts to support lesbian mothers, it unwittingly replicates heteronormative presumptions.

Chapter 5 discusses the major findings of this study and elaborates on its implications and limitations for both rhetorical and critical legal theory. I also propose a strategic expropriation of the lesbian mother oxymoron and offer concrete suggestions for social change, thus exploring the radical potential of lesbian motherhood.

Journalistic, legal, and academic rhetorics construct lesbian maternal identities in multiple and often contradictory ways. Such ideological conflicts and constitutive inconsistencies are significant to any attempt to posit a meaningful critical intervention. This project engages such contestation in the hope that lesbian mothers will one day soon enjoy freedom, justice, and full citizenship.

"My mother made me a homosexual."

"If I get her the wool, will she make me one too?"

Graffiti

"REAL LESBIANS AND SPERM DON'T MIX"

Ms. columnist Lindsy Van Gelder once observed that "the battleground . . . has now shifted to the culture beyond the courtroom, where the very concept of a 'lesbian mother' still computes about as well as 'ice-pick-wielding First Lady' or 'Mother Theresa centerfold.'"[1] Van Gelder's amusing observation regarding common responses to lesbian maternal identity draws attention to at least two distinct senses in which lesbian motherhood is characterized as an oxymoron. The first analogy, to the "ice-pick-wielding First Lady," highlights the sense of criminality undergirding lesbian identity and is particularly revealing for its attitude toward agency. The depiction of the First Lady as an *active* agent—and a criminal one at that—conflicts with conventional expectations surrounding her role. So too for the sodomitical lesbian, whose very existence signifies criminality. The analogy to the "Mother Theresa centerfold" underscores the sense in which lesbian identity is construed by many as little more than a set of perverse sexual practices. Western Christianity (in particular, Catholicism) prohibits both lesbians and nuns (not to mention lesbian nuns!) from the legitimate expression of erotic desire; thus to imagine a "Mother Theresa centerfold" is practically impossible.

The criminal and pathologic depictions of lesbians, as Van Gelder implies, occur in domains outside the specific realm of sexological research—or, as she notes, the law. Public contestation of identity occurs, for instance, in journalistic discourse, which includes the voices of various advocates, each advancing claims and arguments either to certify or to oppose lesbian motherhood. These advocates are positioned differentially according to their relative authority. Some journalistic outlets tend to publish primarily the "expert" voices of scientists, psychologists, and scholars, while other publications include the voices of ordinary citizens, including lesbian mothers themselves.

In this chapter I explore how rhetorical ambivalence about lesbians is implicated in both the lesbian and the straight press. I argue that the ambivalence manifests itself in the straight press in accounts of lesbian identity as an illusory concept or a material threat to "real" American families, while the lesbian press characterizes lesbian motherhood as an act of either feminist revolution or feminist betrayal. It is important to include analysis of material from the lesbian press because straight journalism tends to neglect news that affects members of particular cultural subgroups such as lesbians and gay men. While the lesbian press renders lesbian maternal identity more visible (simply by granting it legitimacy as a topic of discussion), it occasionally reifies the oxymoron by constructing motherhood as a form of female agency outside the realm of respectable lesbian identity.

Straight Press Accounts: "The Great American Family"

Understanding how lesbian maternal identity has been contested since the 1970s necessitates comprehension of the broader cultural discussion of families and, more recently, of "family values." These debates often demonize lesbians and gay men (among others) by scapegoating them for the ostensible breakdown in family values. Racist, homonegative, and antifeminist advocates never seem to tire of characterizing the American family as a fragile institution in grave danger of ruin by black teenage single "welfare" mothers, homosexual child molesters, and selfish, career-oriented mothers. While advocates pay occasional lip service to "alternative" family forms such as single-parent homes and blended stepfamilies, the heterosexual nuclear family remains idealized and hegemonic. Contemporary discourse about the ideal family teaches us that the social organization of gender in American culture remains patriarchal. Moreover, the ideological family is decidedly heterosexual, is the building block of society, and is fundamentally opposed to any insidious influence such as homosexuality. In a speech delivered before the Allied Education Foundation in 1994, Mark Draper, president of the National Education Taskforce, warned that "never before in its million year history has the family faced a more vicious and powerful alliance of enemies. . . . The family is under assault by a militant deviant minority out to undermine the family's privileged status." Fearful of this "militant deviant" influence, Draper argued that "the greatest social good is a secure and loving family."[2]

In the sample I studied, the straight press consistently characterized the family as presumptively heterosexual and functionally procreative, with the rhetorical effect of legitimizing the asymmetrical and gendered social organization of responsibilities within the family. Such representations created the grounds on which "alternative" family forms such as lesbian-headed households and single-parent families could be opposed, as well as those on which oppositional discourses approving such alternatives could be established. Those who promoted the nuclear heterosexual family included D. Bruce Lockerbie, who, in a 1993 Baylor University lecture published in *Vital Speeches of the Day*, defined the contemporary family as "male and female for the express purpose of loving companionship with each other and with God," and for the "natural procreation and responsible nurture of children."[3] Those who propose "alternatives," according to Lockerbie, thus posit "the subsequent displacement of [the] conventional family structure," and thereby exhibit "scorn" and "mockery" for the "conventional family."[4] Lockerbie vehemently opposed plans then pending in the New York City public school system to adopt an elementary-level curriculum titled "Children of the Rainbow," which would include information about gay and lesbian families. This curriculum, Lockerbie argued, while ostensibly "intended to teach tolerance of gay families," was instead meant "to coerce taxpayers into accepting instruction at enmity with their moral principles, offensive to citizen-parents who believe homosexuality to be a perverse and essentially genocidal lifestyle."[5] It is significant that Lockerbie places lesbians and gay men *outside* the taxpaying citizen–parent population. Such placement illustrates the ways in which a hegemonic heterosexual public is constructed so that alternative families lack legitimacy in the larger culture.

Others have challenged the heteronormative construction of the nuclear family. In his contribution to the 1990 special issue of *Newsweek* devoted to the "21st Century Family," Jerrold K. Footlick recognized that "the traditional family retains a profound hold on the American imagination." He continued, "The historical irony here is that the traditional family is something of an anomaly," since the mother-at-home and father-at-paid-work model thrived for only a brief sixty-year span between 1860 and 1920.[6] But there are other factors that affect this cultural struggle, as public dialogue continues to address social, legal, and economic policies regarding American families. Anxiety about and ambivalence toward shifting gender and sexuality norms also become evident in societal debates about contemporary homosexualities.

The Invisible Lesbian

The most striking feature of the straight press coverage is that it renders lesbians invisible while simultaneously drawing attention to the effacement of lesbians from the landscape of American public culture. In a 1990 special issue titled "Women: The Road Ahead," *Time* magazine devoted only three quarters of a page to American lesbians; the subtitle of the article highlighted lesbian invisibility: "Though they may be as numerous as gay men, they remain America's invisible women."[7] The author, William Henry III, recognized the sexist elements in such treatment, noting that "when homosexuals are discussed in the media, men are almost always the focus, with women at best an afterthought." Such invisibility will continue, Henry argued, "unless they proclaim themselves vehemently."[8] An article in the December 1993 *Los Angeles Times* headlined "Lesbians Work to Shed Label as 'Invisible Gays'" examined the ways in which "lesbians have the double challenge of being female and gay in a world that has preferred both to be silent."[9] Conditions had not improved significantly by the time *Newsweek* devoted a special issue to "Gay America" in March 2000. Interviewing a lesbian couple about their co-parenting experiences in Maryland, Pat Wingert and Barbara Kantrowitz focused on the anxiety-producing situation of being lesbian mothers in a culture that generally despises lesbians.[10]

Vehement proclamations aside, these typical representations minimize the role that social institutions such as the media play in the various processes of "othering," whereby certain citizen populations are almost simultaneously marked and rendered invisible. Claiming that invisibility is a problem to be solved through the heroic actions of an individual belies the fact that "vehement proclamations" often fall on the wrong or deaf ears, or are directed to audiences that already support lesbian rights (preaching to the choir), don't care (policy makers who lack the courage to support basic civil rights for gay people), or care but are not in a position to lobby effectively for civil rights and humane treatment. Attempts to gain visibility occur in the context of multiple rhetorical obstacles, including audiences who lack necessary decision-making power, hostile media outlets that wish to avoid offending a heteronormative public, and practical restrictions on the ceremonial podium.

Characteristic invisibility, of course, only reinforces the status quo and delays the enactment of positive social change. So long as the *existence* and *size* of a population can itself be the primary subject of debate, the denial of civil rights can continue. Thus, various popular discussions of lesbians and gay men continue to be framed around topoi such as "Who Are You?" "Do You Really Exist?" and "Okay, You Exist, but How Many of You Are There, Really?" The rhetorical effect of such framing is significant, for it constitutes gays as a "special interest" group or potential voting bloc rather than a minority suffering widespread discrimination and struggling for social justice and the rights constitutionally guaranteed to all citizens. My observation here, of course, begs the question whether and under what conditions gay and lesbian people count as "citizens." On good days, citizenship seems just around the corner. On most days however, true citizenship status for lesbians and gay men is a mirage.

Like sexologists, contemporary writers and advocates of various types speak of lesbianism as the female version of homosexuality, an implicitly male construct. I found many more sources that dealt with homosexuality than those that focused exclusively on lesbians, lesbian mothers, or lesbianism. Most articles that chronicled public attitudes toward homosexuality collapsed gender in the sense that while the category "homosexuals" on the face of it included both women and men, in effect it applied exclusively to the latter. Lesbians were thereby rendered invisible as homosexuals *while simultaneously* included in the category for purposes of regulating identity.[11] Thus, while "gay" sometimes may be used as a gender-neutral term, it functions more often than not as a masculine signifier. One such regulative function involves the characteristic disbelief that greets the notion of lesbian/gay parenthood.

"Gay? Lesbian? You Can't Be a Parent!"

I found that the straight press employed three identity-related characterizations of lesbians: as potential child molesters or recruiters, as distinctly nonprocreative, and as a threat to the family. The characterization of lesbians as potential pedophiles or "recruiters" surfaced most often in debates concerning lesbians as elementary school teachers. "Is there a chance that even without overt action such a teacher [a lesbian or gay man] would become a 'role model' for some children?" asked a *New York Times* editorial in May 1977. "Parents" were portrayed as *always* heterosexual, as when the same editorial asserted, "Feelings of repugnance and hostility toward homosexuals continue to run deep, especially among parents concerned about their children's development." In addition, the editorial argued, "society has a stake in the continuing strength of the family, and parents naturally put the health and happiness of their children before the welfare of any group."[12] Although, by the time the editorial appeared, at least two custody cases involving lesbian mothers had been the subject of much media attention, the *Times* writer chose to ignore the existence of queer parents, thus exacerbating the problem of invisibility.

"Opponents" of homosexual identity (to the extent that one can morally oppose an ontological category) enact a double standard of sexual orientation identity formation. While homosexuality is construed as a matter of recruitment, heterosexuality is represented as the timeless essence of natural sexuality, even as it is propagandized, inculcated, and enforced in various sectors of society such as religion, education, law, and the media. This double standard becomes all the more fascinating when we recall that "heterosexuality," as an identity concept, actually postdates "homosexuality."[13] An anonymous letter to the editor of the *Times* expressed the fear that gay/lesbian teachers would pose an "inevitable detrimental influence" and should thus be barred from being "teachers of malleable youth."[14] The characterization of "detrimental influence," of course, depends on enthymematic claims of criminality, sinfulness, or proselytical tendencies that will *necessarily* corrupt youth, who themselves are presumptively heterosexual.

Those who opposed gay teachers inevitably depicted young people as impressionable, malleable, and the like. In a speech, the psychoanalyst Melvin Anchell ventured to claim that gay folk do more than exert a negative influence on impressionable children. A homosexual, he insisted, "will use a child as a sex object if he has a sexual urgency and an adult member of his own sex is not readily available—thus, a homosexual is at the same time a potential pedophile." Anchell's conflation of homosexuality and pedophilia led him to claim further that "1,000s of children are stolen from parents to meet the sexual needs of homosexuals." He concluded that since gay men and lesbians are "abnormal," and "destructive to life," they pose a "danger to society" when they occupy powerful positions such as teaching school, for "from these positions [they] can easily influence and recruit others into homosexuality."[15] Anchell's published comments could be dismissed easily as the words of a demagogue, but such a dismissal would not serve my purposes here.

Anchell delivered this address *not* in a deliberative context, as one might expect, but on a ceremonial occasion: a college commencement. Ceremonial oratory, conceived traditionally, typically functions as a discourse of praise and/or blame and reaffirms (though occasionally it may challenge) a community's prevalent ideological commitments. Evidentiary standards differ from one rhetorical context to another. The affirmative function, coupled with the ceremonial context, may exempt orators from providing evidence to support controversial claims, especially evidence that would certainly be required in a deliberative context. Thus, the ceremonial context in which Anchell spoke gave him the opportunity to capitalize on the heteronormative American public's deepest fears about lesbians and gay men without providing verifiable proof. Given the ceremonial context of Anchell's attack, he was able to certify and recirculate characterizations of gay folk as criminal, neurotic, and pedophilic.

Fears that lesbians and/or gay men would harm children by "recruiting" them or exploiting them sexually also surfaced in the debate over whether lesbians and gay men should be allowed to function as adoptive and/or foster parents. In 1987 the Massachusetts Department of Social Services decided to place foster children only in "traditional family settings," and specifically excluded lesbians from such formulations of "family."[16] New Jersey took a different path and determined that openly gay teenagers could be placed with gay foster parents. Should a child be in the process of questioning her or his sexual orientation, however, psychiatrist Aaron H. Esman warned that a gay foster family might not be the best choice. "For young adolescents," he told reporters, "the pattern of sexual orientation might not be fixed, and that kind of placement might tend to fix it as homosexual"—and that, of course, would not be a good thing.[17] Esman's warning reified heterosexuality as the ideal objective of human sexuality through the dual construction of homosexuality as arrested development and as a temporary condition that could be "cured" through the love of a married heterosexual couple. These advocates thus characterized sexual orientation as a matter of persuasion: children and youth were presumed to be naturally heterosexual yet vulnerable to the evil rhetorical influence of lesbians and gay men, demon rhetors who ostensibly had to exert such influence over other people's children because they were incapable of reproduction themselves.

The straight press typically characterized gay men and lesbians as intrinsically non-procreative. An early 1970s report on the feminist movement, for instance, cited Betty Friedan's sentiment that "lesbians, for whatever reasons, have repudiated two aspects—sexual feelings for men and child bearing."[18] Others were even more fervent in their assertions that gay men and lesbians could not function as parents. A letter to the editor of the *Washington Post*, for instance, contended that if homosexuality "were to become a dominant practice, it would threaten the very existence of society itself. Why? Because it preempts our most important national resource—children."[19] Even gay-positive advocates circulated characterizations of gays as non-procreative. Betty Fairchild, then the coordinator of the Washington, D.C., chapter of Parents of Gays, replied to the letter by asserting that "legalizing (or not legalizing) marriages between homosexual couples will have little effect on the number of children born into this already over-populated world. For, even if gay couples continue to be denied the benefits available to heterosexually married couples, they would hardly start producing children."[20]

Others cited a common reaction to an offspring's revelation that he or she was homosexual: "When the homosexual child is an only child," Judy Klemesrud wrote, "some parents feel distraught mainly about the fact that they probably won't have any grandchildren."[21] Parents' expectations that their children will and should reproduce arise in a profoundly pronatalist culture, but those expectations and hopes, conventional wisdom tells us, are automatically subverted when homosexuality enters the picture. Reassurances to parents that one's queerness does not necessarily dissolve the desire or the capacity to procreate may be met with consternation—"Yes, but do you want to subject an innocent child to your lifestyle?" Lesbians are thus caught in a double bind. They can resist pronatalist ideology and risk being characterized as selfish and immature, or they can fulfill the cultural mandate to reproduce and risk a lifetime of additional stigma, possible custody litigation, and other obstacles to peaceful living. "When I thought about having a child," feminist attorney and law professor Nancy Polikoff noted in a discussion with Tacie Dejanikus of the Washington, D.C.–area Off Our Backs Collective, "part of what I thought about was that I felt like a freak and an outcast as a lesbian and that having a child would give me this great thing in common with other women." But, she asked, "to what extent is that an unanalyzed motivation to have children and what does it say about our feelings about ourselves as lesbians?"[22] Moreover, are "lesbians any less subject to that culture and socialization and do we have kids for any different reasons than other women have children? Can any woman, including a lesbian, make a *free* choice to have a child in a society that makes childbearing virtually mandatory to be considered a real, normal, or true woman? When lesbians start to have children and are really gung-ho about it, as a lot of us are, does that feed into the socialization?"[23]

Because of their supposed inability to fulfill the biblical mandate to procreate, then, it followed that lesbians and gay men necessarily resorted to "recruiting" techniques and thereby posed a threat to the stability of the heterosexual nuclear family. In 1974 the Roman Catholic Archdiocese of New York printed an editorial titled "A Menace to Family Life" in its official news organ, the *Catholic News.* "Homosexuality," the editorial argued, "is an increasing threat to sound family life in our city today. We must make every effort to promote the principles and values of the family as the basic unit and foundation of society."[24] Other advocates construed gay men and lesbians as such a severe threat to the family that they advanced public definitions of parenthood that specifically excluded them. The second White House Conference on Families, held in 1980, for instance, "approved a definition of families that excludes homosexual relationships," and in 1992 the president of a community school board in Queens, New York, sent a memo to parents swearing that "we will not accept two people of the same sex engaged in deviant sex practices as family."[25] Constituted as a non-citizen class outside the institution of The Family, lesbians are thus effectively disallowed participation in one of the few legitimate social roles held out to women: motherhood.

To summarize, the ambivalence of the straight press toward lesbian maternal identity manifested itself in two primary ways. First, straight journalists exhibited doubt as to whether lesbians really even existed as a separate class. Such doubt surfaced through discussions of homosexuality as a primarily male domain. When the category "lesbian" was included, it was either as an afterthought, as the *Newsweek* article on the future of gay America,[26] or as a novelty that, like other fashionable trends, would eventually fade from public consciousness and therefore posed little threat to the natural order of things.[27] At other times, lesbians as a class were portrayed as a threat to heterosexual society, worthy of legal punishment and social ostracism.

We turn now to lesbian-owned or managed periodicals, as well as other periodicals targeted to lesbian audiences. I found that they were sometimes just as likely as the straight press to attack lesbian maternal identity, although for somewhat different reasons and in markedly different ways.

Lesbian Press Accounts: Lesbian Mothers as Vanguard or Betrayal

Examination of lesbian and feminist periodicals against the straight press reveals a rhetorical resistance to hegemonic characterizations of lesbian maternal identity (although it may constitute its own form of hegemony). As Rodger Streitmatter points out in his outstanding history of the queer press in the United States, "the lesbian and gay press has published a distinctive brand of journalism committed to affirming the values of the community it serves, while documenting a shocking record of society's homophobia."[28]

The queer press began in 1947 with the initial publication of *Vice Versa* by an author writing under the pen name "Lisa Ben," who created the small publication (usually fewer than twenty pages) to provide a community forum for Los Angeles–area lesbians. Published for approximately nine months, *Vice Versa* created a place where lesbian issues could be discussed in a positive tone. Lisa Ben rejected the metaphoric characterizations of lesbians as sick and criminal, so popular in the hegemonic straight press, and, as Streitmatter notes, she did not "apologize or communicate a sense of guilt or shame to [her] readers."[29]

Other early lesbian periodicals, however, were not always so successful in resisting or rejecting such characterizations. *The Ladder*, published in San Francisco from 1956 until 1972, often sounded guilt-ridden and communicated a sense of shame about lesbian identity; nonetheless, it made an important contribution to the development of a discourse of lesbian identity separate from gay male identity. The magazine's first issue contained a brief article titled "Raising Children in a Deviant Relationship," which characterized such arrangements as problematic: "It is surprising to learn how many women are raising children in a deviant relationship. . . . To be of any assistance to those who are meeting this problem, we need more data and more research into the various facets of such a relationship."[30] Widespread concern for motherhood-related issues within the lesbian community, however, did not emerge until the early 1970s, the pinnacle of lesbian-feminist publishing.

Articles published before the "gayby boom" of the mid-1980s and 1990s structured an ideological ambivalence toward lesbian maternal identity by constituting it as either the preeminent expression of lesbian feminism or the supreme example of co-optation by a demonized heterosexual majority. The lesbian press recognized the existence of "families" headed by one or more lesbian mothers, faithfully reported news of custody cases from every corner of the nation, and was generally supportive (editorially, at least). Yet the lesbian media also did their part to reify the oxymoron by sometimes representing lesbian motherhood as a practice undeserving of community support. One commentator noted the difficult position of the lesbian mother by outlining two major positions in the controversy over the legitimacy of lesbian motherhood:

[Position 1]: [R]aising children is an issue of heterosexual domain. . . . the fact that we raise children tests the limits of [heterosexuals'] tolerance. Pushes people a bit too far. Crosses the line. Got it?

[Position 2]: The fact that we raise children tests the limits of tolerance for some lesbian members of our own communities. Their perspective is that we are joining the mainstream, going (heterosexually) native by parenting. . . . [W]e are accused of playing into women's socially acceptable role, and we are suspected of using this legitimacy to avoid the worst of homophobic oppression.[31]

Lesbian-feminist periodicals tended to symbolize the family either as the hegemonic force of heterosexuality or as a flexible structure that could include "alternative" family forms. "When a society becomes homophobic and screams about how homosexuals threaten the family unit," Rebecca Dixon maintained in *Harvest Quarterly,* "the charges must be examined in specifics, not in sweeping terms of 'God and Country' or 'natural' idealism." Rather, the "contemporary American family" remained "the basic unit of production and consumption as well as the primary group affiliation for the individual."[32] Jeanne Cordova, co-founder of the classic periodical *Lesbian Tide,* argued that "survival of the species is patriarchies' oldest and most sacred excuse for binding women to men, to the institution of the nuclear family, to monogamy, to heterosexuality, for denying women the love of their own sex, and for keeping women bound to men in a manner that is becoming as outdated and unnecessary as it is cruel and debilitating."[33] Jane Melnick echoed Cordova's sentiments, noting that "the spectre of lesbian motherhood casts its shadow across questions about the family with a peculiar cutting edge. Proponents of the traditional nuclear family talk about lesbianism as if it is one of the causes of the decline. Issues about possible alternatives it offers, and light it may shed on the embattled nuclear family get lost in the maze of issues of survival, and defense against attacks from all sides."[34] Finally, "the fight for custody," one member of the Seattle-based Lesbian Mothers National Defense Fund argued, is an "exaggeration of what all lesbian mothers face in this society, which in turn reflects the distorted image of 'motherhood.'"[35]

Any residual ambivalence toward lesbian-headed families dissolved, however, in the face of dramatic custody battles. Lesbian and feminist periodicals documented these custody cases and rallied support for women caught in lengthy, expensive litigation. Lesbian periodicals constituted a crucial resource for lesbian mothers and their advocates, who needed to remain current on other cases in order to prepare their own. This information-sharing function was especially important in light of the fact that straight periodicals seldom publicized custody disputes, and those that were publicized were atypical rather than representative.

The media brouhaha that occurred in 1994, when Sharon Bottoms lost custody of her son Tyler to Tyler's grandmother in Virginia is such an example. The majority of custody disputes involving lesbian mothers do not involve third parties but instead are disputes between two parents (either the mother and father or the two mothers). On the one hand, while it is not inappropriate to report disputes between lesbian mothers and third parties, "mainstream" journalism's tendency to focus on the atypical misrepresents the issues that the majority of lesbian mothers face. On the other hand, such coverage may be useful in reminding us that fathers and sperm donors are not the only external threat to lesbian maternal practice. The lesbian-feminist press also embraced the atypical from time to time. For instance, three cases that received sustained attention in the lesbian press (more than five articles per case) were atypical of the majority of custody proceedings lesbian mothers face. The first concerned a lesbian couple and their respective ex-husbands. A second case occurred in 1973, when Larraine Townend's ex-husband broke into the home she shared in the Seattle area with her partner, Vicky Dickenson, and then later tried to murder his ex-wife.[36]

Lesbian press coverage of the two cases typically accomplished one or more of five tasks: to introduce the facts of the case; to provide updates for regional audiences; to publicize pleas for financial support to offset attorneys' fees; to editorialize regarding the legal system's prejudice against lesbians in general and lesbian mothers in particular; and, perhaps most important, to advance a strategic legal agenda whereby lesbian identity could no longer function as an a priori factor for denying women's petitions for custody and/or visitation rights. Lesbian-feminist periodicals functioned as a vital source of information for coverage of custody disputes involving lesbian mothers. Some advocates critiqued the legal system through the lesbian-feminist media. One writer identified as "Barb Wire" noted in 1987 that "our legal rights as lesbians planning parenthood are very limited at this point, and we remain barely visible, let alone recognized as hopeful co-parents entitled to equal rights regarding a child's custody."[37] More than a decade later, non-biological lesbian mothers still face legal obstacles in gaining visitation and custody privileges as co-parents.

Several proponents rejected explicitly the judiciary's use of criminal and/or mental illness metaphors to constitute lesbian maternal identity. Melvyn A. Berke and Joanne Grant argued in the *Gay Community News* that custody determinations were often based on judicial homonegativity rather than "an evaluation of [a] particular person's skills as a mother"; courts focused mostly on evidence regarding the "tendency to commit homosexual acts."[38] The "commission" of "homosexual acts," of course, implies criminal activity as a central feature of lesbian identity. The June 1978 *Out and About* reported a ruling that removed one mother's custodial and visitation rights completely to protect her children from being "exposed" to lesbians. The custody hearing concluded with the judge announcing, "I may be prejudiced but I think homosexuality is an illness." Moreover, he advised the mother to identify her lesbian identity as an illness; if she chose to characterize it otherwise, he would disallow any future visitation.[39]

In this particular case, even the mother's communication with her children was subject to judicial discipline. She was effectively silenced unless she was willing to say, "Sweetie, Mommy suffers from a horrible sickness," and thereby pass the conventional perception of lesbians as neurotic to the next generation. Of course, one might wonder about the extent to which this admonition could actually be enforced—supervised visitation for surveillance of mother-child conversations? Taped telephone calls? Video cameras installed throughout the home? The mother's visitation rights had already been curtailed severely. Was she to don a heterosexual mask during visitation? The possibility of state regulation of private communications is daunting indeed. And while it is difficult to imagine the practicability of enforcing such a sanction, the rhetorical effect is the same: unless the parent does not care about visitation or custody (which was not the case here), she is in no position to contest judicial authority. Judges can therefore enact a variety of punishments against lesbian mothers with wide latitude.

This particular rhetorical context enabled "Tryna," in her contribution to the popular 1970s publication *Lavender Woman,* to criticize the legal advice commonly offered to lesbians fighting for child custody. Family attorneys, she argued, give lesbians two choices:

> One: to humiliate myself by denying my lesbianism and going back to the closet for the rest of my life—and if it can be proven that I'm indeed a lesbian, I can be held for perjury. Two: I can say yes I'm a lesbian, it's too bad I'm a pervert but I will do everything in my power not to expose these ideas to my child either through words or actions, and hope to god (because we'd better believe in god) that she's not harmed by my unfortunate lifestyle. . . . We've been told that when asked if we're lesbians we should take the fifth amendment on the grounds that our answers might *incriminate* us.[40]

Faced with such hostility, the lesbian press tended to foster lesbian solidarity against judicial homonegativity. Some commentators proposed a reconstruction of motherhood by attending first to the negotiation of lesbian identity.

Challenging Images of Sickness and Perversion

Lesbian-feminist advocates rejected psychopathologic characterizations of lesbians as sick, neurotic, or perverse. Such challenges were important for the rhetorical purposes of drawing attention to normative heterosexuality and challenging it. "A Redstocking Sister," for instance, argued that so "long as Lesbians are still treated as perverts, and 'sick,' it means that any woman who wants to live as she sees fit" will be subject to "harassment" and "ridicule," and will live "in the shadow of fear."[41] Eleanor Cooper, reporting on the persecution of lesbians at a Speakout on Sexual Crimes against Women in 1976, held that "the institutions of the law and the church and the so-called social sciences" as well as other "authorities of the patriarchy" often "declare us and our entire lives tainted because we are categorized as illegal, sinful, or sick," and such "fraudulent" declarations are wielded as mechanisms of social control.[42]

Various lesbians expressed doubt as to the negotiability of lesbian identity beyond its hegemonic characterizations. In her chronicle of various homophobic practices, Rebecca Dixon observed that others "may only deny us housing, employment, and the legal right to love—at least according to the letter of the law. But the spirit of the law is to deny our existence." Moreover, she argued, the effect of such notions was that while "doctors decide homosexuality isn't a disease and churchmen are adjusting their notions of it as sin, legislators all over the country are passing anti-gay laws."[43] These anti-gay laws, along with the cultural context that nurtured and certified their enforcement, are eventually woven into the fabric of lesbian maternal existence itself. Everyday life for lesbian mothers includes the fear of losing their children. The Lesbians with Children Support Group in Boston noted that the "spectre of a custody fight is one of the most devastating crises we have discussed. Some women in our group have gone through or are now facing custody battles. For others, it is a constant but as yet unrealized threat. And for others, it is only the shadow of an unlikely fear."[44] Ruth Mahaney noted in her review of *In the Best Interests of the Children,* a documentary about lesbian mothers and their children, that the "quality of a lesbian's mothering is under constant scrutiny. The threat of losing her children is very real to any mother who is a lesbian."[45]

Sometimes the specter of custody denial was enough to force a woman to masquerade as heterosexual in court. Linda Duck employed this strategy during her three-year court battle for custody. "'I had to establish my priorities,' said Duck, 'and my children are number one. I'm sad that I can't be who I am and have my children too.'" Duck "consistently maintained" throughout custody proceedings that she was "not lesbian," despite the fact that she had had a lesbian partner for five years.[46] Denial and the subsequent effacement of lesbian identity as a rhetorical strategy for maintaining custody (or preventing the loss of custodial rights) marks one important dimension of the rhetorical ambivalence. While such denial or silence may function as a political expedient for legal purposes, it also legitimates the heteronormative characterizations of lesbian identity as a shame-based subjectivity. Such denial and/or strategic effacement of lesbianism often correlated to the explicit reification of the lesbian mother oxymoron, and sometimes functioned as the rhetorical grounds on which it could occur.

Certification of the oxymoron took three primary forms in lesbian periodical literature: (1) speaking explicitly of lesbian motherhood as a contradiction in terms, (2) communicating hostility toward lesbian mothers generally and toward lesbian mothers' male children in particular, and (3) advancing the thesis that children should not be exposed to lesbianism or homosexuality. Lesbian advocates who were not mothers often mimicked the heteronormative notion that lesbians and mothers occupy mutually exclusive identity categories. Such characterizations are significant rhetorically both because they demonstrate how hegemonic ideologies can work their way into an oppressed group's rhetoric, and because such characterizations demonstrate that the lesbian community is by no means monolithic in either its support or its rejection of other lesbians, especially when the "other lesbians" are mothers.

Lesbian periodicals sometimes reported instances of the seemingly widespread perception that homosexuality and lesbianism excluded the possibility of child raising. In a 1963 lecture before the Philadelphia chapter of the Janus Society, the Reverend Robert W. Wood held that there "can be no question that permissive homosexuality is another effective means of birth control," and it "appears to be a built-in escape valve provided by an all-wise creator."[47] At a workshop sponsored by various Episcopal dioceses, the Reverend L. Robert Foutz declared that "homosexual acts must always be regarded as perversions because they are not part of the natural process of rearing children."[48] The anthropologist Margaret Mead stated in a speech before the Washington Press Club that "homosexuality appears to be increasing because 'we decided we don't want so many children.'"[49] *Lesbian Connection* reported in 1976 that a gay male advocate at the Gay Academic Union Conference, "in response to a complaint that the needs of certain groups (i.e. Lesbian Mothers, poor, etc.) in the gay community were not being taken into consideration, said 'If they were really Lesbians, they wouldn't be mothers.'"[50] These reports documented societal attitudes toward lesbianism generally, but also reinforced the notion that lesbian motherhood was logically implausible.

While Mead and Wood failed to recognize that gay men and lesbians did in fact choose to parent, numerous lesbian advocates portrayed such a choice as a betrayal of the gay/lesbian community or a concession to "breeder" ideology. "Ann Nemesis," for example, claimed: "Lesbians' lifestyle totally frees them from the breeding farms of heterosexual 'family.' Yet some lesbians are so totally out of their minds that they go to great lengths to replicate and create women's essential oppression. . . . Worldwide, heterosexual women don't know how to stop their own breeding apparatus. Lesbians go to extremes of artificial insemination to add to the problem! And what great innovations have these dyke moms created? They have pseudo-marriages of two 'Mom' families. . . . The truth is, the 'broad' (pregnant cow) is denying her role designed by the Fates who made her a lesbian in the first place."[51] Sylvan Rainwater agreed in principle that "our roles as lesbians is not, and should not be, to replicate the heterosexual nuclear family; and the sometimes-sickening romanticizing of motherhood," especially since motherhood is "highly overrated."[52] At a conference on motherhood, one lesbian mother noted that "we get criticized by the goddamned lesbians too when they say 'Well, if you're a mother you can't be a lesbian.'" Another mother chimed in that other lesbians "don't accept us. They didn't even think of us, for God's sake!" Yet another mother responded, "Oh no, they thought of us. They thought of us and they cut us out."[53] Lesbian mothers thus faced bias from heterosexuals as well as other lesbians and gay men.

Lesbian periodical literature is replete with accounts of lesbian animosity toward lesbian mothers. Dana Morrison tried to explain at a panel discussion on lesbian separatism in 1974 that she endured "oppression from Lesbians for my maternity. . . . This oppression is very real, very constant, and so well known to all Lesbian mothers."[54] Noy Dublex was one such "oppressive" lesbian. Dublex declared in the pages of *Dyke: A Quarterly*, "I will not support the fights for the right to be a Lesbian mother," even though she herself had children.[55] Lesbian mothers bespoke the pain of such animosity. In *Momazons*, one mother wrote, "We're not real lesbians. (Real lesbians and sperm don't mix)."[56]

If their children were male, lesbian mothers often experienced particular hostility. "'No boys! No boys!' shouted one woman in a code that was immediately understood around the circle," reported Pam McAllister in her coverage of a lesbian mother roundtable.[57] One woman recounted that "another fear I have about having a boy child is that other lesbians will condemn me or give me grief about it."[58] Social ostracism of lesbians mothering sons could be particularly insensitive and cruel. At the Third Annual Lesbian/Gay Town Meeting of Boston, Louise Rice told the audience that she had "received condolence calls from lesbians" when "her first son was born."[59] Karen Burr of the Lesbian Mothers' National Defense Fund noted that their "oppression as mothers of male children has been compounded by both the lesbian community, many of whom feel that we are 'raising the enemy,' and by courtrooms where judges are most concerned that we will rear healthy, happy, normal heterosexual males."[60]

While some lesbian advocates construed lesbianism as a threat to children's safety or psychological stability, others focused instead on the sheer hypocrisy of such claims by other lesbians. The *Lesbian Contradiction* exchange between Ann Nemesis and Sylvan Rainwater characterizes these disparate positions. After haranguing lesbian mothers for their complicity with breeder ideology, Nemesis complained that "some" lesbians "create the personal suffering of a child who discovers s(he) is marginal by having two 'queer' parents instead of 'normal heterosexual' ones."[61] Rainwater called this "such a classic case of victim blaming that I shouldn't even have to comment on it." She continued: "Do black parents *cause* personal suffering to their children by bringing them forth into a racist society. . . . Who causes homophobia? Not lesbian parents."[62]

The majority of lesbian periodical articles, however, did not echo heteronormative notions that lesbians "harm" children; rather, they documented homophobic responses from ex-husbands and legal officials in an effort to support lesbian mothers. One father, a psychologist, decided to sue his exwife for custody of their two children, arguing, according to the journal *Sister*, that "her lesbian lifestyle is stressful on her daughter and will be on her son, living among 'a bunch of man-hating women.'"[63] Other articles documented court decisions that lesbians could never function as positive role models, that lesbianism was some sort of dread disease to which children "should not be exposed," and that lesbian-headed households "can make little or no contribution" to children's "spiritual or intellectual growth and development" or would "create an element of instability that would adversely affect" the children's well-being.[64]

Lesbian periodicals also contained news reports that rejected the narrative of harm. *Gay Community News* reviewed a study published in *Science News* which found that "37 children being reared by either lesbians or by parents who have changed sex shows that 36 of the youngsters are heterosexually oriented with behavioral patterns indicating attraction to the opposite sex."[65] A 1976 UCLA study reported similar results, finding that "young children of lesbian mothers do not develop the 'deviant traits' that judges have been warned about in recent court battles."[66]

The tendency to valorize research that vouched for children's heterosexual "normalcy" in spite of their mothers' lesbianism is problematic, since such valorization implicitly supports the notion that lesbians are defective in some way. Harassment of lesbian mothers and their children, as well as court decisions that revoke mothers' custodial rights, are often based on the premise that lesbianism is "wrong." From another perspective, the valorization may serve expedient ends when legal advocates use the results of such studies as evidence that mothers should retain custody of their children. If one accepts the major premise, one consequently argues from a subordinate and already defensive position. In the long term, however, it would be more useful to *reject* that premise and begin with a new one reframing the debate in essentially lesbian-positive terms.

That some lesbians participate in the reification of the lesbian mother oxymoron should come as no great surprise, however, given that most lesbians exist in a social and cultural milieu that despises lesbian identity. Inculcated with anti-lesbian attitudes through various discourses, lesbians themselves can experience self-loathing. The struggle to resist such socialization, with the goal of developing a positive sense of lesbian identity, can sometimes carry with it the rejection of other dominant cultural traditions, such as the valorization of motherhood.

Rejecting the Lesbian Mother Oxymoron

Strategic rejection of the oxymoron typically fell into three broad categories: (1) explicit rejection of the oxymoron, (2) vows of support and acceptance for lesbian mothers and their children (including male children), and (3) characterizations of lesbian motherhood as the quintessential feminist revolutionary act. While other strategic characterizations were employed, they were idiosyncratic rather than representative.

Various lesbian advocates called attention to the supposedly oxymoronic cast of lesbian motherhood in order to critique and reject it. An article titled "Lesbian Mothers' Custody News" in a 1977 issue of *Leaping Lesbian*, for instance, introduced the topic with the following: "MYTH: LESBIANISM AND MOTHERHOOD ARE CONTRADICTIONS IN TERMS. FACT: ALTHOUGH MOST LESBIAN MOTHERS ARE HIDING BECAUSE THEY MAY LOSE THEIR CHILDREN, ABOUT ONE OUT OF EVERY THREE LESBIANS IS A MOTHER AND MORE LESBIANS ARE EXPRESSING THE DESIRE TO HAVE CHILDREN. THERE ARE AT LEAST 4 OR 5 MILLION LESBIAN MOTHERS IN THE U.S. TODAY!"[67] Fran Boyce concurred in a 1978 issue of *Gay Community News*, hoping that "other lesbian women accept the reality that we [lesbian mothers] are dykes too!" She emphasized that being a "gay parent is not alien to being a homosexual."[68] In 1983 another lesbian mother commented: "It's ironic to me that folks on two different sides of the sexual orientation fence can both identify our choices as testing the limits of their [heterosexuals' and lesbians'] tolerance. It's ironic to me that in this era of advanced reproductive technology, both camps inextricably link parenting with heterosexuality. Both groups would perceive the term lesbian mother to be an oxymoron—a contradiction in terms."[69] In 1993 "Lori" from Tennessee shared her own experience of harassment: "I had a boss who made advances to me, and I shunned him. He went around for some reason, he kept telling everybody that I was a lesbian, so people wouldn't like me. In a way, it was nice I got pregnant, I could say ha ha in his face. Because most of those people didn't think of a.i. [artificial insemination] unless they need it themselves. I had to laugh a little bit after that, because people came up to me for a while, telling me that he had called me a lesbian. That pissed me off. They told me this story because they figured if I was pregnant, it couldn't be true. So I really had the last laugh."[70]

Lesbian journals periodically included declarations of support for lesbian mothers generally, and for lesbian mothers of sons in particular. "Neva," writing for the Denver-based feminist publication *Big Mama Rag*, recounted how one lesbian "mother was refused housing in a predominantly homosexual commune-type house because she would have a child with her." She remarked that lesbian mothers often face a "double bind." The "outside world [the heterosexual regime] asks us—demands, sometimes, it seems—that we hide our sexuality," while the queer world "asks us to hide parenting, saying basically, 'give away your male children,' or 'it's okay if you have kids, but I don't want to hear about it.'"[71]

Other writers encouraged lesbians to overlook individual political or ideological differences in order to foster a sense of community. Lois Gilbert of the Ann Arbor Lesbian Mothers' Defense Fund made a sweeping plea for solidarity: "Who we are, how we choose to define ourselves individually is secondary to the real fact that sisters are losing their beautiful children to a legal system in which hatred and fear masquerade as justice."[72] The editors of *Leaping Lesbian* encouraged lesbians who were not mothers to support those who were by volunteering child care services, donating money to lesbian mother defense funds, raising child care issues at political meetings, and befriending children.[73]

Lesbian advocates occasionally rejected separatist claims that lesbians should not mother male children. Xenia Williams wrote in *Lesbian Contradiction* of her affection for her friend's son: "I know that Joshua is very dear to me, and that I do not at all buy the exclusion of male children from lesbian events. I won't go to anything from which Joshua is excluded for being male."[74] Terri Poppe, reporting on a lesbian mothers' retreat in Massachusetts, wrote of conferees' agreement "on the importance of trying to build support for male children (and women with male children) in the women's community."[75] Such characterizations were central to the development of a lesbian-feminist agenda affirming lesbian motherhood as a political act.

While advocates such as Ann Nemesis characterized lesbian motherhood as a "sellout" and a symbol of illusory lesbian identity, others argued that lesbian motherhood was *the* definitive expression of radical feminism. "The situation of the lesbian mother," Ellen Agger and Francie Wyland argued, "epitomizes the weakness of the position of all women in this society. She threatens the 'natural' role of women by refusing to be a sexual, physical, and emotional servant to a man."[76] Legal strategists Nan Hunter and Nancy Polikoff agreed, observing that "the attempts to deprive lesbian mothers of custody must be considered in the perspective of an historical pattern of punishing independent or political women by declaring them to be unfit mothers and taking their children."[77]

Advocates such as Baba Copper argued that lesbian motherhood was the *only* form of maternal practice that had any chance of challenging the patriarchal social order. "As much as any other institution I know," Copper wrote, "motherhood needs feminist transformation."[78] Moreover, "while it is true that lesbian motherhood cannot be equated automatically with good daughter-rearing or separatism or even feminism, *lesbian mothers are the only category of women sufficiently alienated from patriarchal traditions to sustain radical modifications in the socialization of daughters.*"[79] While one may be tempted to interpret Copper's claim as mere wishful thinking, it does foreground strategically the professed radical potential of lesbian motherhood. But it is not clear *how* lesbian maternal practice could be reconstructed positively as transgressive or transformative. It is also unclear *how* and to what extent lesbian mothers could be "sufficiently alienated" from patriarchal ideology. How does such alienation occur? Under what circumstances? Is membership in an identity category adequate grounds for alienation? "Radical modifications" are thwarted by courts, pundits, and politicians who consistently attack lesbian motherhood. As Judith Halberstam puts it, rejecting criminal characterizations of lesbian identity necessarily entails rejecting the notion that lesbian identity is necessarily transgressive—unless transgression means the violation of social norms rather than laws.[80] Copper's statements thus illustrate the utopian notion that members of subcultures can somehow escape the machinations of hegemonic ideologies of gender, race, or sexuality.

Several lesbians who organized a Mother's Day Rally for Boston-area lesbian mothers reported that the demonstration was "part of our struggle as women to have the right to have a family *if we choose, when we choose, and how we choose.*" They thereby cast lesbian motherhood as a reproductive rights issue, a concern central to liberal feminism.[81] Del Martin and Phyllis Lyon, two San Francisco–area lesbians who founded the Daughters of Bilitis, argued that the lesbian mother often faced an anti-lesbian and sexist court system: "The judge has wide discretionary powers in determining the merits and 'best interests' in each individual custody case. What is at stake then is the judge's frame of reference. Usually *he* is older, white and heterosexual. Usually *he* is conservative in his concept of family, marriage and divorce. Usually *he* is bound to traditional stereotypes of femininity and masculinity and of wife and mother roles."[82]

Lesbian maternal identity was also represented as a direct challenge to sexism. A 1975 *Lesbian Tide* profile of the Lesbian Mothers National Defense Fund noted that one of its primary goals was "fighting against the attitudes and judgements of courts in this country and throughout the world where women have been enslaved and victimized for centuries by the patriarchal system."[83] In a follow-up two years later, members noted that in "the months we have functioned as a defense fund, we have come to understand how central an issue lesbian custody is to the feminist movement. When men have the power to take our children away from us because of choices we make without their participation, the basic rights of all women are threatened."[84] In the context of addressing lesbian mothers' relationship to feminism, then, nonmother lesbian-feminist advocates tended to characterize lesbian maternal identity as a failure to resist patriarchal ideology and authority. Mothers, however, represented lesbian maternity as the ultimate symbol of feminist resistance to patriarchal authority.

In both the straight and lesbian press, construction and reification of the lesbian mother oxymoron typically occurred within the larger cultural debates about the meaning of family and family values. The hegemony of heterosexual motherhood was strong enough effectively to disallow the enactment of a legitimate maternal identity. Specifically, advocates of heteronormativity constructed The Family in such a way that lesbians and gay men were placed outside it and, more important, portrayed as inimical to it. To the extent that lesbians and gay men were mentioned in discussions of the family, they were characterized as threats, as enemies who would, if given the chance, corrupt the sanctity of conventional family life by recruiting children into the "homosexual lifestyle."

The straight press manifested the rhetorical ambivalence by relying on a set of binaries that placed lesbianism and motherhood at distinct odds with each other: the heterosexual = family / lesbian = threat opposition, and the heterosexual = procreative / lesbian = recruiter opposition. Families were constituted as *always* and *naturally* heterosexual and therefore functionally procreative. Even though the straight press tended to portray lesbians as an invisible portion of the gay community, it did not hesitate to represent lesbians as a clearly visible threat to the family.

Such representations obviously patrol the borders of The Family. If lesbians constitute a threat, then they should not be part of the family. The first binary works in tandem with the second, which specifies the threat lesbians pose: they are recruiters or potential child molesters because they cannot possibly have children of "their own." Such representations were plentiful in the straight press. Moreover, the binary oppositions employed by the straight press limited the debate's framing: those rare advocates, for instance, who tried to reject the lesbian mother oxymoron could do so only through a strategy of negation. Such a strategy in this case would have contested the lesbian-as-recruiter characterization, for example, but doing so would have meant, at least temporarily, granting provisional credence to the claim that lesbians are recruiters in the first place. In essence, the strategy of negation cedes the terms of the debate rather than restructuring the debate itself.

Constitution, negotiation, and regulation of the lesbian mother oxymoron within the lesbian press manifested itself a bit differently. Lesbians were not placed outside the domain of the family, since many lesbian advocates at least acknowledged the material existence and participation of lesbians within the domain of American family life. The lesbian press structured and maintained the rhetorical ambivalence through its binary characterizations of lesbian mothers either as feminist revolutionaries or as traitors to the lesbian nation—especially if the traitors were mothers of sons.

Neither the straight press nor the lesbian press presented entirely monolithic characterizations of lesbian maternal identity. While the straight press denied, minimized, or ignored lesbians, it also patrolled the borders of legitimate maternal practice by characterizing lesbians as alien both to the family and to motherhood. The lesbian and/or feminist press did not necessarily doubt that lesbians could also mother, but the boundaries of lesbian identity were often characterized as impermeable to maternal agency.

The rhetorical ambivalence is the symbolic ground on which lesbian maternal identity can be constituted and negotiated. It also has a regulatory function: once "lesbian" and "mother" have been constituted through the residues of American journalistic discourse as concepts inherently at odds with each other, the material history of the terms themselves influences and constrains any present or future negotiation. Competing ideologies of family, sexuality, and gender within each journalistic community provided fertile ground for discussions of how "lesbian" and "mother" could coexist within an individual body. Taken together, voices of the straight and lesbian journalistic spheres reinforced the lesbian mother oxymoron as a particular effect-structure of rhetoric, one that overdetermines the boundaries of legitimate motherhood as off-limits to lesbians.

The rhetorical regulation of lesbian maternal identity in American journalistic discourse, then, has occurred within two major debates: the debate about family and family values, and the debate over the creation of a lesbian identity not predicated on narratives of criminality or sin. These debates, of course, have taken place in discourse communities other than journalism. In addition, the communities often collude through their particular enactments of the rhetorical ambivalence to negotiate and certify the lesbian mother oxymoron. To understand better how the oxymoron is constituted and contested in other symbolic arenas, we now turn to another discourse community that exerts a significant rhetorical influence on the lives of Americans: the law.

The sexual preference of the mother in this case is known and openly admitted. . . .
Robin shares a home with her partner. . . . [W]e must conclude that the trial judge's
award of primary custody to Jim was appropriate in light of the adverse impact
on the children resulting from Robin's unconventional living arrangement.

Scott v. Scott (1995)

NEUROTIC, CRIMINAL,

AND A DANGER TO CHILDREN

We saw in the previous chapter that straight journalism marked the lesbian
mother as a threat to traditional family values even as it tried to render lesbians invisible, while lesbian/gay periodicals complicated these characterizations by depicting lesbian mothers either as revolutionary feminists or as traitors to the feminist cause. Threads from each argumentative strand become
manifest in judicial opinions concerning lesbian maternal identity. In this
chapter I explore how lesbian maternal identities are constructed, negotiated,
and regulated in the legal rhetoric of child custody cases. I argue that narratives of the lesbian-as-criminal, lesbian-as-neurotic, and lesbian-as-
proselytic formalize the lesbian mother oxymoron, thereby subverting the
potential legitimacy of lesbian maternal agency. It is precisely at the site of the
law, as a specific ideological state apparatus, that a formal oxymoronic mean-

ing is structured. The meaning of "mother" is not negotiated by itself; the court assumes a commonsense meaning for motherhood that excludes lesbians, at least within the context of custody disputes between heterosexual fathers and lesbian mothers.

Family law structures and limits intimate social relations among members of American society. Zillah Eisenstein argues that the law "is a collection of symbols and signs that structure and effect choices, options, consequences."[1] The discussion in this chapter illustrates the material rhetorical consequences of legal representations of lesbian mothers. Judicial rejection of single-parent lesbian households in divorce cases typifies the rhetorical ambivalence, although judicial acceptance of dual-mother lesbian households in second-parent adoption cases ameliorates such renunciation. Two strands of argument demarcate the ambivalence: one strand reifies the oxymoron by accepting and employing criminal, neurotic, and proselytic narratives of lesbian identity, while the other creates a rhetorical space for the legitimacy of dual-mother lesbian households. The ambivalence in judicial discourse differs significantly from the ambivalence in journalistic rhetoric. I found that the straight press sometimes ignored the existence of lesbians, and many lesbians who were not mothers doubted the veracity of mothers' claims to dual citizenship in lesbian and mother communities. How legal advocates constitute, represent, and regulate lesbian maternal identity has a material effect on women's agency as mothers, for it is within the state's power to affirm or deny a woman's claims for custody and visitation.

The Legal Frame of Acceptance: The "Best Interest" Standard

In *Attitudes toward History*, Kenneth Burke writes that "philosophers, poets, and scientists act in the code of names by which they simplify or interpret reality. These names shape our relations . . . [and] prepare us *for* some functions and *against* others, *for* or *against* the persons representing these functions." A "frame of acceptance" refers to the rhetorical process by which we interpret, construct, and name our various social realities—or "the more or less organized system of meanings" through which people understand their contingent historical placement and to which people will respond.[2] In contemporary family law, custody decisions are framed within a discourse of "interests," whereby the judge balances the interests of the children against those of the parties petitioning for custody.

Since the inception of no-fault divorce statutes in the early 1970s, child custody disputes have been adjudicated under the "best interests of the child(ren)" standard.[3] The legal rules that define these "interests" vary from state to state, though the Uniform Marriage and Divorce Act provides general guidelines for states to follow in the construction of statutes governing child custody adjudication. Such variance notwithstanding, most states have identified factors that courts must consider in child custody determinations. The Michigan legislature, for example, identified eleven factors, including valuation of "love, affection, and other emotional ties existing between the parties involved and the child," the ability of "the parties involved" to "provide the child with food, clothing, medical care," the "moral fitness" of the disputants, and "any other factor considered by the court to be relevant" to the custody dispute.[4] The actual practice of determining the best interests can be relatively complex, since the courts must weigh the facts of the case and then apply statutory and case law to them. In each case, the court must interpret the "best interests" statute.

Generally, best interest statutes "control the outcome of all child custody disputes," and are thus the gold standard of adjudication in statutory and case law.[5] The best interest standard, however, is not always the sole standard, especially in post-divorce modification petitions. In such situations some judges employ the "established custodial environment" rule as an additional standard.[6] This presumption holds that custody modifications should not disrupt the continuity and stability of the environment in which the child usually resides. As a rule, changes in custody arrangements can be granted at the appellate level only where there is "clear and convincing evidence" that custody modification would meet the best interest standard. It may appear that courts do not attend to such lofty issues as lesbian identity formation in their pragmatic attempts to determine custody awards. As I show in the next section, however, the regulation and occasional punishment of lesbian identity is a central factor in the way judges negotiate custodial arrangements.

State trial and appellate courts rely on existing case and statute law to guide their decision making in child custody disputes. I draw on a series of seventy-two cases of child custody disputes between a heterosexual father and a lesbian mother to illustrate judicial ambivalence. The cases represent fairly detailed opinions concerning the legitimacy of lesbian motherhood as well as divergent interpretations of statutory and case law. The cases also represent a temporal and geographic distribution of decisions made between 1970 and early 2000. Legal contestation of identity is a rather disorderly affair, negotiated at various court levels. While one could argue that such decisions are important only at the appellate level, I am concerned primarily with the *rhetoric* of the decisions rather than the specific legal outcomes (though of course those count, too). I examine judicial opinions rendered at both the trial and appellate levels because the rhetorical contestation of lesbian maternal identity occurs at both levels.

Negotiating Lesbian Identity

Courts negotiate lesbian maternal identity by punishing and trying to inhibit the enactment of lesbian sexuality. The courts fetishize sex by reducing lesbian identity to a discrete set of perverse sexual practices. As in the broader journalistic discussions of homosexuality, three primary characterizations of lesbian identity emerge in legal discourse: lesbians as criminal, lesbians as neurotic or psychopathological, and lesbians as proselytizers. When such depictions dominate a particular case, judges advance a stigma argument to hold that a parent who is sick or criminal should not secure custody of her child. Courts consider a mother's lesbianism relevant to custodial and visitation arrangements to the extent that sexual orientation is construed to have material effects on one's children. Courts typically employ one of two methods for assessing such "effects." The per se approach assumes that a mother's lesbian identity will in some a priori fashion harm the child(ren). The nexus approach requires the presentation of evidence to support a claim of possible harm. The primary difference between the two approaches, then, is a matter of evidentiary standards.

In the cases I surveyed, several justices relied on the nexus approach to render their decisions. The court in *S.N.E.* held, for instance, that "consideration of a parent's conduct is appropriate only when the evidence supports a finding that a parent's conduct has or reasonably will have an adverse impact on the child and his best interests."[7] The *Kallas* decision found "manifestation of one's sexuality and resulting behavior patterns are relevant to custody and to the nature and scope of visitation rights." At issue, then, was "whether or not homosexuality of a parent renders such parent unfit *per se* to have custody of his or her children."[8] The *D.H.* decision held that "homosexual conduct" constituted "relevant" and "admissible" evidence in custody disputes, but "whether such evidence is controlling in a custody determination" remained unspecified.[9]

Hegemonic appeals to "traditional families" and to dominant social mores undergird characterizations of lesbians as sick, criminal, or some combination thereof. Justice Tamilia of the Superior Court of Pennsylvania argued that "the essence of marriage is the coming together of a man and woman for the purpose of procreation. . . . [I]f the traditional family relationship (lifestyle) was banned, human society would disappear in little more than one generation. . . . [T]he concept of family is essential to society, homosexual relationships are not."[10] Where custody disputes arise between one heterosexual parent and a homosexual parent, "*the presumption of regularity applies to the traditional relationship* and the burden of proving no adverse effect of the homosexual relationship falls on the person advocating it."[11]

Appeals to public morality or normative heterosexuality also populated the child custody discourse. Justice Tamilia argued that "the national bias, which cannot be ignored," functioned as an important factor in the dispute. The social acceptability of lesbianism became a crucial dispositive factor in many child custody disputes. Witnesses such as the psychologist Tom Biller testified that "homosexuality . . . is not a socially acceptable practice" and "would be damaging to a child" owing to the "peer pressure" the child would encounter.[12] A Missouri judge based his decision to deny custody on a desire to "protect" the children from "peer pressure," from "teasing," and from "other possible ostracizing" they might experience because of their mother's "alternative life style."[13] Another Missouri judge held in *L. v. D.* that "homosexual practices have been condemned since the beginning of recorded history," and can thus be a legitimate factor in determining custody.[14] A New Jersey lesbian mother allowed to retain custody of her two children was subjected to the following dissenting opinion: "The stability of a family is most important. Children should not be victims of an avant-garde tolerance that does not represent the thinking of the vast majority of society."[15]

These representations rely on problematic bandwagon appeals. The per se approach is predicated on the erroneous assumption that lesbianism is "in fact" bad and harmful to society. The Missouri judge in *L. v. D.*, appealing to a version of majority opinion, may have been more or less accurate in characterizing heteronormative societal sentiment about lesbianism. One must ponder, however, the legitimacy of such characterizations. Appeals to "majority opinion," when employed by these justices, tended to override any evidence presented in favor of specific mothers in specific cases. One must therefore be wary of bandwagon appeals in custodial rhetoric, for they create the grounds on which the judges can then employ one or more of the three "lesbians are bad" characterizations.

Lesbians as Neurotic/Immoral

Most state best interest standards do not mention parental sexual orientation as a factor for adjudication. Many states, however, find a parent's "moral fitness" relevant. Characterizations of lesbian identity as a neurosis sabotage lesbian maternal agency by collapsing mental health with the "moral fitness" criterion in various best interest statutes.[16] Justice Tamilia characterized the mother's "lesbian relationship" as indicative of her "moral deficiency."[17] Other judges depicted lesbian households as "unhealthy" or "unwholesome environments" that would expose the children to a "questionable" or "immoral influence."[18]

In such cases the court collapses identity and morality to occupy the same conceptual terrain. This rhetorical move places lesbian mothers in the defensive rhetorical position of having to refute the notion that they are inherently immoral or lack moral fitness. More important, it places on mothers' advocates the burden of having to refute the notion that lesbian identity itself is a moral matter, whereas the mothers' heterosexual counterparts are found to lack "moral fitness" only if evidence proves that their participation in indiscreet sexual behavior has had a demonstrably adverse effect on the child's welfare. So, for example, the Missouri Court of Appeals in *G.A. v. D.A.*, stating that "a court cannot ignore the effect which the sexual conduct of a parent may have on a child's moral development," held that a lesbian household *necessarily* constituted an unhealthy environment for children.[19] Evidentiary standards thus differ for heterosexual and homosexual parents: homosexuality per se is indicative of immorality, while heterosexuality is morally suspect only if practiced unwisely. The inculcation of disparate evidentiary standards is not easily rectified, though some legal activists may contest the discriminatory conditions.

At least one case from the 1990s exemplifies the contestation of lesbianism as a moral matter. In a 1996 case, *Maradie v. Maradie*, a Florida trial court took judicial notice that a "'homosexual environment' could 'adversely effect [*sic*] a child.'"[20] The concept of judicial notice is significant here for understanding the larger rhetorical context in which morality-related identity claims work against the collective interests of gay parents. Under Florida evidentiary rules, courts may take judicial notice in a narrow range of matters without benefit of expert evidence or testimony to reach conclusions. The *Maradie* court reviewed the circumstances under which judicial notice could occur. Such circumstances included the introduction of "facts that are not subject to dispute because they are generally known within the territorial jurisdiction of the court" and "facts that are not subject to dispute because they are capable of accurate and ready determination by resort to sources whose accuracy cannot be questioned."[21] Valerie Maradie's lesbianism constituted sufficient grounds on which the court could deploy the rules of judicial notice to deny custodial and visitation rights. The trial court used the per se approach by reference to judicial notice: that is, it took evidence of adverse impact for granted. Although the appellate court ultimately rejected this ploy, it should not escape our notice that the tactic has potent appeal. The claim that lesbian-headed households are "bad" curries favor in many quarters, from the anti-gay Family Research Council to various halls of justice themselves. Courts may capitalize on anti-lesbian sentiment in order to micromanage the family lives of countless lesbian citizens.

Lesbians as Criminal

In addition to facing sanctions based on perceptions of lesbian identity as a neurosis and/or moral failure, lesbians also face judicial wrath for their "inherently" criminal propensities. Judges in the cases surveyed consistently represented lesbians in criminal terms: mothers "admitted" lesbian status by engaging in "illicit" homosexual relationships. "Admission" implies action-oriented guilt rather than a mere statement of fact; one's moral and legal "fitness" as a parent becomes tied to perceived sexual practices. As the *Kallas* court held, lesbian status is "directly relevant to the issue of the nature of visitation rights which should be accorded."[22] Judge Cooper of the Arkansas Court of Appeals held in *Thigpen v. Carpenter* that the public had "declared" any lesbian "conduct" to be "so adverse to public morals and policy as to warrant criminal sanctions."[23]

Judicial references to sodomy laws punish lesbians for any "performance" of their lesbian identity. Once a woman acknowledged her lesbianism, anti-lesbian advocates reduced her identity to a set of "practices" or "conduct" that made her an unfit parent. A memorandum decision handed down by the Appellate Division of the New York State Supreme Court criticized a lower court's failure to find Maureen DiStefano "unfit as a parent" though she was "an admitted practicing homosexual" and though "deviate sexual intercourse remain[ed] a crime" in New York. The published opinion contained no record of any criminal indictments (for sodomy or deviate sexual intercourse) against DiStefano, yet it assumed that her relationship with Nancy Wilson was *necessarily* sodomitical.[24]

Lesbians as Proselytic

The presumption of a necessary relationship between lesbian identity and criminal behavior patterns also surfaced with judicial conflation of lesbianism and pedophilia. As my discussion of journalistic rhetoric illustrated, many anti-lesbian advocates capitalize on anti-gay bias by characterizing lesbians as proselytizers whose primary interest resides in "recruiting" children into the corrupt ranks of lesbianism/homosexuality. One Pennsylvania court, for instance, expressed fear that a lesbian would "proselytize [her] children" should she reveal her lesbian identity to them.[25]

In the context of disclosing one's lesbian sexual orientation to one's progeny, the judicial community reworks the communicative rules of self-disclosure to assume that the parent's mere *mention* of identity will be enough to make the children "become" gay. Judges and ex-husbands thus sometimes admonish the mother to remain closeted "for the sake of the children." Some may assume that I necessarily advocate the disclosure of one's sexual practices to one's children ("Who would want to talk to their children about what they do in the privacy of their own bedroom?"). The self-disclosure of which I write is not the same thing, however, and must be understood within the larger context whereby a heterosexual parent's self-disclosure of orientation would never be taken as an attempt to "proselytize the children." It would be an innocent factual statement. Judicial and popular fears reflect the fact that the mere mention of lesbian *identity* (again, I do not envision parent and child talking about specific sexual/erotic practices) is interpreted as an attempt to recruit.

The faulty assumptions of a direct relationship between disclosure and "recruitment" bear a striking resemblance to conservative arguments against sex education and attempts to include information about gay/lesbian history and culture in high school and college curricula. Detractors portray such efforts as "promotion" rather than "education." The *root* problem is that such portrayals do not foster productive dialogue but instead are designed to silence a significant number of individuals ("If we don't mention the fact that gay people exist, maybe their numbers will diminish!"). Even if silence *could* effectively negate the "problem" of homosexuality, judges would find (and, indeed, have found) ways to disallow lesbian mothers legitimacy. (Even the mere *presence* of a lesbian—who remains silent—is seen as proselytical, as when mothers' partners are banned from being present during visitation.)

In a 1976 New York case, a lesbian mother testified that "she never discussed homosexuality" with her daughter, nor did she demonstrate in her presence "any emotion or affection" toward her lover, "Lucy Q." A psychiatrist testifying in the case claimed that although the mother had not revealed her identity to the child, "being close to the mother, the child could emulate her conduct and . . . the present living environment would be harmful to the child."[26] Such fear of emulation was evident in a Kentucky case four years later, when a court-appointed psychologist testified that "it is reasonable to suggest that Shannon [the daughter] may have difficulty in achieving a fulfilling heterosexual identity of her own in the future."[27]

Judicial fears of potential recruitment surfaced in yet another context, when courts disallowed or limited mothers' freedom to enter into or maintain romantic relationships. Lesbian mothers in a significant relationship at trial lost custody or were prevented from having their romantic partners present during visitation. The Supreme Court of Virginia went so far as to admonish one woman, "should it become necessary, for her son's sake," to "sever the relationship with the woman with whom she now lives. There may come a time when the welfare and best interest of her son require that she honor this commitment."[28] She hence had to choose between two ostensibly contradictory identities: she could identify as lesbian and remain in her relationship, or she could deny her lesbian identity in the interests of being a good mother. One Oregon trial judge granted a father's petition for custodial modification, and limited the mother's visitation *"to such times and places that Petitioner [mother] does not have with her, in her home, or around the children any lesbians."*[29] Other courts forced the mother's lesbian partner to vacate their joint residence as a condition for custody and/or visitation awards.[30] The Superior Court of Pennsylvania's review of *In re Breisch* in 1980 noted that the trial court had ordered the mother to "cease living with Nancy Maruschak but made clear that the court was not otherwise interfering with their relationship." When the mother refused to stop cohabiting with her partner, the court removed the child from her home and placed him with a county office of child and youth services.[31]

Many of us would not wish to entertain the haunting possibility of a court dictating the circumstances under which we can legitimately conduct significant relationships. Students in my Contemporary Rhetoric of the "American Family" class have great faith that American culture embraces and enacts a "live and let live" attitude toward family relationships. Many students hate to think that a court of law or a legislature could dictate the grounds on which they could cultivate and maintain romantic partnerships. When I mention cases like *Scott, Breisch,* and *Jacobson,* and when I mention that cohabiting heterosexuals with children are also sometimes punished, I am met with looks of shock and incredulity. I capitalize on their doubt to pose the question now central to my concerns: What is a state's legitimate interest in determining, dictating, or formulating the grounds on which "families" can be formed and maintained, free of state intervention?

The state does not hesitate to intervene in lesbian family relationships when it forbids the mother's partner to be present during visitation.[32] Once a lesbian performs her identity by desiring or maintaining a romantic relationship, the court punishes her by regulating or forbidding the performance. Such judicial opinions raise the issue of performance as *constitutive* of sexual orientation. It is one thing, such reasoning holds, to simply name oneself as "lesbian"; it is quite another to actually *do* anything or to embark on any form of human interaction in the interest of *living* one's identity. "Living with another person of the same sex in a sexual relationship is not something" beyond one's control, the North Dakota Supreme Court claimed in *Jacobson v. Jacobson*. Sandra Jacobson's respectability as a mother was contingent on her willingness, as a "concerned" parent, to make "sacrifices of varying degrees" for her two children.[33] What we thus find is the legal equivalent of the Christian dogma to "love the sinner, hate the sin." The regulative effects on lesbian identity are severe: lesbians cannot speak of their identities, nor are they to enact their criminal, sinful, and substantially immoral desires. Though the courts may acknowledge the existence of lesbians, judges nonetheless seek to eradicate lesbians' inhabitation of contemporary family life. The message of judicial rhetoric is thus: "It may be tolerable for you to be lesbian *and* to have custody/visitation rights, but those rights will be contingent on (a) silencing yourself and/or (b) dumping your lover. Again, the question must be posed: What ideological interest does the state have in reifying criminal characterizations of lesbian identity?

Stigma and Custody Denials

The conflation of lesbian identity and immorality surfaces in legal rhetoric when judges entertain the possibility that a mother's lesbianism will traumatize the child. Sometimes the state will claim an interest in protecting minors from the terrible "stigma" attached to lesbianism. In the cases I examined, such claims often made passing reference to scholarly research, especially in the domain of psychology and the expert testimony of psychological professionals. Judges invoked stigma claims to protect children from the supposed disgrace of growing up in a lesbian household. Characterizations of lesbian identity as "unnatural" and "deviant" provided, in their eyes, an unquestionable presumption that a mother's lesbianism stigmatized her children. Several judges accepted stigma arguments to deny lesbians custody or visitation. The *Jacobson* court represented Sandra Jacobson's "sexual preference" as the "burning issue" in her custody modification appeal. Leading Justice Vande Wall ruled that "living in the same house" with a lesbian couple "may well cause the children to 'suffer from the slings and arrows' of a disapproving society."[34]

Judge Kennedy's comments in the 1980 Missouri case of *N.K.M. v. L.E.M.* are instructive for understanding the scope of stigma-related claims. The appellate summary of the trial court opinion included a narrative regarding the mother's relationship to "Betty," a co-worker and ostensible romantic partner. The original divorce decree granted Kathy, the mother, custody of her ten-year old daughter Julie, but made the award contingent upon Kathy's "immediately discontinuing any relationship whatsoever" with Betty; Betty was also excluded from Julie's presence.[35] The appellate judge's opinion regarding stigma is worth quoting at length: "There emerges from the evidence a picture of Betty as a powerful dominant personality. She had befriended Julie and had won her affection and loyalty. She had broached the idea of homosexuality to the child. Allowing that homosexuality is a permissible life style—an 'alternate life style,' as it is termed these days—is voluntarily chosen, yet who would place a child in a milieu where she may be inclined toward it? She may thereby be condemned, in one degree or another, to sexual disorientation, to social ostracism, contempt and unhappiness."[36] The judge's narrative portrays the mother's alleged girlfriend (and, by implication, the mother) as potential pedophiles. In the popular imagination, pedophiles win the trust, admiration, or friendship of their victims before any untoward behavior occurs—in this case, simply by referring to homosexuality. At trial, a co-worker testified that Betty had asked Julie "if she would still feel the same even if there were allegations that she was the kind of person who would be harmful to be with, not good for her and she said she went about it in a roundabout way, trying to tell Julie that there were allegations about her being a homosexual and Julie said, according to Betty, that, 'I would still love you even if you were.'"[37]

It would be easy to dismiss this narrative as the worst kind of sophistry, whereby an advocate capitalizes on a community's "common sense" to make specific claims of probability. Indeed, on the surface, judges exploit existing constructions of lesbian identity to make claims about the probable or possible effects of a mother's lesbianism on her children. Obviously, however, there is a wide gap between the realm of the probable and the domain of certainty. The deliberative rhetoric enacted by judges in custody cases faces a generic constraint, for it is extremely difficult to make any *certain* claims in the context of a *single* case regarding specific effects. The best the judge can do is listen to witnesses, read any briefs filed on behalf of the interested parties, review relevant statutes and sources of common law, and try to render a prudent and just decision that serves the children's best interests. More crucial questions emerge, however: What circumstances make it possible for *speculation* regarding stigma to function as a *necessary conclusion?* In other words, when are probability and certainty conflated rhetorically? What standards of evidence are required to hold that the merest possibility of stigma is enough to deny a mother's claims to custody and visitation?

Although many judges exploited homonegative beliefs regarding "recruitment" and "stigma," other courts ruled that lesbian families had no negative effect on children. Indeed, at least one justice ruled that lesbian-headed families were model households. In 1987 the *Stroman* court determined that the mother had raised a "properly adjusted and healthy" daughter who was "heterosexual, intelligent, and well-mannered after having lived with the mother and the other woman for a five-year period."[38] In a 1983 case a Massachusetts appellate court found no evidence to support the "adverse effect" hypothesis and rejected explicitly any stigma argument: "The trial judge specifically found, and we think this an important fact, that David [son] 'has not been tormented by his friends in regard to his mother's lifestyle.'"[39] In these and other cases stigma claims failed for one of two reasons: expert psychiatric testimony or lack of convincing evidence.

In sum, I found that criminal, neurotic, and proselytic characterizations of lesbian identity subverted lesbians' claims to any legitimate maternal identity. In these cases, however, the courts faced the fact that the female parent standing before them embodied lesbian *and* maternal identities. Judges thus could not presumptively dismiss lesbian mothers as fictive subjects as journalists often did. Instead, the courts circumscribed lesbian agency. Judges construed lesbianism as an unnatural condition from which children must be protected. Obsessive concern for the material effect of lesbian relationships on the children's health was predicated on heteronormative logic that cast lesbianism as a moral threat to families. Courts bracketed discussions of the potential ontological status of lesbianism to focus on its *effect* on children.

Whereas the *Stroman* court entertained the possibility that a lesbian mother could run a model household and raise healthy children, the possibility that a child of a lesbian mother would also "become" homosexual terrified most judges. Such fears diverted attention from discussions of the child's best interests, even when the prurient discussion of lesbianism's effect on children was couched within judicial claims that *only* those interests mattered.

Lesbian Maternal Identity in Planned Lesbian Families

If judges have difficulty managing child custody disputes between divorcing heterosexual couples, imagine their distress when faced with a custody contest between lesbian couples who had planned a family and raised children as "co-parents." Throughout the legal system in general, exclusive definitions of family status prevail whereby a "family" is composed of one female parent, one male parent, and one or more children. The legal system grants minimal legitimacy to heterosexual family structures that contain more than one same-sex parent, as in the case of stepfamilies. The system has been even more remiss in granting widespread legitimacy to families headed by two parents of the same sex residing in one household.

The dissolution of lesbian relationships is no less painful, but tremendously more complex, than the dissolution of heterosexual relationships, at least from a legal standpoint. Lesbian couples are not permitted the option of legal marriage (except in Vermont, which allows "civil unions" for gay and lesbian couples). Absent that right, courts typically deny non-biological mothers' custody and visitation requests on the basis that such women have no legal standing to press the claims. Lesbian families face numerous legal obstacles in disputes over custodial and visitation privileges. In addition, the non-biological lesbian mother who "divorces" her female partner faces a specific rhetorical problem in that the birth mother rejects her partner's custody and/or visitation claims on the basis that the partner has no biological connection to the child. As I will discuss later, the biological mothers' claims may serve expedient individual needs, but only at tremendous cost to the numerous lesbian co-parents who have performed the laborious duties of mothering. Such a result undermines attempts by both legal scholars and gay/lesbian rights advocates to expand American notions of family and parenthood.

Not all is lost for the non-biological lesbian mother, however. Just when it appears that the non-biological mother will always be at a legal and rhetorical disadvantage for custody and visitation claims, a different type of legal case emerges: the second-parent adoption. Developed originally for heterosexual stepparents, second-parent adoptions acknowledge the valuable role that non-biological parents play in contemporary family constellations. Like the planned lesbian family, second-parent adoptions by lesbian partners are relatively recent in the domain of family case law. In this section I examine the rhetorical negotiation of lesbian motherhood in cases where lesbian couples engage in a custody dispute after their relationship dissolves. I also analyze the contestation of maternal identity in cases where a non-biological mother petitions to adopt her partner's biological child. The need to develop a rhetoric of motherhood that recognizes and values lesbian families has been called for by both legal scholars and members of the lesbian community. Law professor Nancy Polikoff, for example, argues that "a new definition of parenthood is necessary to adapt to the complexities of modern families," and that judges need to "tailor legal rules that reflect the reality" of planned lesbian families.[40] Paula Ettelbrick urges other legal scholars and practitioners "to propose solutions and guidelines to the courts that reflect [lesbians'] experiences, rather than trying to fit ourselves into the already confusing matrix of heterosexual family rights."[41]

In general terms, legal scholars posit that a clear and definitive "nexus" must exist between a mother's lesbian identity and the potential adverse effect of such identity on her children. That is, the nexus approach requires proof of a link between a mother's lesbian identity and any harm to the child before her claims for custody and visitation can be rejected. The approach exemplifies the type of legal strategy that may be used to preempt or discredit stigma claims. Philip Kraft, for instance, notes that courts typically exhibit three concerns regarding the nexus requirement: (1) Will granting the lesbian mother custody be tantamount to sanctioning child molestation? (2) If the mother is lesbian, will her child(ren) also become homosexual? and (3) If the lesbian mother has custody, will her children suffer stigma and harassment?[42]

In their groundbreaking 1976 exploration of the legal status of lesbian mothers, Nan Hunter and Nancy Polikoff argue that American judicial resistance to granting lesbians custody or visitation claims is founded on the erroneous assumption that a mother's lesbianism *causes* harm insofar as judges assume that "lesbianism is equivalent to, or tantamount to, unfitness."[43] The focus on a mother's sexual orientation, they argue, diverts attention from the central issue: determining the child's best interests. "Absent a showing of relevance to the particular case," Hunter and Polikoff claim, a mother's lesbianism has little if anything to do with her children's welfare. Nevertheless, Steve Susoeff observes, "the courts overwhelmingly accept the assertion that a child will suffer harm in the custody of a gay or lesbian parent, without requiring any proof of such harm."[44] Judicial temptation to base decisions on erroneous assumptions and negative stereotypes of gay/lesbian parents, he claims, could be offset by adopting a due process standard whereby courts "would be obliged to articulate specifically what clear and convincing evidence showed detriment to the child."[45]

Noting that the U.S. Supreme Court's 1984 ruling in *Palmore v. Sidoti* held that "denying custody because the child might feel stigmatized by societal prejudice is constitutionally impermissible,"[46] David Dooley also argues that the custody claims of gay/lesbian parents might be more successful if such claims were subjected to a due process analysis. Under such a system, courts would be required to follow the *Palmore* ruling and could no longer rely on stigma arguments to deny custody. Although legal scholars such as Susoeff, Dooley, Kraft, Hunter, and Polikoff agree that the American legal system grants little if any legitimacy to planned lesbian families, they differ as to the most effective approaches to legitimating lesbian maternal identity.

Functional Approaches to Redefining Motherhood

A functional approach to motherhood views mothering as a set of discrete and identifiable practices. Several legal scholars favor this approach as it pertains to the efforts of lesbians to secure their parenting rights and obligations. This focus on maternal *practice* or *performance* differs significantly from how lesbian identity is usually constituted in performative terms. Judges typically construe lesbianism as little more than the enactment of perverse desires. This perversity, so the logic goes, necessarily prevents lesbians from being good mothers. But motherhood is sometimes depicted as an inherently biological identity, whereby women mother by "instinct." It is this focus on maternal identity as a biological given that pro-lesbian advocates must contest and negotiate in their attempts to secure legal recognition for planned lesbian families.

Nancy Polikoff defines a parent as "anyone who maintains a functional parent relationship with a child when a legally recognized parent created that relationship with the intent that the relationship be parental in nature."[47] She stresses that courts must balance parental autonomy with the best interests of the children. Judges, she claims, should recognize that children in lesbian families have an interest in maintaining relationships with both their biological and non-biological mothers, and the state has a legitimate interest in preserving those ties. Recognizing the interests and rights of the non-biological mother is a simple necessity. "In the context of a lesbian-mother family dissolution," Polikoff notes, "the child will continue to live with a lesbian regardless of who has custody, and regardless of whether the legally unrecognized mother has visitation rights." Therefore, the "only issue in these cases is whether the court will recognize that the child has two lesbian mothers."[48]

William Rubenstein echoes Polikoff's concerns, and emphasizes the tenuous legal status of non-biological lesbian mothers. He advocates statutory redefinition of "parent" and "family" as such terms apply to lesbian mother custody cases, second-parent adoptions, and other "nontraditional" family structures. Recognizing the rights and interests of the non-biological parent, he argues, does not *necessarily* entail the rejection of the biological parent's rights and obligations: in other words, putting together a family is not a zero-sum game. Such statutory redefinition, I think, is a key step toward securing lesbian parental rights and duties, especially since courts must follow legislative definitions (in addition to common law) in their adjudication of cases. As Paula Ettelbrick contends, "The world would not come to an end if two parents of the same sex are recognized as having a parental relationship with a child."[49] Ettelbrick proposes a four-part test granting lesbian mothers legal status as parents: "(1) Is the woman seeking legal recognition as a parent the partner of the biological/adoptive mother? (2) Was she involved in the initial decision to conceive or adopt the child? (3) Was it the agreement of both women that they be co-equal parents to the child? (4) Has the woman seeking recognition abided by this agreement by living with the child and actually provided care to the child on a daily basis?"[50] This four-part test could be applied to both second-parent adoption cases and custody disputes between dissolving lesbian couples.

Legal scholars thus agree that "parent" should be redefined. As Polikoff asserts, "Neither biology nor legal adoption is sufficient to establish who is a parent in a complex world affected by cultural norms, technology, and patterns of sexual behavior."[51] A functional approach transcends blood connections between mother and child to recognize particular *practices* that might constitute motherhood. Such an approach to redefining motherhood is useful, and Ettelbrick's approach is particularly valuable. Legal scholars, however, tend to neglect the rhetorical and ideological constitutive elements of parenthood that place lesbians and gay men at a distinct disadvantage for gaining legal standing as legitimate parents. The efficacy of the functional approach is therefore limited by the epistemological framework within which the legal scholar operates. In what follows I attempt to overcome the rhetorical limitations of current functional definitions of parenthood by identifying, through case analysis, the rhetorical ingredients of a lesbian-affirmative discourse of motherhood that draws on existing theories of parenthood even as it tries to subvert the heteronormativity of such theories. This affirmative discourse will be treated in detail in the final chapter. To understand the rhetorical circumstances under which lesbian families negotiate the legal system's murky terrain, a brief review of reproductive technology is necessary.

Reproductive Technology and the Rhetoric of Motherhood

The alternative reproduction technology known as artificial insemination has been practiced in the United States at least since 1884.[52] Appropriating a technology developed originally for breeding farm animals, medical professionals seized an opportunity to provide legitimate offspring to women married to infertile men. Under conditions of strict confidentiality, and perhaps anonymity, a donor provided the necessary sperm to a doctor. The doctor then performed a simple insemination procedure (using a turkey baster!). Successful inseminations, of course, resulted in pregnancies and births. The infertile husband could present the child to the community as his own, an acknowledgment that was critical as medical professionals struggled to legitimate the practice. As Gena Corea points out, fears about the "legitimacy" of the practice derived from a complex set of social values predicated on patriarchal notions of parenthood and family: "A woman can never legitimate her own child because 'legitimacy' is a concept invented by men for men. . . . This is the key question AID [artificial insemination by donor] posed to the patriarchy, the one to which courts devoted their attention: Is an AID child a 'legitimate' child? Even when delivered by a man's wife, the child does not spring from the man's own loins. If an AID child is 'illegitimate,' has the mother committed adultery in conceiving it?"[53]

Professional medicine's fears relative to the social, legal, and moral implications of artificial insemination resulted in the decision to deny unmarried women access to the technology.[54] Doctors were particularly reluctant to provide donor semen to lesbians, but such reluctance has not prevented single lesbians or lesbian couples from seeking, obtaining, and using the technology in order to start their own families.[55] The practice of artificial insemination, of course, carries entirely different implications for the lesbian population, for it means that lesbians can become pregnant without engaging in heterosexual intercourse. The opportunity to become pregnant, bear a child, and raise a family free from any significant male involvement (except, of course, for the necessary sperm) creates the functional grounds on which lesbians might craft a novel maternal identity as well as create a family.

Lesbian family constellations are as complex and varied as the individual lesbians who create them. One lesbian might decide to raise children without the presence of a romantic partner. Another lesbian couple might decide to raise a family through donor insemination. Yet other lesbians might decide to raise their families in a communal atmosphere. How the legal system responds to such constellations depends, of course, on its views of whether the particular family form serves the children's best interests. Here I explore the rhetoric of motherhood as exemplified in seven custody disputes between dissolving lesbian couples. In each case the lesbian couple entered a romantic relationship and decided at some point to have and to raise children. In each case, one partner gave birth to one or more children conceived through donor insemination. At some point the lesbian couples' romantic partnerships dissolved. In each case, the non-biological mother petitioned a court for custody and visitation privileges. In all but one case the courts rejected such petitions.[56]

The court faces one central issue: Does the biological mother's partner qualify as a "parent" under relevant statutory and case law? In each case the court answered "no." This case rhetoric regulates lesbian maternal identity by constructing parenthood as a legal consequence *only* of state-sanctioned marriage and *only* of biology. The decisions thus characterize motherhood *primarily* as a biological function: if a particular woman lacked a biological relationship to a child, then she could not qualify as its "mother" or, more broadly, its "parent." As I mentioned previously, lesbian couples in the United States are not allowed the legal right of marriage. Planned lesbian families are denied legal status both as they attempt to form and as they dissolve. Courts are thus faced with a mismatch between existing law and a heretofore unrecognized family form.

The inability of lesbian couples to form state-sanctioned family relationships is one reason for the difficulty faced by the non-birth mother in planned lesbian families on dissolution of the relationship. In a 1995 case the Wisconsin Supreme Court noted that the petitioning mother "knew that Wisconsin did not recognize same sex marriages. Thus, she could not have had a reasonable expectation that she would eventually acquire legal parental status in this state."[57] In a similar case, the New Mexico Court of Appeals affirmed a district court's findings that "no valid legal marriage existed between the parties, there was no adoption of the child by the Petitioner, and thus, Petitioner had no standing or enforceable rights."[58] The Third District Court of Appeals for California held in *Curiale v. Reagan* that its legislature "has not conferred upon one in plaintiff's position, a nonparent in a same-sex bilateral relationship, any right of custody or visitation upon the termination of the relationship."[59] Moreover, the court ruled, "jurisdiction to adjudicate custody depends upon some proceeding properly before the court in which custody is at issue such as dissolution."[60] In other words, since the parties were unmarried, Angela Curiale had no legal standing to press her custody and visitation claims.

Judges also conflate a lesbian mother's lack of a biological relationship to a child with legal "nonparent" status. An Appellate Division of the New York Supreme Court found in *Alison D. v. Virginia M.* that while Alison had "apparently developed" a "close and loving relationship" with "the child," she was nonetheless a "biological stranger" to the child and therefore not a "parent" under the meaning of the extant New York domestic relations law. Alison and her partner, Virginia, had been a couple for approximately two years when they decided to raise a child as "co-parents." Virginia conceived a child through artificial insemination and gave birth to their son in July 1981. Their partnership dissolved in 1983, but Virginia granted Alison visitation until 1987. When Alison accepted temporary employment overseas in 1987, Virginia decided to end visitation permanently.[61] Alison argued that she stood in loco parentis to the child, a legal term most jurisdictions use to describe one who functions "in the place of a parent" or "instead of a parent," or is "charged, factitiously, with a parent's rights, duties, and responsibilities."[62] The court rejected her claim, explaining that although the relevant statute "does not explicitly define the term 'parent,'" her relationship "does not come within the meaning of that term." Specifically, the court rejected the claim that a person serving in loco parentis could have legal standing as a parent. A California appellate court advanced a similar opinion relative to a lesbian partner's in loco parentis claim, holding that the doctrine was not intended for use in custody actions and therefore was inapplicable in *Nancy S. v. Michele G.*[63]

Other justices also rejected attempts to expand the legal meaning of "parent" through use of the in loco parentis doctrine. Using the term "in loco parentis" to "describe an individual with a parent-like relationship with the child for custody purposes," the Wisconsin Supreme Court conceded in the case of *Z.J.H.* that Wendy L. Sporleder had a "parent-like" relationship to her partner's adopted son.[64] Yet the court ruled that the doctrine could not apply in custody disputes.[65] "To the extent that we award custody rights to one who stands in loco parentis as Sporleder urges," the court held, "we diminish the rights of legal parents such as Hermes [Sporleder's estranged partner and the adoptive mother of their son]."[66] Judicial rejection of the in loco parentis doctrine as a means to expand the definition of "parent" is significant insofar as it entails a rejection of a functional approach to parenthood or motherhood. Lesbians are thereby denied access to existing legal doctrine to qualify as legally recognized "parents."

The exclusion of non-parents leads to another quandary for lesbian mothers. In *Curiale,* the court found that Angela Curiale, who was "neither the natural mother, stepmother, nor adoptive mother of the child," could not qualify as a legal parent.[67] The court in *Nancy S.* advanced a similar opinion, holding that since Michele G. was neither the birth nor the adoptive mother, she was therefore not a legal parent.[68] The Wisconsin Supreme Court held in the *Z.J.H.* case that "a non-parent may not bring an action to obtain custody of a minor child unless the natural or adoptive parent is unfit or unable to care for the child, or there are compelling reasons for awarding custody to a third party."[69] Absent a biological relationship to a child, a lesbian mother can have no legal expectation that she qualifies as a parent. The presumption that granting custody to the "natural" parent will serve the child's best interests thus renders the non-biological lesbian mother invisible, in a position where she might function as a "parent" but is not recognized legally as such.

Finally, legal rejection of non-biological lesbian mothers' claims for de facto or in loco parentis status reflects judicial fear that granting such status would open avenues for other "non-parents" to press custody and visitation claims. The *Z.J.H.* court, for instance, realized the "public policy consideration" implicit in its decision to deny Sporleder standing to obtain custody of her son when it held that "limiting the number of individuals with whom a child is placed" would "promote stability in that child's life." Granting Sporleder parental standing "would open the doors to multiple parties claiming custody of children by virtue of their in loco parentis status." The court thus concluded that "without limitations as we have discussed today, a child could have multiple 'parents,' and could find himself or herself subject to multiple custody and visitation arrangements."[70] When judges deny the non-birth or adoptive partner in a planned lesbian family legal status as a parent on the basis of this fear, they place such mothers on a par with baby-sitters, housekeepers, nannies, day care workers, and other individuals who may interact with the child on a day-to-day basis. This definitional rhetorical strategy denies and displaces the significance of the relationship that existed at one time between the two women; it also disregards the couple's intention, desire, and practice of raising a family as "co-parents." Indeed, such rulings reject the possibility that two women could function as mothers within a single-family unit. Day care providers and other similar categories of individuals are *not* on par with partners, because the biological mother neither has a significant "marriage-like" relationship with the day care provider, nor does she intend the day care provider to function as a parent.

Judges in some lesbian dissolution cases, however, have wished to preserve the non-biological mother's relationship with her child. Dissenting opinions typically expressed such wishes. Justice Bablitch of the Wisconsin Supreme Court began his dissent in *Z.J.H.* by observing that "everyone agrees that children of a dissolving traditional relationship deserve and need the protection of the courts. Yet the majority opinion holds that children of a dissolving non-traditional relationship are not entitled to the same protection. What logic compels that result? The legislature could not have intended such an absurd and cruel result, but that is what the majority of this court has determined."[71] The children of dissolving lesbian partnerships, Bablitch continued, "need" and "deserve" the "protection of the court."[72] His opinion was thus an attempt to recognize a legal ground on which "non-traditional" parent-child relationships could be preserved after dissolution of the parental partnership.

The rhetoric of lesbian dissolution cases posits a fundamental inflexible meaning for the term "parent." These cases demonstrate that even though a biological mother's lesbian partner might *function* as a mother within her specific family, courts will be reluctant to grant her legitimate legal status as a mother or a parent. Exclusive appeals to biology, however, are not always successful, and did not work for many of the mothers in their divorce cases involving heterosexual husbands. Which rhetorical circumstances make it possible, and perhaps even plausible, for judges to recognize biology in one type of case but not in another? Is it possible that judicial recognition of biological mothering in lesbian dissolution cases is actually a decoy? Does judicial support somehow deflect attention from the predominantly anti-lesbian attitudes that inform most custody decisions? Might the rhetorical ambivalence in lesbian dissolution cases be resolved in favor of "traditional" or biological kin–based definitions of The Family? On what grounds do the functional approaches fail? The rare dissenting opinions may signal rhetorical hope for the non-biological mother. Judicial recognition of the non-biological lesbian mother creates the grounds on which lesbian mothers, both as individuals and as members of planned lesbian families, can craft a legally recognized lesbian maternal identity.

Whereas courts typically declined to recognize the value of parenting in lesbian dissolution cases, they embraced planned lesbian families when the non-
biological mother petitioned for adoption of her partner's child, conceived
through donor insemination. A woman's lack of a biological connection to a
child became unimportant in these cases, in which the courts tried to recognize the role that the non-birth mother enacted as she and her partner raised
their children. By granting legal recognition to the term "co-parents," courts
affirmed the existence of two-parent planned lesbian families. The second-
parent adoption cases thus negotiate kinship terminology by accepting a
functional approach to parenthood.

As in most family law matters concerning children, the child's best interests serve as the measuring stick by which parental rights and duties are cal-
culated in second-parent adoptions. The first published second-parent adoption involving a planned lesbian family occurred in 1992, in the *Matter of
Adoption of Evan*. "Valerie C." and "Diane F." had been together approximately seven years when they decided to have a child through donor insemination. Their son, "Evan," was born in 1985. In January 1992 the Surrogate's
Court for New York County granted the couple's petition to recognize "their
mutual status as parents."[73] The court described the couple as "coparents,"
and noted that Evan referred to both women as "Mama."[74]

The court held in this case that it was necessary to create legal rules to
match the setting. Since Evan was "a part of a family unit that has been functioning successfully for the past six years," permitting "continuation of the
rights of both the natural and adoptive parent where compelled by the best interests of the child" was "the only rational result."[75] In the 1994 *Matter of
Adoption of Caitlin*, a New York court advanced a similar holding. "The issue
before this Court," Judge Anthony Sciolino maintained, was "whether, given
the realities of the relationship between the children and the petitioners and
between the petitioners and the biological mothers, would the children herein
be better or worse off if the adoptions were approved?"[76] Sciolino thus held
that the court had a duty to interpret the law to reflect the realities of the
case, rather than attempting to fit the family into existing legal structures.
The Kings County (New York) Family Court, in granting a lesbian mother's

pre-certification for adoption petition, noted that "courts should not be blind to modern day realities in giving definition to statutory concepts."[77]

Most adoption laws require the natural parent to terminate his or her rights upon adoption. The Surrogate Court in *Evan* rejected this requirement: "If this provision were strictly enforced it would require termination of the parental rights of Valerie upon granting the adoption to Diane. This would be an absurd outcome which would nullify the advantage sought by the proposed adoption: the creation of a legal family unit identical to the actual family setup."[78] Indeed, judges often nullified the requirement for the natural mother to terminate her parental rights and duties. Justice Johnson of the Vermont Supreme Court held in the *Adoption of B.L.V.B.* that "when the family unit is comprised of the natural mother and her partner, and the adoption is in the best interests of the children, terminating the natural mother's rights is unreasonable and unnecessary."[79] At least one lesbian mother's second-parent adoption petition, however, was rejected on the basis of the traditional termination requirement. The non-biological mother in the *Matter of Dana* case petitioned to adopt her partner's child. Under the "plain meaning" rule, the court held, her petition had to be denied since an adoption would require termination of the biological mother's legal rights and obligations.[80] The opinion criticized recent decisions that had granted second-parent adoptions to lesbian mothers, characterizing the cases as "impermissible judicial legislation" and "ultimately unpersuasive."[81]

The five jurisdictions that granted the published second-parent adoptions argued that such adoptions created legal advantages both for the children and for the lesbian mothers. The Chancery Division of the Essex County (New Jersey) Superior Court, for instance, reasoned that the adoption would "provide critical legal rights and protections for [the child's] safety as well as her physical and emotional well-being. This adoption will provide additional economic security."[82] The Vermont Supreme Court contended that to "deny the children of same-sex partners, as a class, the security of a legally recognized relationship with their second parent serves no legitimate state interest," and found, moreover, that the Vermont legislature *intended* to "protect the security of family units by defining the legal rights and responsibilities of children who find themselves in circumstances that do not include two biological parents." Finally, the court reasoned, the state had a legitimate interest in granting second-parent adoptions so that "any problems that arise later may be resolved within the recognized framework of domestic relations laws."[83]

Other jurisdictions took pains to specify the legal advantages relative to second-parent adoptions in planned lesbian families. Such advantages included inheritance rights, social security benefits, and the right to be supported by the adoptive parent. The court in *Evan* noted that such "formal recognition" would mean that Evan's connection with two involved, loving parents "will not be a relationship seen as outside the law, but one sustained by the ongoing, legal recognition of an approved, court ordered adoption."[84] In such instances courts recognized the lesbian couple as "mutual parents" or "co-parents," thus supporting lesbian couples' struggles to craft a *legal* family identity. Such recognition, in turn, depended on the flexibility of the term "parent," whereby the practice of parenthood did not become a zero-sum game.

Finally, the rhetoric of motherhood in these adoption cases often included a rejection of an idealized heterosexual traditional family. Justice Freedman of the New Jersey Superior Court for Essex County concluded his opinion in the case of *J.M.G.* by noting that "while the families of the past may have seemed simple formations repeated with uniformity (the so called 'traditional family') . . . [w]e cannot continue to pretend that there is one formula" that "should constitute a family."[85] In the case of *Caitlin*, the Monroe County (New York) Family Court held, similarly, that "most children today do not live in so-called 'traditional' 1950 television situation comedy type families," and "it is unrealistic to pretend that children can only be successfully reared in an idealized concept of family, the product of nostalgia for a time long past."[86] Judicial rejection of the idealized patriarchal nuclear family was significant for second-parent adoptions because such rejection created the rhetorical grounds on which a different family discourse could emerge. Once courts determined that "real families" did not necessarily have to include one mother and one father, lesbian couples had a better chance of obtaining legal recognition for their planned families.

Judicial acceptance of second-parent adoptions stands in stark contradiction to lesbian dissolution and lesbian mother–heterosexual father divorce cases. Given the pervasive condemnation of lesbian mothers, why were the second-parent adoptions accepted so readily? One crucial difference between adoption cases and the dissolution/divorce cases is that adoption cases are not adversarial in nature: none of the biological mothers contested their partners' petitions. The second primary difference resides in the fact that judges did not question the partners' maternal identity. Instead, they renegotiated the meaning of "family" to include more than one mother. Adoption rhetoric thus turns on "family" rather than "biology." Finally, judges may be more amenable to granting second-parent adoptions when the child was conceived through artificial insemination rather than heterosexual intercourse. In the latter case, the "father" may have grounds to contest custody or adoption rights. In the adoption cases examined here, however, all children were conceived through donor insemination in lesbian partnerships; there was no "outside" party to contest the adoption, unless the sperm donor was known to the couple.

By contrast, in the divorce cases, "two-mother" families were disallowed. Judges forced lesbian couples to maintain separate residences and often restricted the partner's freedom when the children resided with the mother. Judges knowingly disregard the importance of family bonds in divorce and dissolution, but they highlighted those bonds in adoption cases. How can this contradiction be explained? The usual criminal, neurotic, and proselytical characterizations of lesbians are virtually nonexistent in the (non-adversarial) adoption rhetoric. Judges typically did not build their opinions on those characterizations, choosing instead to focus on the value of "alternative" families. Several judges saw no reason to use outdated definitions of "the family" to punish lesbians. They used their judicial power to ignore heteronormative conceptions of the family and lesbian identity, and instead certified the couples' desire to protect their families legally. Given that second-parent adoptions are relatively new in lesbian family law, analysis of future cases will help determine whether negative representations of lesbians continue to be rejected in the interest of constructing and negotiating broader meanings of the word "family."

I have argued that the rhetoric employed by judges in custody disputes between heterosexual fathers and lesbian mothers reified and legally regulated the lesbian mother oxymoron by drawing on characterizations of lesbians as neurotic, criminal individuals interested ultimately in proselytizing or recruiting their children into a subversive "lifestyle." The rhetorical ambivalence manifests itself in this set of child custody disputes by questioning the negative characterizations that ordinarily are taken as evidence of maternal unfitness. In cases pertaining to planned lesbian families, the rhetorical ambivalence acts to reify the biological aspects of motherhood so that non-biological lesbian parents typically lack standing to press for custodial and/or visitation privileges. Yet the ambivalence affirms the formation of two-parent lesbian families in cases granting second-parent adoption.

Advocates in the disputes between divorcing couples negotiated and regulated lesbian maternal identity (and the legitimacy thereof) by debating claims that lesbian identity is necessarily criminal, neurotic, or proselytic. When such claims prevailed, judges denied lesbian mothers custody and buttressed their opinions by maintaining that a lesbian's "inherent" status as an outlaw, a neurotic, or a recruiter would stigmatize her children. These characterizations anchor the lesbian in a rhetorical space marked out-of-bounds for legitimate maternal agency. Moreover, they are strengthened by judicial appeals to heteronormative morality to deny custodial and visitation claims. Such anti-lesbian assumptions could be held to be purely rational, since few reasonable people would want criminals, psychopaths, or pedophiles anywhere near children, much less raising them. The rhetorical ambivalence thus reproduces the oxymoron in divorce cases by reifying the constructions of lesbianism as an outlaw identity or a moral deficiency.

The ambivalence also became manifest through the construction of mothering as a *necessarily* biological phenomenon. The judges in lesbian dissolution cases could not deny the existence of lesbian mothers, nor could custody and visitation rights be granted or denied because of a mother's lesbian identity. Instead, judges accepted the notion that a child should remain in the custody of his or her blood relatives, with little regard for the nurturing role played by the non-biological mother. The oxymoron became reified in the use of "blood" as a litmus test for custody. The cruel irony here, of course, is that appeals to genetic connections would be of little service to lesbian mothers in custody disputes with heterosexual fathers, where the supposedly unnatural status of lesbian identity is outweighed by the father's biological tie to the child.

Two poles of argument thus characterize the types of cases examined in this chapter. One, primarily involving custody disputes, reproduces and reifies the oxymoron through repetitive articulation of lesbian identity as *essentially* sick, criminal, or proselytic, and therefore outside the bounds of acceptable or legitimate maternal practice. Such characterizations are complicated by additional appeals to biological connections between mother and child in the lesbian dissolution cases. The other pole, involving second-parent adoption cases, represents an oppositional rhetoric that rejects characterizations of the lesbian as bad to legitimize lesbian motherhood within the context of a dual-mother household structure. In these cases judges' rejection of anti-lesbian rhetoric enabled them to grant second-parent adoption requests.

Reproduction of the oxymoron in judicial rhetoric thus disallows the legitimate enactment of lesbian maternal identity *unless* such agency occurs within the context of second-parent adoption. While such an outcome is beneficial for lesbian couples who raise their children together, it does little for lesbians who wish to raise children on their own. Nor does the rhetoric of the dissolution cases serve the interest of non-biological parents—including heterosexual stepparents, if we follow the judicial arguments to their logical conclusion.

The rhetorical ambivalence in judicial rhetoric, then, also serves a regulatory function, but a bit differently from journalistic regulation. While both discursive communities engage the broader question of which women shall "count" as mothers, the lesbian dissolution cases underscore how essentialist arguments can be used both for and against the enactment of legitimate lesbian maternal identity. The boundaries of lesbian identity are characterized, in the heterosexual divorce cases, as fundamentally at odds with good mothering. But lesbian identity takes on a shadowy existence in lesbian dissolution cases when the cases become arguments about maternal *nature* rather than maternal *function*. The "alternative family" is certified in the second-parent adoption cases, as judges reward a particular formation, the stable two-parent family structure. The ideological commitments to some sort of "essential" motherhood (through a woman's biological connection to her children) and to the family occur, of course, in other discursive communities. Such questions, for instance, have concerned academics since the 1970s. It is to this scholarship that we now turn our critical attention.

The great danger of analogy is that a *similarity*
is taken as evidence of an *identity.*
KENNETH BURKE, *Permanence and Change*

"STOP! YOU'RE MAKING ME SICK!"

In "every society," Michel Foucault argues in "The Discourse on Language,"
the "production of discourse is at once controlled, selected, organised, and
redistributed according to a certain number of procedures."[1] Cultures develop rules to govern discourse production, rules to govern which individuals or groups may speak about particular topics, and rules that govern the relative suitability or taboo nature of those topics.[2] While culturally bound
external rules limit discourse production and speaker agency, there also exist
internal regulations, "concerned with the principles of classification, ordering, and distribution."[3] This regulatory system influences the development of
academic "disciplines," whereby a "discipline" is both a categorical scheme
for organizing knowledge *and* a rule system that regulates the types of information or the areas of inquiry allowed legitimate space within any particular
location in the categorical scheme. Thus, as Foucault notes, "disciplines are

defined by groups of objects, methods, their corpus of propositions considered to be true, the interplay of rules and definitions, of techniques and tools."[4] Moreover, specific disciplines "constitute a system of control in the production of discourse, fixing its limits through the action of an identity taking the form of a permanent reactivation of the rules."[5] Particular disciplines enact "fellowships of discourse," thereby coordinating the development of rules that affect what will remain secret within the discipline and what shall be disclosed.[6] Of course, such rules are always produced in specific historical and social contexts, and dominant cultural values are likely to be reproduced within ivory tower walls. For instance, homonegativity and patriarchal values may operate as specific mechanisms for authorizing or de-authorizing speech about particular topics.

This authorizing function, in conjunction with the disciplinary rules, is significant for understanding the conditions under which certain topics become more or less legitimate as grounds for scholarly inquiry. As Foucault notes, the "modes of circulation, valorization, attribution, and appropriation of discourses vary with each culture and are modified within each."[7] Institutionalized rules govern what any specific "author" can say about a topic. "The author is not an indefinite source of significations which fill a work; the author does not precede the works; he is a certain functional principle by which, in our culture, one limits, excludes, and chooses; in short, by which one impedes the free circulation, the free manipulation, the free composition, decomposition, and recomposition of fiction."[8] Foucault concludes that the author is "an ideological product," because it is the universe of discursive structures or the multiple webs of meaning that make possible the appearance of the author in the first place. These discursive structures regulate not only the production of texts or rhetoric, but also the relative authenticity or ethos of the author's voice within particular disciplines. It is therefore more important, according to Foucault, to inquire about the "modes of existence" of a particular rhetoric, and to ask, "Where has it been used, how can it circulate, and who can appropriate it for himself? What are the places in it where there is room for possible subjects? Who can assume these various subject functions?"[9] The critic's task is to "mark out and distinguish the principles of ordering, exclusion, and rarity in discourse," as well as to pay attention to the rules for "effective formation of discourse."[10]

Robert Hariman has observed that the "professional ethic" exacts specific "institutional pressures" from the academic writer, so that the "rules of decorum," including the rules of "disinterestedness" and of "political neutrality," constrain not only the objects of scholarly inquiry but also the scholar's voice in speaking to such issues.[11] University culture thus declares itself to be apolitical and not "affiliated with any one political interest, community, or doctrine," even though "the disciplinary system is the means for recruiting, training, authorizing, and rewarding the political agents of the dominant class. Knowledge is by definition apolitical, yet the body of knowledge was created as an agency of social control."[12] It is in this sense that the academy generally, and the disciplinary system specifically, functions as an ideological state apparatus. Critical examination of academic discourse becomes all the more crucial, then, because such discourse is a primary site at which conditions of social domination are reproduced and reified through certain disciplinary and authorizing practices. Specifically, it is crucial to understand how academic rhetoric reproduces and legitimates the lesbian mother oxymoron, since academics are granted "expert" or "authority" status in the larger culture of which they are a part.

In this chapter I analyze contemporary psychological approaches to the study of lesbian motherhood. I trace how characterizations of lesbianism as a mental disorder, neurosis, and/or pathology have been negotiated within psychological studies of lesbian mothers since the 1970s. I focus on two primary categories of research. First, I analyze how one significant feminist-psychological theoretical model of motherhood, Nancy Chodorow's *Reproduction of Mothering*, is predicated on problematic assumptions about human sexuality. I then perform a rhetorical criticism of several social scientific studies of lesbian mothers and their children. I show that rhetorical ambivalence toward lesbian motherhood in this particular strain of academic discourse (with the exception of Chodorow) is marked by a desire to "help" lesbian mothers retain custodial and visitation rights, but such intentions are essentially undermined through the rearticulation and circulation of anti-lesbian understandings of gender.

The notion that the related disciplines of psychoanalysis, psychiatry, and psychology function as mechanisms of ideological control has been the subject of much academic and political commentary. Indeed, these disciplines have themselves been the site of ambivalence and dissent where homosexuality is concerned. Although lesbianism as such is no longer *officially* considered a mental illness, the lesbian-as-psychopath is a concept that still enjoys authorial and ideological dominance. This dominance emerges in the methodological frameworks and assumptions of studies of lesbian mothers and their children. Before one can assess how contemporary psychological research plays a role in the contestation of lesbian maternal identity, however, one must understand the historical circumstances under which homosexuality and lesbianism were conceptualized in these disciplines.

I have selected six representative studies that attempt to determine the probable "effects" of being raised by a lesbian mother. I contextualize the analysis within a brief history of lesbianism as a mental illness or psychopathology and critique how the pathological character of lesbian identity within the professional discourses of psychiatry, psychology, and psychoanalysis function in the studies themselves. While the studies self-consciously try to subvert the medicalization of identity by attempting to "prove" that children of lesbians are not likely to "become" homosexual themselves, they inadvertently lend credence to, if not reify, the oxymoronic cast of lesbian motherhood.

Historical Context of the Studies

The Stonewall riots of June 1969 ushered in a new period of civil rights activism for lesbians and gay men. The American Psychiatric Association's December 1973 decision to declassify homosexuality as an illness represented a second potential turning point, whereby emancipation from hegemonic characterizations of lesbianism as psychopathology might facilitate social acceptance and freedom from discrimination. The declassification, however, did not guarantee liberation from pathological characterizations, as in the case of numerous judicial, academic, and popular advocates who still think and speak of lesbianism as a specific set of repugnant neuroses. As I will show, such depictions and assumptions formed the basis of psychological studies well into the 1990s.

Critical analysis of the studies is crucial and potentially beneficial in two senses. This type of study is common in the literature. More important, many of the studies are motivated by an explicit desire to improve the likelihood of positive legal outcomes for lesbian mothers. Scholars have conducted this research to provide "scientific" evidence that lesbian mothers pose no "danger" to their children. In 1994, for example, a coalition of scholars represented by the American Academy of Child and Adolescent Psychiatry and the American Psychological Association (among others) urged the Supreme Court of Virginia to accept the conclusions of numerous studies that found children of lesbian mothers to be "normal" (read: properly masculine or feminine, with a presumed heterosexual orientation). Advocates urged the justices to find that "an individual's sexual orientation does not correlate with the person's fitness as a parent," and to "consider such scientific research in view of the widespread prejudice and stereotyping that exists with respect to gay men, lesbians, and bisexual people in the United States."[13]

My desire to analyze the research comparing lesbian mother households to heterosexual mother households (or "normal populations," as they are identified in the academic literature) stems from a pragmatic concern. If study after study finds no ill effect from lesbian mothers on children, *and* the studies are motivated in part to respond to lesbian mothers' legal problems, why do lesbian mothers still experience discrimination in the judicial sphere? The failed efficacy of the researchers' stated desire to use their research to combat discrimination could be explained in at least two ways. The simplest explanation is that one study, two studies, or even a multitude of studies cannot reasonably be expected to surmount a century of negative attitudes toward and discrimination against lesbians. In other words, the psychological studies are discounted or outweighed by the sedimentation or reification of the lesbian mother oxymoron, whereby many decades' socialization in believing that the oxymoron is intractable undermines the studies' putative power. In such a conceptual scheme, no amount of research could ever "disprove" the "fact" that lesbians pose a danger to children and should thus be barred from mothering. In this sense, social change is incremental, and the more the academic community can do to combat stereotyping and discrimination through "scientific" research, all the better. The lack of efficacy could also be explained by the notion that academic and legal discourses do not actually overlap or interpenetrate one another. This explanation lacks persuasive power, however, given the considerable overlap between the journalistic and legal spheres. It is clear in several cases that judges attend to psychological research in the process of deliberation; it is also clear that psychological researchers are well aware of legal discursive characterizations of lesbian mothers. To claim that lesbian mothers still experience discrimination because of a lack of transference or interaction between spheres of public argument, then, is to deny the existence of plentiful evidence to the contrary.

The problem actually goes much deeper than these explanations acknowledge. I refer loosely to what I call the "yardstick" problem, whereby the studies attempt to legitimate lesbian mothers by comparing them to heterosexual mothers (or by comparing children of lesbians to children of heterosexual women). The practical and ideological limitations of academic discourse in the legal sphere is, at root, a function of the fact that all of the comparative studies (and even some of the noncomparative ones) are predicated on heteronormative and sexist assumptions and research questions. The studies are thus doomed to rhetorical failure in the legal and popular spheres of public deliberation because they unwittingly replicate anti-lesbian attitudes.

A century ago, sexologists and other interested academicians constructed a complex taxonomy to explain variations in human sexuality. The taxonomy itself could not be shorn of the historical and social circumstances that gave rise to it, however, as the moral authority of the church gave way in the latter half of the nineteenth century to vested authority in scientific expertise. The initial construction of homosexuality as a particular neurosis, as we saw in chapter 1, had its historical roots in these historical circumstances. Psychiatry's ascendance as a source of cultural authority has been the subject of much scholarly commentary; my purpose here is to sketch the broad contours of the intradisciplinary debates regarding homosexuality and lesbianism as specific mental illnesses or neuroses. Ronald Bayer's historical account functions as the exemplar; I summarize his argument here and supply other contextual information to explain how contemporary psychological studies of lesbian mothers fail to escape replication of the idea that lesbianism is an insidious illness.

In 1981 Bayer published *Homosexuality and American Psychiatry: The Politics of Diagnosis,* in an impressive effort to account for the historical, social, and institutional conditions that made it possible for the American Psychiatric Association to remove homosexuality from its official diagnostic manual of mental illnesses in December 1973. He traces the transformation of homosexuality from a religious typification of abomination to a scientifically classifiable disease.[14] Western religion itself had fostered and encouraged psychiatry's role in policing homosexual behavior, and the "most heated response in the removal of homosexuality from the diagnostic system came from orthodox religious groups and orthodox psychoanalysts. The reason is that they share the same philosophical system, one rooted in Judeo-Christian morality."[15] Indeed, Bayer notes that sexologists, psychoanalysts, and others developed a scientific paradigm of homosexuality *within* the bounds of "moral opprobrium."[16] The medicalization of lesbian identity thus took root and flourished while the sciences of psychiatry, psychoanalysis, psychology, and sexology gained both moral and scientific authority in public culture. Within the psychoanalytic tradition, for instance, figures such as Irving Bieber and Charles Socarides became powerful advocates of the perspective that homosexuality (and its implied female equivalent, lesbianism) *as a matter of necessity* must be defined as a "profound psychopathology."[17]

Speaking generally, conventional psychoanalytic theory is predicated on a teleology that assumes heterosexuality to be the inevitable outcome of "normal" human sexual development. This teleology produces a concurrent theoretical fixation on the causative agents of homosexuality. In 1972, for instance, the *International Journal of Psychiatry* published a forum exploring the illness model. The forum's first article, authored by Richard Green, questioned the depiction of homosexuality as an "illness, a disorder, a defect, or unnatural behavior."[18] Green raised fundamental queries regarding Freudian psychoanalysis, social learning theory, and other models of homosexuality as a deviation from heterosexual normativity. He rejected the major psychoanalytic claim representing heterosexuality as *the* natural state of human sexuality, whereby heterosexuality and procreativity were one and the same.

Other professionals in the forum tended to concur with Green's approach. Alan Bell called for a more complex theoretical model of human sexuality free of the rigid binary distinctions between heterosexuality and homosexuality. Judd Marmor and Martin Hoffman noted how psychoanalysis measured conformity to social norms: while Marmor argued that the illness paradigm was a "moral judgment" with "no basis in fact," Hoffman observed that psychiatry had "quite unreflectingly carried over" the "moral views of the culture from which it arose."[19]

Charles Socarides, however, did not concur with Green's critique. He characterized homosexuality as a necessarily pathological arrested development. Whereas heterosexuality is "determined from birth by anatomy and then reinforced by cultural and environmental indoctrination," homosexuality is "based on the fear of the mother and the aggressive attack on the father, and is filled with destruction and self-deceit."[20] Socarides's position, as Bayer notes, was not a solitary one in the disciplinary debates regarding the proper classification of homosexuality. Other men, including Sandor Rado and Irving Bieber, occupied the illness paradigm camp, characterizing homosexuality, respectively, as a phobia and as a failure to follow nature's dictate.[21]

Mid-twentieth-century constructions of homosexuality arose during the period of psychiatry's growth as a scientific-moral enterprise. Drawing on popular notions of homosexuality as deviance, inversion, or abnormality, psychiatric clinicians and researchers formalized such views and authorized them with a scientific voice. In 1952 the American Psychiatric Association published its initial official compendium of mental disorders. Its pages contained the haunting classification of homosexuality as a "sociopathic personality disturbance."[22] One might ask how gay people at mid-century responded to the medicalization of identity. Bayer found that many gay men and lesbians throughout the 1950s and early 1960s "publicly welcomed the psychiatric effort to wrest control of the social definition of their lives from moral and religious authorities. Better sick than criminal, better the focus of therapeutic concern than the target of the brutal law."[23] The rhetorical and historical lesson of this complicity, obviously, is to choose one's allies carefully. The decisions of groups such as the Mattachine Society and the Daughters of Bilitis to trust psychiatry may have seemed prudent under the circumstances, given psychiatry's authorial voice as a scientific and therefore objective and bias-free enterprise. Bayer found that these early homophile organizations placed unquestioning faith in scientific authority, hoping that psychiatry's "scientific neutrality" might be advantageous to the cause of integrating and assimilating gay citizens into American culture.[24]

The hegemony of psychoanalytic, psychiatric, and psychological construction of the illness paradigm cannot be understated. The battle to declassify homosexuality was fought bitterly over a period of several years. Professionals such as Green, Marmor, and Thomas Szasz questioned the orthodoxy, while members of the nascent gay liberation movement took pains to contest their own classification as psychopaths.[25] The contestation of the illness paradigm, however, required an attack on psychiatry's status as a legitimate authority. Vocal advocates such as Franklin Kameny argued that the "corpus of clinical studies of homosexuality was flawed on methodological grounds. Lacking statistically verifiable evidence that homosexuality constituted a pathological condition, psychiatric researchers had *defined* homosexuality as a disease."[26]

The first organized assault on the APA by gay liberation activists took place in 1970 during the APA's annual meeting. Over the next three years, sympathetic clinicians joined forces with gay activists to secure a voice within professional debates regarding homosexuality. Finally, at the 1973 convention a panel of researchers, clinicians, and gay activists convened to explore the potential removal of homosexuality from the *Diagnostic and Statistical Manual (DSM)*. Opposition within the professional organization was fierce, as many clinicians had materially vested interests in keeping homosexuality in the *DSM* and their "patients" on the account books. The only gay activist on the panel, Ronald Gold, listened patiently as other panelists and audience members continued to endorse the hegemonic view. In Bayer's account, Gold made an "impassioned appeal" to the APA demanding abandonment of the "clinical stance." "Stop it," he declared. "You're making me sick!"[27]

Within the broad contours of this institutional history, two research trajectories emerged. One path challenged the implicit sexism of psychoanalytic theories of mothering. The other attempted to use psychological research to "help" lesbian mothers.

Equal Opportunity Parenting: Chodorow on Mothering

Nancy Chodorow's study *The Reproduction of Mothering* is typically characterized within the feminist academic community as a highly influential work for the theorizing of motherhood. Michèle Barrett, for instance, contends that Chodorow provides a "refreshing formulation of psychoanalytic theory" with her call "for a conscious break in the cycle of 'mothering' by which contemporary femininity and masculinity are reproduced."[28] Patricia Hill Collins characterizes Chodorow's text as a "groundbreaking work," because it has "been highly influential in framing the predominant themes in feminist discourse."[29] The text functions as a site of struggle for negotiating the meanings ascribed to maternal practice and identity. Chodorow analyzes the institution of motherhood as it is constructed within contemporary Western societies generally, and twentieth-century American culture in particular. She places her research in a feminist framework which holds, minimally, that gender and sexuality constitute central problems for scholarly analysis and any effort to improve the condition of women's lives. Written from within the object relations tradition of psychiatry, *The Reproduction of Mothering* examines how asymmetrical gender relationships become reified in "traditional" families. Chodorow thus reformulates psychoanalytic theory to explain how motherhood reproduces systems of domination based on gender inequality. She argues for a restructuring of parenthood so that men and women share equal responsibility for child care and child rearing. Chodorow notes that "families create children gendered, and ready to marry. But families organized around women's mothering and male dominance create incompatibilities in women's and men's relational needs."[30]

The institution of motherhood, and the practice of motherhood itself, she asserts, is maintained through an asymmetrical social ordering of gender that places the majority of responsibility for child raising on women. Chodorow situates her own research within feminist practice, noting that "questions of gender and sexual inequality" have "led feminists to focus politically on questions of personal life, on women's control of their sexuality and bodies, on family relations, [and] on heterosexual bias and discrimination against lesbians and homosexuals." Chodorow begins by observing that "women's mothering is a central and defining feature of the social organization of gender and is implicated in the construction and reproduction of male dominance itself." She questions how asymmetrical power relations, organized along lines of gender and sexuality, reproduce the systems through which women continue to mother and shoulder an unequal burden of labor for child rearing. What counts as mothering? "Being a mother," Chodorow explains, "is not only bearing a child—it is being a person who socializes and nurtures. It is being a primary parent or caretaker." She then asks: "Why are mothers women? Why is the person who routinely does all those activities that go into parenting not a man?"[31]

Her argument excises lesbians even as it attempts to subvert the patriarchal organization of gender in contemporary Western society. Chodorow crafts a space for fathers' equal participation in and responsibility for parenting, and in so doing explicitly casts lesbian motherhood as a distinct threat to the re-structuring of family life. To her credit, however, Chodorow offers a trans-gressive discourse in that she explains how heterosexuality is constructed and enforced to maintain gender asymmetry. At first glance it appears that Chodorow has not much to say about lesbian motherhood, for the word "les-bian" is used only a few times in the two hundred-odd pages of her book. The text exemplifies, however, how heterosexuality, constructed and maintained by and through ideological force, limits the potential legitimacy of lesbian maternal identity and agency.

The fact that women mother, and not men, is, for Chodorow, "central to the sexual division of labor." Moreover, the "maternal role has profound effects on women's lives, on ideology about women, on the reproduction of masculinity and sexual inequality, and on the reproduction of particular forms of labor power." Chodorow reviews and subsequently rejects various arguments that have been advanced to justify and perpetuate the asymmetri-cal construction of parenting in contemporary Western societies. The argu-ment from nature assumes that women mother because women give birth, or that women mother owing to some biological maternal instinct; thus it is "natural" for women to mother, and therefore women "*ought* to mother." Chodorow concludes that this biological/natural argument for "women's mothering is based on facts that derive, not from our biological knowledge, but from our definition of the natural situation as this grows out of our par-ticipation in certain social arrangements."[32] The argument from biology is thus inadequate for explaining the perpetuation of asymmetrically structured parenting relationships.

The notion that women mother because of sex-role training is also defi-cient, because it is overly individuated and conflicts with Chodorow's conviction that "women's mothering does not exist in isolation." While Chodorow acknowledges "an intentional component to gender role socialization in the family, in schools, [and] in the media," she finds that the "social reproduction" of mothering "comes to be independent of individual intention and is not caused by it." More specifically, "sexual inequality is itself embedded in and perpetuated by the organization of these institutions, and is not reproduced according to or solely because of the will of the individual actors." This socialization takes place through ideology: "Legitimating ideologies themselves, as well as institutions like schools, the media, and families which perpetuate ideologies, contribute to social reproduction. They create expectations in people about what is normal and appropriate and how they should act. Society's perpetuation requires that *someone* rear children, but our language, science, and popular culture all make it very difficult to separate the need for care from the question of who provides that care." Insofar as conventional accounts, such as those offered by anthropologists (who advance arguments from nature), or social psychologists and some feminist theorists (who advance role-training arguments), are "inadequate," she sets out to explain "mothering as an institutionalized feature of family life and of the sexual division of labor [which] reproduces itself cyclically."[33]

Chodorow situates her work within the domain of psychoanalysis, and allows space for explaining how cultural ideologies exert particular influences on psychological development. She makes clear that she follows a particular tradition within psychoanalytic theory—the object relations school—to advance her argument about the social production of gender generally, and the reproduction of mothering specifically. Within psychoanalytic argot, an "object" refers to "people, aspects of people, or symbols of people." Object relations theory takes as a foundational assumption that individuated senses of identity are inherently influenced by the social systems of which they are a part, and do not develop in isolation. Psychoanalytic theory, to Chodorow's mind, explains how individuated bodies and psyches internalize ideology. Her approach and specific subject of inquiry are innovative, since object relations theory had previously failed to address gender, and because psychoanalysts presumed that gender and sexuality had roots in biology and natural instinct. The constitution and enforcement of heterosexual maternal identity is of central concern to Chodorow. Within her object relations perspective, a child develops a core sense of self primarily in relation to her or his mother, given the fact that mothers typically function as the primary caretaker. But the core sense of self develops asymmetrically along gendered lines, such that boys will develop a sense of self different from the sense of self developed by female children.[34]

The reproduction of heterosexual relations is, she believes, a central constitutive feature of contemporary family life: "The psychoanalytic account not only shows how parents act and children respond. It also assumes that mothers and fathers *should* play certain kinds of parental roles *in order to* make their children heterosexual. Polar orientation (active and initiating versus passive and receptive) should emerge in heterosexual relationships whose goal is reproduction." Chodorow explains that within traditional psychoanalytic theory, especially that view offered by Freud and his followers, "the normative definition of the situation is an assumption that heterosexual genitality is a major desired developmental goal." And while this theoretical domain characterizes a girl's heterosexuality as "biologically normal" and therefore dictated by nature, "there is nothing inevitable, natural, or preestablished in the development of human sexuality." In addition, "a reading of cases, and the theory derived from them, suggests that sexual orientation and definition is enforced and constructed by parents. Parents are usually heterosexual and sexualize their relationship to children of either gender accordingly, employing socially sanctioned child-rearing practices." These practices require that girls eventually reduce their identification with their mothers and transfer their energies to men (first to the father, then, later, other boys and men). But this developmental phase is not without problems. Chodorow claims that females' early adolescence is "characterized by bisexual wavering" and "indecisiveness about the relative importance to the girl of females (mother/girlfriends) and males (father/boys)." It is only during the later stages of puberty that "most girls" will stop wavering.[35]

Of course, the phrase "most girls" leaves open a space for girls who may identify as primarily bisexual (but are less likely to identify as lesbian, according to Chodorow, because of Western societal taboos against homosexuality). The rhetorical characterization of heterosexuality as a model of natural linear progression implies that lesbian identity (and bisexual identity as well) is a form of "arrested development" and thus a kind of psychopathology. Heterosexual identity for girls typically includes, according to Chodorow, interest in men as "erotic objects," but their primary emotional object attachments continue to be with other girls and women. Chodorow describes this state as one of "triangulated" heterosexuality. Given the taboos against lesbianism, women will fulfill their emotional needs by having children. "Contradictions in heterosexuality," however, guarantee that "women will seek relations to children and will not find heterosexual relationships alone satisfactory." Mothering is reproduced, then, when women have children in order to fulfill "the relational triangle."[36] The construction of women's desire for children is thus produced, at least partially, as a result of the prohibition of lesbianism.

The implied outcomes of Chodorow's argument are problematic because they perpetuate the characterization of lesbianism as a neurosis. While her treatment does acknowledge the material existence of lesbians, some of whom also mother,[37] and while her argument also depicts heterosexuality as a socially constructed identity, the argument nonetheless restricts lesbian maternal agency. Her argument implies that if fathers were to become more equal participants in the parenting process, female children would have less trouble "resolving in favor" of heterosexual orientation, and would thus have greater capacity to develop a "strong heterosexual object love." Heterosexuality remains *the* objective ideal. If men and women parent equally, then girls will develop a more resolutely heterosexual identity. Chodorow makes this clear: "Any strategy for change whose goal includes liberation from the constraints of an unequal social organization of gender must take account of the need for a fundamental reorganization of parenting, so that primary parenting is shared between women and men. . . . Fathers must be primary masculine role models for boys, and heterosexual objects for girls. . . . Fathers are supposed to help children individuate and break their dependence on their mothers. But this dependence on her, and this primary identification, would not be created in the first place if men took primary parenting responsibilities." Chodorow carries the argument to its only possible conclusion: we must have two-parent households (composed of one male parent and one female parent), and men and women must share parenting responsibilities equally.[38] While Chodorow argues commendably that heterosexuality is constituted and negotiated through parenting, the potential legitimacy of lesbian maternal practice is eclipsed through a rhetoric that portrays lesbian identity either as taboo or in strict relation to heterosexuality, as heterosexuality's inferior "other" along asymmetrical lines. This asymmetry limits the radical potential of her claims.

One is left rather dissatisfied upon finishing the text. Although a radical restructuring of motherhood is possible, whereby heterosexuality is itself a construction and not "essential," "transhistorical," "immutable," or "natural," the book's radical potential is co-opted by a larger ideological commitment to the two-gender, two-parent family structure. Of course, to free women from the bondage that is mothering, Chodorow necessarily has to argue for a two-parent household in which fathers share equal responsibility. Left out of her equation, however, is any sustained acknowledgment that lesbians do in fact mother, and that perhaps the fact that they do says something about the ways in which hegemonic constructions of gender and sexuality can be disrupted. Lesbian motherhood could thus be interpreted as a specific form of resistance to patriarchal authority, one with the potential to restructure the "institution" or the "nature" of motherhood. Although Chodorow's engagement of psychoanalytic theory fails to account for lesbian disruption of the hegemonic ideal, a second avenue of research draws explicit attention to lesbian mothers and their children. It is to this research that I now turn.

Comparative Studies, Social Control, and Bad Mothers

A significant body of discourse exists in the field of psychology which argues for greater tolerance of lesbian mothers by showing that the children of lesbian mothers or gay fathers have no more likelihood of "becoming gay" than children with non-queer parents. The attempt to legitimate lesbian motherhood in this manner is flawed, for the approach grants hegemonic legitimacy to heterosexual parenthood and to heterosexuality in general. In other words, the research takes for granted that "becoming gay" is necessarily or inherently *bad*. In her research on lesbian mothers, the psychologist Laura Benkov found that

> virtually no one had written about lesbian and gay parents prior to 1979. The only studies I found were done in response to an increasing number of custody battles emerging during the 1970s. For the most part, these studies compared children of divorced lesbians and children of hetero-

sexual mothers, sometimes also divorced, sometimes not. They asked whether children of homosexuals were more likely to have emotional problems, be confused about gender identity and sex roles, or to grow up to be gay. Researchers found no differences with respect to these issues. . . . Homophobic questions shaped the inquiries, and heterosexual parents constituted the norm against which lesbian and gay parents were measured.[39]

My own analysis confirms Benkov's findings. The framing of the studies raises several crucial questions: How are psychological discourses of lesbian motherhood disciplined? What are the epistemological limits of the studies? How does an ideological tension between sameness and difference become a distinct rhetorical problem within this body of research? How do academics negotiate the lesbian mother oxymoron through an agenda advocating greater tolerance?

In this section I perform a critical analysis of six academic studies that focus on the psychological health of American lesbian mothers and/or their children as compared to heterosexual mothers and their children. Plentiful research has been conducted in this area, and I focus on those studies cited most frequently in published reviews of the related literature. The fundamental rhetorical problem facing the researchers is that they are working within a disciplinary framework in which only certain forms of research can be conducted. Although the studies painstakingly make clear their concern for legal problems and other forms of discrimination affecting lesbian families, they nevertheless betray those concerns by casting lesbian motherhood as an implicitly inferior alternative to heterosexual motherhood. The comparative approach reproduces the notion that queer experience is best understood from a heterosexual perspective, and the approach is essentially conservative, for it fails to question the dominant paradigm. In speaking to the development of a lesbian-centered ethics, for instance, the philosopher Sarah Lucia Hoagland writes that even if one tries to reform or rebel against a particular system, one is necessarily "operating within the system's parameters and [is] thus giving the system meaning by helping to hold its axis (what goes unquestioned) in place." Moreover, "to engage, to participate, in a situation or in a system is to affirm its central values."[40] These studies operate to such ends.

The six studies included here are empirical in nature, based on data from sample populations through various research methods: open-ended interviews, structured interviews, questionnaires, and other survey instruments. They were published between 1981 and 1996, with initial research conducted from the mid-1970s to the early 1990s. The articles were structured in the same way most empirical research is reported: an introduction including a review of relevant literature, a statement of rationale, and an explanation of purpose or hypothesis. The articles explained participant selection methodology, specific research procedures, and methods employed, and reported research findings in statistical and narrative form. The articles typically concluded with a discussion of results, including acknowledgment of limitations and suggested directions for future research. All studies were motivated by a concern for lesbian mothers' legal problems. For example, as David Flaks and his colleagues noted in their study, "Should research demonstrate the viability of lesbian and gay families, this would necessitate a reformulation of extant theories, such as psychoanalytic and social learning, which prescribe that healthy development requires two opposite-sex, heterosexual parents for the developmental tasks of identification and rejection on the one hand and modeling on the other."[41] Although the authors all profess similar concerns, they employ different research methods and ask different research questions.

Noting that "alternative family forms have emerged as a significant social phenomenon during the past decade," Beverly Hoeffer justifies her 1991 study on two pragmatic grounds. She claims that empirical study of "lesbian-mother families is necessary to provide the public and professionals with an understanding of lesbian mothers and their children based on empirical reality." Moreover, the study is necessary given the various legal and social problems facing lesbian-headed families.[42] Her study addresses one primary research query: How does a mother's sexual orientation influence her children's "acquisition of sex-role traits and behavior, one component of sexual identity?" To answer that question, Hoeffer compared the children of twenty white lesbian mothers to the children of twenty white heterosexual mothers in the San Francisco Bay area. Mothers were matched according to socioeconomic class, with educational levels and occupations identified as class markers. To maintain a manageable sample, Hoeffer included only one child from each household—either the only child or the eldest child, aged six to nine years old. Children were matched according to age and gender. Hoeffer's study measured sex-role conformity through interviews regarding mothers' and children's toy preferences.[43]

Like Hoeffer, Martha Kirkpatrick and her colleagues Catherine Smith and Ron Roy conducted research as a means to respond to the custody battles facing lesbian mothers. The research team—a female psychologist, a female psychiatrist, and a male child psychiatrist—noted that "custody proceedings have been hampered by a lack of judicial and clinical experience and a lack of research data on the development of such children." The researchers compared the "psychological status" of forty children of lesbians and heterosexual women. They noted that tests and interviews were conducted in conditions under which the mothers' sexual orientation was unknown.[44] One procedure analyzed the mothers' psychosexual development.[45] Several others tested the children's intelligence and psychological health through measures such as the Wechsler Intelligence Scale for Children (WISC), human figure drawing, and the Holtzman Inkblot Technique, which were administered to determine the children's "psychological functioning," with special attention paid to "gender development." Kirkpatrick, Smith, and Roy measured "gender development" by interviewing the children about toy preferences, friend and playmate preferences, "special interests," cross-dressing or sex role nonconformity, and drawings. The discussion of findings pointed out that "measures of gender identity, object choice, or indices of future sex role behavior in childhood are not well established [so that] a developmental stage may be mistaken for established personality structure. The fluidity of developmental process, which makes new levels of integration possible, mitigates against any measure or any single evaluation being definitive. These concepts should be kept in mind in appraising any childhood gender measures."[46] Moreover, the researchers found both groups of mothers to exhibit highly similar "maternal interests, current life-styles, and child-rearing practices." Finally, the study found no significant correlation between mothers' sexual orientation and children's psychopathology. Instead, when children did manifest emotional difficulties, such problems were most likely related to their experience of family strife and divorce.[47]

Daniel Patrick Moynihan and Dan Quayle are not the only men obsessed with the effects of single motherhood on children. Psychological research is also fascinated with discovering what happens to children's sexual identity development "in a father-absent household." Richard Green and four other researchers set out in the late 1970s to "assess aspects of the psychosexual and psychosocial development of prepubescent children living [only] with their mothers."[48] Comparing fifty-six children of fifty lesbian mothers to forty-eight children of forty heterosexual mothers in ten states, Green and his colleagues studied the psychological health of both mothers and children. Mothers completed questionnaires concerning child rearing, romantic relationships, and parenting experiences. Researchers measured mothers' attitudes toward divorce, sex roles, and their children's sex education. Mothers also completed the Bem Sex Role Inventory and two other measures designed to test "general personality variables" and "psychological sex typing." Their children, ages three through eleven, submitted to two separate Wechsler Intelligence tests and other examinations assessing "sexual identity and family relationships," and answered interviewers' questions regarding "play preferences, friendship, television preferences, and thoughts about life as an adult." Green also measured the extent to which the lesbian mothers participated in "lesbian activist groups." He found no significant differences in children's sexual identity, and no children "met the criteria of gender identity disorder in childhood." Finally, the study revealed "no psychopathology related to the mothers' sexual orientation."[49]

Barbara McCandlish's article "Against All Odds: Lesbian Mother Family Dynamics" did not explicitly compare lesbian mother households to heterosexual families, but instead focused on the "health of children raised from birth in lesbian families." Characterizing her work as a "preliminary study," McCandlish contacted five lesbian couples who had borne children through donor insemination. "The purpose of the investigation," she wrote, "was primarily to develop a theoretical model of normal lesbian mother family structure, which would lead to more appropriate clinical services to these families and to future research." Using a two-hour interview format, McCandlish's approach included open-ended questions regarding the couples' romantic relationships, parent-child interactions, and extrafamilial support systems. Her study found, among other things, that the couples' relationships underwent significant changes subsequent to the birth of their children. McCandlish also noted that none of the children exhibited signs of gender identity disorder.[50]

Lesbian couples raising children born through donor insemination also sparked the research interests of David Flaks, Ilda Ficher, Frank Masterpasqua, and Gregory Joseph at the Institute for Graduate Clinical Psychology at Widener University. Concerned initially with lesbian mothers' legal status, Flaks and his colleagues compared the children of thirty lesbian couple households to the offspring of thirty heterosexual parent households. The researchers focused on the first child between the ages of three and nine in each family. The children were matched by birth order, sex, and age, and families were matched by educational level and income. All the families were white. Measurement instruments included the Wechsler Intelligence Scales for Children, a Parent Awareness Skills Survey, Dyadic Adjustment Scales for parents, and other questionnaires. The researchers noted that each area measured "was chosen because it has been the subject of negative judicial assumptions about lesbian-mother families." The researchers found no significant differences in the children's general behavioral and cognitive functioning. They also found that the lesbian mothers tended to be more highly aware of parenting skill guidelines.[51]

Charlotte Patterson, a researcher from the University of Virginia who developed the Bay Area Families Study in response to the lesbian "baby boom," examined the lives of sixty-six lesbian mothers and their children—a total of thirty-seven households. "Despite psychological, judicial, and popular prejudices," she observed, "a substantial body of research now attests to normal adjustment among mothers and normal development among children in these families." Patterson's study addressed mothers' mental health and their children's psychological development. Mothers completed the Rosenberg Self-Esteem Scale, a Child Behavior Checklist, and the Derogatis Symptom Checklist, which measures psychological distress (including "anger/hostility, anxiety, depression, interpersonal sensitivity, obsessive/compulsiveness, paranoid ideation, [and] phobic anxiety)." She found all mothers in the study within the "range of normal functioning," with "generally positive views about themselves."[52]

Patterson studied and evaluated children's mental health through standard interview and questionnaire techniques. The interview focused on matters related to "sex-role identity," or "preferences for sex-role behavior," with questions addressing four topics: "peer friendships," "favorite toys," "favorite games," and "favorite characters on television, in movies, or in books." Children's responses in each area were coded for "sex-role relevant qualities." Patterson found children of lesbian mothers similar to the "normal sample." In other words, most children conformed to traditional sex roles and gender identities.[53]

Contemporary psychological academic discourses of motherhood are constituted as always already heterosexual. While granting marginal visibility to lesbian mothers, the research nonetheless unwittingly casts lesbian motherhood as a silhouetted identity overshadowed by a hegemonic heterosexual maternal identity. All six studies confirmed the researchers' oft-cited hypothesis that children of lesbians were no more likely to "become homosexual" than children of heterosexuals. The problem with such claims, however, as I will attempt to show in the next section, is that such notions are predicated on the idea that "becoming gay" is necessarily bad. As earlier chapters exemplify, lesbian mothers are often criticized for exposing their children to "immoral" and "unhealthy" influences and are accused of attempting to "recruit" their children into homosexuality. Trying to demonstrate that lesbians' children are for the most part heterosexual does little to subvert the hegemonic characterizations of lesbians. In fact, the six representative studies effectively reproduce the lesbian mother oxymoron by granting implicit credence to the notion that "becoming homosexual" is something that must be avoided at all costs. The studies are flawed on epistemological and methodological grounds and are of little value to lesbian mothers. The studies *may* serve short-term practical concerns by providing information that lawyers need in their advocacy for lesbian mothers, and they may also provide resources for social workers and mental health practitioners; but serving *only* those interests works against the long-term ideological interests of emancipating people from compulsory heterosexuality. The argument from expedience is not necessarily negative, but it does little to disrupt or subvert the reification of lesbianism as a pathology or neurosis.

Sex Role Conformity and Latent Homosexuality

Psychiatric and psychological discourses of lesbian motherhood pose a grave rhetorical danger to the struggle for queer equality generally and justice for lesbian mothers and their children in particular. The studies I have outlined are all predicated on the assumption that heterosexuality equals psychological health, whereby "normal" gender identity or compliance with gender norms is characterized as an a priori or "natural" predictor of future heterosexual orientation. The literature characterizes children's noncompliance with hegemonic sex role norms as a dispositive factor in the development of latent homosexuality. Since researchers would be hard-pressed to ask children what their sexual orientation "is," they instead seek to correlate compliance with gender and sex roles to progress toward a healthy heterosexual future. If it can be demonstrated that lesbian mothers engage in specific nurturing practices that encourage such compliance, then "naturally" the children will develop into "normal," "healthy," and "successfully developed" heterosexual adults.

The Hoeffer study, for instance, deploys this rhetorical strategy in its well-intentioned attempt to "normalize" lesbian families. The study makes much of social learning theory's characterization of parent-child role modeling. Social learning theory suggests that children's performance of "stereotypical" sex role behavior is often encouraged and modeled by adults, including but not limited to one's parents. If the models exemplify and "directly encourage less stereotypic" behavior, children's behavior will also be "less stereotypic."[54] It should not escape our attention that social learning theory presumes that lesbian identity is "naturally" an outcome of violating normative sex role expectations. More important, if lesbians cannot as a matter of nature "fit" into a culture's norms for gender-appropriate attitudes, appearance, and behavior, then lesbian mothers will *automatically* role model inappropriately—in Hoeffer's terms, in "less stereotypic" ways.

Such assumptions are not limited to professional psychiatric discourses. The idea that lesbians are inappropriately feminine—not feminine "enough," "butch," with or without a latent wish to "be" a man—pervades popular and legal discourses, too. Lesbians and gay men, such reasoning holds, should be barred from employment as elementary school and high school teachers owing to their own problematic role behaviors. Nor should a lesbian mother's partner be allowed near the children, for she might teach her partner's daughters that playing with Lincoln Logs not only is fun, it's acceptable! The recruitment metaphors that infiltrate journalistic and legal representations of lesbian maternal identity are thus complicated within the academic sphere by the assumption that it is in the character of lesbians to proselytize. This logic suggests that recruitment is an *innate* aspect of lesbian identification rather than a "behavior" as such. Moreover, such logic dictates the inference that if lesbians are proselytical by nature, then children must be protected at all costs, since the last thing American culture needs is a new generation of "queers."

The implied claim that "successful" child development will result in fixed adult heterosexuality is not unique to the Hoeffer study. In their 1995 *Developmental Psychology* article, David Flaks and his colleagues made similar claims. Their review of relevant research found "no significant differences between the children of lesbian and heterosexual parents, suggesting that sexual orientation of custodial parents is not an important predictor of successful child development." In addition, "Healthy development outcomes for the children in this and other studies of lesbian families," Flaks and his associates write, support other research findings "that neither father presence nor parental heterosexuality is crucial for healthy child development. Such a conclusion, although uncontroverted in the research literature, remains controversial because it challenges widely accepted psychoanalytic and social learning theories of child development."[55] Patterson's report of findings from her study of Bay Area lesbian families noted similar results: "Despite psychological, judicial, and popular prejudices, a substantial body of research now attests to normal adjustment among mothers and normal development among children in these families." Patterson's study found that "preferences for sex-role behavior among the children of lesbian mothers" was apparently "quite typical" for preadolescent children.[56] As with the Hoeffer study, Patterson's research approach included a focus on children's toy preferences. Is it reasonable to assume, however, that a child's toy preferences are indicative of or correlated to sex role conformity?

One dangerous rhetorical effect of such characterizations and assumptions is the severe constraints they place on human agency in the negotiation and performance of gender as such. Lesbian mothers, if they are to enjoy the support of professional psychiatric discourses, had better do all they can, despite their "nature," to teach their children that only little girls may play with tea sets and that only boys can play with model cars. If not, the wrath of an angry heteronormative majority will be unleashed, and their custody rights will be in question. Psychiatric discourse in this sense (re)produces broader socio-political constructions of lesbian identity and deploys them with pernicious rhetorical effects.

Hoeffer's study attempts to demonstrate the theoretical possibility that lesbian mothers might be able to overcome their inappropriate gender identifications to serve their children's best interests. Hoeffer administered a toy preference test to mothers and children; data coders then rated the toy and activity preferences on a masculinity-femininity scale. She found that while "lesbian mothers preferred a more equal mixture of sex-typed" toys than heterosexual moms, lesbian mothers were, like their heterosexual counterparts, more likely than not to raise boys who preferred toy rockets, gorillas, snakes, and tool kits. Daughters tended to select gender-"neutral" objects such as seashells, marbles, and whistles, though they also liked to play with feminine toys in their preparation for future homemaking: tea sets, cradles, baby dolls, and kitchen items.[57]

Why do studies like Hoeffer's fail to question the reification of gender-role norms? Why is gender-role conformity constructed rhetorically in such studies as an ideal? What ideological interests do these studies serve? Hoeffer's study claims to create an "understanding of lesbian mothers and their children based on empirical reality instead of stereotypes and myths."[58] One must inquire as to the specific stereotypes Hoeffer had in mind. While it may appear as if her study, and others like it, are the key to legal protection for lesbian mothers and their children by presuming that compliance with gender norms equals heterosexuality, such approaches and characterizations effectively do more harm than good. These studies both reify stereotypical characterizations of lesbians and preclude the disruption of normative ideals that constrain children's abilities to play with toys of their own choosing. Such "disruption" would theoretically place lesbian mothers in danger of social censure and accusations of recruitment, and at risk of suffering the legal system's wrath. Nevertheless, *compliance with gender norms does not guarantee heterosexual development, nor does the contestation of such norms automatically produce transgressive sexuality.*

Parental nonconformity to sex and gender norms is characterized rhetorically by researchers as a significant correlative factor in the development of queer tendencies. Richard Green's study, for instance, measured lesbian mothers' "frequence of participation in lesbian activist groups." In addition, Green and his colleagues made special note of their findings of lesbian mothers' nonnormative gender behaviors. In their survey of fifty lesbian mothers' "psychosexual development, they found that as children, 69 percent had "frequently" or "usually played with masculine toys," 67 percent had at some point dressed in boys' clothing, and 68 percent had been called "tomboys" during childhood. To make matters worse, 92 percent of the women "usually dressed in slacks," and slightly more than half "never wore makeup." The deployment of such statistical claims raises at least one question: What set of rhetorical and historical conditions encourages psychological professionals to focus on such matters in their efforts to protect lesbian mothers from unjust legal maneuvers? One might argue that the professional discourses of academic psychiatry are disciplined in such a way as to reproduce normative expectations and thus to reproduce anti-lesbian assumptions. Such an inference is reasonable in light of the fact that Green's (and others') statistical claims about lesbian mothers are always already contextualized within a heteronormative framework: heterosexual mothers function as the ideal yardstick population against which lesbians are measured. The Green study found, for example, that less than 40 percent of their sample heterosexual mother population had engaged in any presumptively gender-transgressive behavior as children or as adults: 77 percent usually avoided wearing slacks, and 90 percent tended to wear cosmetics.[59]

One crucial feature of the comparative studies deserves further critical consideration. As the Green study concludes, "There are few, if any, data pointing to a role-modeling influence of a parent's homosexual orientation on the sexual orientation of the child."[60] But how, then, can heterosexuality function as the grounds for determining adequate role modeling if its "other," homosexuality, does not? Can the researchers have it both ways? Green implies that parental heterosexuality can and does play a role in child development. On what reasonable grounds can the researchers claim that one sexual orientation and not another will influence child development? How is it possible for lesbian mothers to role model properly when their own sexual orientation is tied so closely in the literature to the transgression of normative gender role preferences, attitudes, and behaviors?

Green's conclusion indicates a slightly different interpretation of role modeling than the Hoeffer study, but the result is the same: "Our study," Green writes, "revealed no psychopathology related to the mothers' sexual orientation." But why "should there be no major demonstrable effect on sexual identity development of children being raised by homosexual mothers? [citation omitted]. If homosexual behavior reflects a fundamental conflict or confusion over anatomic maleness and femaleness, and/or reflects disorder in gender-role sexual expression by children, why do our groups of children look so similar?" Green answers his own query with the following conventional wisdom: "It may appear facile, but nevertheless is accurate, to state that nearly all homosexuals had heterosexual parents." Moreover, Green and his colleagues conclude, the "child does not live in a social vacuum with its homosexual parent."[61]

If most lesbians had heterosexual mothers, were their mothers "bad" role models in some way? Heteronormative logic appears to dictate such an inference, though the researchers in these six studies excluded such questions from critical consideration. Such exclusions effectively exempt presumptively heterosexual parents of future lesbian children from any perception of wrongdoing. Within the heteronormative conceptual framework, lesbians must learn their transgressive roles outside the heterosexual family. Parents of gay children everywhere can now stop asking the futile question, "Where did we go wrong?" But why are lesbians presumed to engage in transgressive role modeling while heterosexual parents of homosexual children are not?

The studies reproduced homonegative and sexist characterizations of lesbians as "too" masculine in appearance and behavior by reporting their "shock" at some findings. Kirkpatrick, Smith, and Roy, for example, finding "no evidence of 'role-playing' of heterosexual marriage stereotypes in the lesbian couples," were "surprised to discover that the lesbian mothers tended to be more concerned with providing male figures for their children than were the comparison mothers."[62] This "surprise," I think, is contingent on the researchers' unstated *doxa*-based assumptions about gender, sexuality, and lesbian identity.

In classical rhetorical theory, a claim is *doxastic* when it constitutes or typifies conventional wisdom within a particular collective culture or community. *Doxa* thus indicates a community's prevailing ideological commitments.

Once a doxastic claim is made, however, the claim does not function once and for all as a "truth"; such a rhetorical effect would be contingent on any number of factors, including an audience's receptivity to such claims. Social, political, and rhetorical conditions must be "ripe," in other words, for the production, circulation, and reception to occur. Doxastic knowledge, in Aristotelian terms, often constitutes one or more of the premises on which deductive claims are made. Doxastic claims are sometimes codified into a culture's legal doctrine (as in the assertion that only opposite-sex partners may marry legally); other claims circulate widely in popular or journalistic culture (as in the claim that presidential election contests are "really" between two— and only two—legitimate candidates).

Regardless of the doxastic claim's specific site of production, circulation, and consumption, however, the (re)production of unexamined claims limits the possibilities for progressive social change. Unquestioned *doxa* preserves and conserves a community's hegemonic ideological commitments. As Robert L. Scott observes, "Silence symbolizes hierarchical structures as surely as does speech. Agreements as to what doesn't count may be verbalized, but they may be observed also silently. The latter may be stronger; that is, verbalizing a negative calls attention to a possibility. It becomes thinkable, whereas silence leaves it in the realm of the unthinkable."[63] "Ironically," Scott notes, "the most powerful rhetoric for maintaining an existing scheme of privilege will be silent. The voice that covers will tend to sound beneficent."[64] Using rhetoric in the service of social change, from this perspective, entails uncovering the silent (but powerful and sometimes dangerous) hidden claims that support or form the basis of policy deliberations. So, one may ask, how does *doxa* play a role in the "shock" and "surprise" noted by researchers such as Kirkpatrick?

Kirkpatrick's "surprise" rests on four unstated doxastic claims. The first is that lesbian relationships mimic heterosexual marriage in some fashion. Why would the researchers search for such evidence? More important, what purpose would the query serve in the researchers' focus on motherhood? The Kirkpatrick study focuses on children's psychological functioning, with special attention directed toward gender development. The comment regarding "role-playing" (or lack thereof) reminds the professional audience that a heterosexual two-parent family is the minimum standard from which successful

child gender development occurs. The claim regarding lesbian mimicry of ostensibly heterosexual roles, however, functions as a precise site of ambivalent
contestation. Kirkpatrick noted "no difference found between the children of
lesbian mothers and those living with heterosexual mothers in the type or fre-
quency of pathology as evaluated by blind psychological testing and a play-
room evaluation."[65] Such results could be explained through a demonstration
that lesbians engage in parental role-modeling behavior similar to heterosexual parents. In this way, the stereotypical assumption that lesbian couples
mimic heterosexual couples may work in lesbian mothers' favor. Yet the character of that mimicry may be contested when a lesbian enacts "masculine" role
modeling and therefore behaves disobediently. The study enacts ambivalence
toward lesbian maternal identity at the precise moment it attempts to explain
the "effect" of lesbians' gender performances on their children. Given that the
children's behavior falls within the "normal" range of the comparative population, studies like this are necessarily caught in a rhetorical bind. Pure mimicry on the part of lesbian mothers would be interpreted as disobedience. Failure to enact mimicry in some sense would also theoretically produce
"abnormal" or "troubled" children. But the problem that lesbian mothers face
in this literature actually goes much deeper: lesbianism is constructed rhetorically in such studies as an automatically transgressive identity.

Researchers made special note of men's presence in children's lives. The
McCandlish study, for instance, found that "all the children had access to
males outside the family," which may have been "a factor in their healthy
gender identity."[66] The Kirkpatrick study also noted "surprise" at the discov-
ery that the sample lesbian mother population provided male role models. At
least three assumptions make such "surprise" possible. First, "lesbian" status
is conflated with separatist or "man-hating" behavior. The idea that lesbians
hate men is not unique to Kirkpatrick's team; this idea pervades the American
hegemonic collective imagination. It is not surprising that the Kirkpatrick
study, among others, would replicate this assumption. Reliance on and reproduction of the assumption, however, undermines the researcher's beneficent interests in helping lesbian mothers retain custody of their children.
Sarah Lucia Hoagland finds it "significant that 'lesbian' is *equated* with 'man-
hating' while 'woman' is not." As Hoagland writes, "Lesbians love lesbians,
so some lesbian energy and focus is not accessible to men. But how is this

manhating? . . . So why are lesbians as a group perceived as manhaters? To hate someone is to direct energy toward them, albeit negative energy, to maintain an aggressive connection. So how is lesbian denial of energy to men such an aggression?"[67]

The unquestioned assumption that lesbian equals man-hater has severely problematic consequences for the comparative psychological approaches to lesbian mothering. In one regard, the false equation may lead to other flawed presumptions: if lesbians hate men, then they should not raise sons; if lesbians hate men, then they will treat male children badly; if lesbians hate men, then they will disallow any role for fathers (if the child is the product of a hetero-sexual union). The presumption that lesbians hate men is tied also to the misconception that lesbians think they can enact both masculine and feminine role modeling. Indeed, most of the studies examined here presume that lesbianism is nothing more than the enactment of a peculiar form of female masculinity, one that is reprehensible for children to witness. If the lesbians are coupled, researchers seek evidence of mimetic role modeling. If a lesbian mother is single, researchers such as Kirkpatrick presume that the children will suffer from a lack of masculine role modeling, even as the research simultaneously presumes that lesbianism is a form of masculinity. In other words, this research reproduces the homonegative idea that lesbian mothers must seize the role of fatherhood because of their naturally transgressive gender identities and performances.

From such a perspective, lesbian mothers simply cannot win. They are "losers" as women because of their innately masculine identities, preferences, appearance, or behaviors. Since they can't "be" men, however, lesbians must resent and literally hate what biological males embody and represent. All four doxastic claims assume maleness, men, and/or masculinity to be central to the constitution and enactment of lesbian identity. Lesbianism is characterized implicitly as a false masculinity, an extreme case of penis envy, mimicry of maleness, a usurpation of fatherhood, or overt misandry. Lesbian identity is *not* constituted in positive or affirmative rhetorical terms. Lesbian mothers are thus on shaky ground when it comes to demonstrating their worthiness to function as proper mothers. If lesbians exist presumptively outside the grounds of femininity, then they can never function as adequate mothers. That is, because "lesbian" is implicitly and repeatedly defined as a psychologically and morally corrupt mimicry of masculinity, then the oxymoron is solidified. Mother = femininity, lesbian = masculinity, therefore mother ≠ lesbian. Lesbian mother households thus represent abnormal family arrangements, subject to judicial and professional psychological scrutiny. Current psychological studies of lesbian mother households—specifically the comparative approach represented here—are doomed to reproduce and reify the lesbian mother oxymoron because of certain presumptions about what it means to be a "lesbian," what it means to "mother," and what it means to develop a sexual orientation. As the Flaks study observes, since psychoanalytic and social learning theories of child development "rely on traditional family structures to define the factors that promote children's development, they are not able to account easily for successful outcomes in nontraditional families, particularly those in which there is no opposite-sex parent in the home."[68]

Psychological studies of lesbian mother families are highly problematic on several grounds, then. The research is predicated on homonegative assumptions and claims, and the research methodologies reproduce and reinforce binary gender-role norms that punish children and adults for noncompliance. The developmental and social learning models, as applied in these studies, hypocritically presume that a mother's homosexuality might correlate more highly to her child's sexuality/gender development than the sexuality of a heterosexual mother, which is presumed not to have such a potentially strong correlation. A closer look at one of the Green study's conclusions may elucidate this rhetorical problem. "Why," it asks, "should there be no major demonstrable effect on sexual identity development of children being raised by currently homosexual mothers?"[69] If the studies are truly comparative in nature, would it not make sense to question whether a parent's heterosexual orientation had any "demonstrable effect" on one's children? Examining the question from another perspective, isn't it possible to conclude that lesbian parents are indeed having a "demonstrable effect" on their children's sexual identity development, that is, that lesbian mothers are indeed socializing their children "appropriately" by enforcing compliance with hegemonic sex role and gender performance norms? Lesbian mothers appear to be caught in an intricate and suffocating bind: if their children exhibit any form of noncompliance with sex role stereotypes, they might be held responsible.

In the sample psychological literature, lesbian identity is constituted as essentially transgressive. How is it that lesbian mothers can role model properly, whereby "properly" entails socializing children into identification with, preferences for, and performances of normatively gender-appropriate behaviors and roles? How is it that when lesbians raise "successfully" developed (read: heterosexual) children, then they have done a "proper" job of parenting, but if their children are gay, lesbian mothers have "recruited"? By what standards shall a profession distinguish between "socialization" and "recruitment"? The hypocrisy of this distinction need hardly be mentioned, but its pernicious effects should be emphasized: the subject position of lesbian mothers in professional psychological and psychiatric discourses is always already wretched and inferior. Lesbians and lesbian families will never "measure up" to the hegemonic heterosexual standard. This failure to "measure up" is a function of at least four correlated factors: the originary definition of lesbianism as a psychopathology, a professional discourse disciplined by its own historical and cultural trajectories, professional failure to examine disciplinary assumptions, and a homonegative culture that rewards those professional discourses that reproduce anti-lesbian *doxa*.

Although lesbianism may no longer *officially* be construed as a neurosis or mental illness, the academic rhetoric examined here illustrates the extent to which psychological professionals continue to conceive of lesbian identity as essentially problematic. The "illness" model, which typically *individuates* the pathological character of homosexuality, appears to have been replaced by the model of social transgression. The articulation represented by Chodorow casts lesbian identity as arrested development; the comparative studies replicate this depiction. The depictions effectively presume that lesbians are somehow less than fully human. For Chodorow, lesbian mothers pose a threat to her goal of fair distribution of parenting responsibilities. If lesbians exist in a state of arrested development because they fail to reach and enact the objective ideal of heterosexuality, then legitimation of lesbian maternal identity is difficult indeed. The comparative studies posit a similar set of problems, because the arrested development paradigm is replicated unwittingly through an obsessive focus on "proving" that children of lesbians will develop "successfully" into happy heterosexuals.

Given that *The Reproduction of Mothering* and the comparative studies are produced in a specific academic context, it behooves one to remember Foucault's warning that knowledge claims will always be subject to discipline. In the current case, it may be unreasonable to expect scholars in psychoanalysis, psychology, and psychiatry to resist their professional socialization. Although critiques of the illness paradigm were evident *before* the 1973 APA decision, it is unlikely that all scholars accepted the decision without reservations. As Bayer's research demonstrates, many contemporary scholars and practitioners still treat homosexuality as a psychological problem. Thus, one might reasonably expect scholarly treatments of homosexuality to contain residual elements of originary constructions, and we have certainly seen such evidence in this chapter. Given the history of the discipline, U.S. social history, and contemporary conditions of widespread discrimination and homonegativity, it is unlikely that academics would be able to resist or subvert the dominant paradigm completely.

At least one major objection to the academic discourse may be raised, however, as to the goals of the research. I claimed earlier that the comparative studies are doomed to rhetorical failure. The studies presume lesbianism to be inherently problematic or transgressive, and the scholars therefore fail to question their own professional assumptions about what it might "mean" to be a lesbian. The studies are misguided in their beneficent attempts to help in the struggle for equality because the studies' methodologies and research questions fail to reject the doxastic claim that *being* or *becoming* gay or lesbian is necessarily *bad*. The psychological research effectively implies that although a degree of tolerance for adult lesbians is necessary, such tolerance is acceptable *only* so long as the children do not "become" gay. The research intends to subvert proselytical characterizations, but the intention is undermined through the deployment of a rhetoric that replicates doxastic assumptions about lesbian identity, human sexuality, gender roles, and child development. The studies fail in spite of themselves through a logic that says, "Look! Lesbian adults exist, and they parent. But see how well they parent! They're socializing their children appropriately by enforcing conformity to binary sex and gender norms!" "Successful" lesbian parents do a different kind of recruiting if they raise "successfully" developed children. Heterosexual parents are not subject to accusations of recruitment, even though some might occasionally encourage their children to violate gender-role norms.

Such parents are "progressive." But any lesbian parent who encourages her children to resist, play with, or otherwise transgress gender roles risks being labeled a "bad mother."

In its interests and intentions the comparative research effectively masquerades as beneficent, but in the final analysis it poses grave rhetorical and practical dangers to lesbian families. Lesbian mothers and their children will not be served adequately by a professional discourse that continues to presume that being or becoming gay is bad. The academic rhetoric here is essentially debilitating, and the constraints on human agency are staggering and horrifying: gender roles, sexuality, and child-rearing practices are all subject to the panopticon of professional psychological surveillance. Unless and until researchers reject the presumption that being lesbian is bad, then the research should be rejected as a tool for advocacy and social change. Lesbian mothers will never achieve equality under the current psychological paradigms and the research that represents the vast ideological interests in preserving heterosexuality as a regime.

Homonegativity operates as a specific disciplinary mechanism in academic psychological discourses. The rhetoric examined here, then, does not (and, in a disciplinary sense, cannot) transcend anti-lesbian ideological conditioning. Instead it is rooted in such socialization. The lesbian mother oxymoron is thus reproduced through scholarly voices that whisper originary constructions of lesbian identity while shouting the praises of constricting sex role standards, compulsory heterosexuality, and conformity to outdated models of human sexuality. The research reifies heterosexual kinship bonds as the standard for comparison; such an approach masks the asymmetrical power relations along lines of gender and sexuality that assign lesbians an inherently disadvantaged status. If it is indeed the case that the types of scholarship represented here foreclose the possibility of a legitimate lesbian maternal identity, where might one turn for emancipation? How might one explode the reified categories of gender and sexual orientation? If my own teleological goal is to disrupt the construction, negotiation, and regulation of the lesbian mother oxymoron, what reformulation might I suggest? It is to these questions and others that I now turn.

The consequence of this tendency toward universality is that the straight mind cannot conceive of a culture, a society where heterosexuality would not order not only all human relationships but also its very production of concepts and all the processes which escape consciousness, as well.

MONIQUE WITTIG, *The Straight Mind*

TOWARD THE LEGITIMATION
OF LESBIAN MATERNAL IDENTITY

My purpose has been to trace the rhetorical development, circulation, and reification of the lesbian mother oxymoron in three major forums of public argumentation. Part of my critical goal has been to expropriate and reinscribe the oxymoronic rendering of lesbian motherhood. Before such a process could occur, however, it was necessary to understand the rhetorical constructions of lesbian maternal identity in American public culture. And before the oxymoron could be redeployed as a strategy for linguistic and social change, it was crucial to understand the complex rhetorical processes through which "lesbian mother" developed as an oxymoron.

The project derives from three related concerns. First, it stems from an intellectual curiosity about *how* ideological discourses, such as journalistic, legal, and academic discourses, construct, negotiate, and regulate individual and group identities, and thereby also craft the bounds of legitimate identity performances. In this context I have attempted to show how advocates deploy hegemonic and oppositional discourses of gender, sexuality, and parenthood to contest the meanings of lesbian motherhood. The project also derives from a desire to demystify the rhetorical and cultural practices that punish lesbians for their attempts to form families and that punish mothers for non-procreative erotic identity performances. Finally, it derives from a commitment to improving citizens' lives. State regulation of identity, when it impinges on the choices of private citizens, poses a threat to individual procreative and associational freedoms regardless of one's sexual orientation. Thus, my specific concern for how lesbian maternal identities are regulated by the state can exemplify the ideological contestation of identity and agency.

In this chapter I review the processes through which the lesbian mother oxymoron became established and reified. I then advance a theoretical reconceptualization of how pro-lesbian advocates might expropriate the lesbian mother oxymoron. In particular, I elaborate my key conclusion that managing the rhetorical problems of identity and agency for lesbian mothers should be based on an eradication of the criminal, pathologic, and proselytic characterizations that anchor the lesbian mother in a necessarily illegitimate rhetorical space. These anchors have been constituted within what I have termed a rhetorical ambivalence, as various public advocates have tried to negotiate and regulate what "lesbian" and "mother" mean as individual words, and what they might or should mean when one woman inhabits and enacts both identities. My proposed redeployment of the oxymoron draws on recent work in critical rhetoric and lesbian-feminist theory. My primary purpose is to call attention to the serious problems posed by retaining the rhetorical anchors that delegitimate the lesbian mother in contemporary American culture. At the same time, I believe that we as a society must construct a cultural space that allows mothers to engage in non-procreative erotic practices.

The ways in which lesbian motherhood functions as a contested identity in American culture reveal deeply rooted cultural ambivalence and anxieties about the meanings and practices of both lesbianism and motherhood. Such anxieties manifest themselves through a rhetorical ambivalence that has two key features. First, the ambivalence becomes articulated through polarized characterizations of lesbian maternal identity. The characterizations themselves rest on a series of binary oppositions that place lesbian identity distinctly at odds with legitimate maternal agency. So, for instance, Chodorow's rhetoric constituted lesbian identity as a kind of arrested development at odds with the teleological ideal of heterosexuality, which could be achieved *only* through heterosexual unions that produced children. Homonegative journalistic rhetoric capitalized on such depictions by casting lesbians as a moral and criminal threat to the contemporary American family. The polarized characterizations structure the debates about lesbian maternal identity so that oppositional depictions become difficult to use successfully. Advocates at each of these discursive sites tend to draw on the fund of negative characterizations of lesbians to advance the hegemonic status of motherhood as a profoundly heterosexual institution and practice.

Second, the rhetorical ambivalence functions as the discursive ground on which the process of identity formation, negotiation, and regulation occur. Rhetorical ambivalence is a structural feature of public argumentation about identity in general, especially in the way it characterizes the debate at large rather than simply functioning as the particular position(s) of individual rhetors. There are some advocates, however, who manifest and reproduce the ambivalence, as in the debates in the lesbian press over lesbian maternal identity as either a form of feminist revolution or a betrayal of sisterhood. This feature emphasizes how the rhetorical ambivalence authorizes or disciplines discourse about specific issues through the binary system, through silent negation, and through pronouncements concerning which speakers have enough legitimate authority to advance their positions in public debates.

In chapter 2 I engaged the rhetorical ambivalence as it has become constructed since the 1970s within the domain of lesbian and straight journalistic accounts of lesbian identity and lesbian motherhood. Within the straight press, lesbians either were rendered invisible or so marginal as to be practically invisible, or were characterized through recruitment metaphors as a serious threat to the family. The rhetorical ambivalence manifest in the lesbian press applied the "personal is political" adage to lesbian motherhood by characterizing lesbian mothers either as revolutionary heroes or as co-opted dupes of the patriarchy. Within the domain of journalism, then, the rhetorical ambivalence functioned both as a symbolic terrain on which lesbian maternal identity could be constructed and negotiated and as a basis for identity regulation. This regulatory function is a crucial feature of rhetorical practice, for it indicates that the meanings of words are not easily renegotiated over short periods of time. The existing rhetorical history of a word will invariably influence and regulate the range of acceptable meanings it may enjoy in the future. In addition, individual advocates cannot easily reinscribe meaning. Linguistic change is a collective practice. As Leslie Feinberg writes so eloquently, "I learned that language can't be ordered individually, as if from a Sears catalog. It is forged collectively, in the fiery heat of struggle."[1]

In chapter 3 I examined the implication of criminal, pathological, and proselytic representations of lesbian identity in child custody cases involving divorcing couples, lesbian couple dissolutions, and second-parent adoptions. I explored the discursive limitations of lesbian motherhood and tried to explicate various dimensions of the process of identity formation. We saw how the rhetorical ambivalence in judicial rhetoric regulated the lesbian mother oxymoron by characterizing lesbians as neurotic or psychotic women intent on recruiting their children into the "homosexual lifestyle." Judicial rhetoric reified the biologic component of maternal identity in such a way as to exclude lesbian co-parents or non-biological mothers from legitimate parental agency. I do not assume that all lesbians who choose to raise children are in fact fit to do so. To be sure, some lesbians are unfit parents, for the same reasons some heterosexual parents are unfit. Many parents, regardless of sexual orientation, fail to provide for the day-to-day nurturing of their children, or they abuse their children or allow them to be abused by others. Not every lesbian who presses a custodial and/or visitation claim should succeed. What we find in the divorce cases, however, is a profoundly anti-lesbian reading of the legal concept of fitness such that a woman's ontological status as a lesbian *automatically* places her in the "unfit" category. Lesbians lose custody not for the same reasons that non-lesbians do, but for being "bad" women. The legal discourse thus creates a structural inequality by making the "fitness" concept a slippery one and by constituting lesbian status as proof of an inherent "unfitness" to parent.

Academic rhetoric, as we saw in chapter 4, also participates in the construction of the lesbian mother oxymoron by perpetuating stereotypic representations of lesbians as masculine, proselytic, and inherently non-maternal. Contemporary psychological research thus reproduces early twentieth-century sexological representations of lesbianism, and does so by failing to problematize the stereotypes that undergird the research. Academic discourse is disciplined in this instance to reproduce prior or originary constructions of lesbian identity even as it proclaims the goal of helping lesbian mothers. One key implication, then, is that to achieve radical social change (i.e., legal and social justice for lesbian mothers), one must identify, contest, and disrupt originary constructions. Failure to do so will perpetuate linguistic and material domination.

Taken together, the analyses in chapters 2, 3, and 4 illustrate that rhetorical ambivalence is *systemic* in the sense that each of the three discursive communities functions simultaneously to (re)produce the lesbian mother oxymoron. The hegemony is not the responsibility of any one individual advocate, but instead is produced, circulated, reproduced, and reified through repetitive articulation at the site of each ideological state apparatus. The fact that the contestation of lesbian maternal identities occurs in multiple public forums may indicate the extent to which hegemony, rather than locating itself at one cultural site, is instead negotiated at various sites. Advocates, working individually and collectively, will struggle to participate in, provide direction to, and ultimately win the contest (even if provisionally or temporarily) for hegemonic control of identity and the forms of agency that may be authorized within that particular identity category. *How* the rhetorical ambivalence is jointly constructed and maintained is important for any theory of social change, for it suggests that critiquing *only* the mass media or the law or the academy is not enough. Instead, it is crucial to understand how each of these discourse communities relies on and contributes to the others recursively so as to (re)produce the hegemony.

To what extent is it possible to reinscribe the lesbian mother oxymoron? Rather than constituting lesbian identity as criminal or pathologic, one might build an affirmative rhetoric of lesbian motherhood with a lesbian-as-function or lesbian-as-agent characterization. In addition, rather than unwittingly continuing to rely on strictly biologic representations of who "counts" as a mother, one might privilege a mother-as-function approach. Relying on functional characterizations will potentially reconstitute the lesbian mother oxymoron in a more affirmative mode, one that allows for simultaneous enactment of lesbian and maternal identities. In what follows I illustrate my proposals by examining how legal and academic discourses (and, by implication, the journalism that reports on them) could change. I then explore the rhetorical limitations of my recommendations.

My attempt to reconceptualize the "lesbian mother" as a legitimate identity exhibits a critical concern for the ways in which ideological discourses, as inherently rhetorical discourses, form and shape cultural notions of gender and sexuality through discussions of what it means to be a lesbian mother in contemporary American society. The form and content of such discussions are shaped by, and in turn shape, broader cultural notions of the acceptable range of gender and sexuality-related identity performances.

Lesbians and Mothers as Affirmative Agents

As I have shown, characterizations of lesbians as *essentially* neurotic, criminal, or proselytical anchor the lesbian in a rhetorical space marked out-of-bounds for legitimate maternal agency. These characterizations are strengthened by judicial acceptance, and in some instances appeals to public morality, as reasons to deny custodial and visitation claims. But the courts face a material dilemma when they encounter lesbian mothers in divorce cases, for judges must acknowledge that the female parent is both a mother and a lesbian. Mothers' advocates address this seeming paradox by arguing that lesbian mothers constitute neither a logical impossibility nor a moral threat to the development of their children; that is, they refuse to concede that the terms "lesbian" and "mother" exclude each other.

There are specific rhetorical tactics that advocates can deploy to contest and reconstruct the oxymoron in affirmative terms. For example, advocates need to contest the collapse of identity and morality that occurs in the concept of parental "fitness." Pro-lesbian advocates must continue to question social constructions of gender, sex, and sexuality; they must also disrupt the notion that gay people are essentially proselytic. The rhetorical practices currently employed by lesbian mothers' legal advocates and legal scholars concerned with planned lesbian families provide fertile ground for both engaging and critiquing the roots from which a rhetoric might emerge that both recognizes and values planned lesbian families. Maia Ettinger writes that "in order to claim an identity free of self-loathing, gay and lesbian people have created discursive strategies that reject and transform the categories produced by a hostile and hegemonic heterosexual discourse."[2] Although I do think it is true that pro-lesbian advocates have achieved important rhetorical goals, some practices undermine the legitimacy of lesbian motherhood by reifying negative characterizations of lesbian identity. Here I review the primary discursive practices used to legitimate lesbian families in the legal rhetorical domain as the basis for a discussion of how greater rhetorical legitimacy might be achieved for planned lesbian families.

The rhetoric of co-parenthood as manifested in both lesbian dissolution cases and second-parent adoption cases is significant because it recognizes the cooperation and mutuality necessary for the successful functioning of all two-parent families. The use of the non-gendered term "parent" is also significant: the cases I examined spoke not of "mothers" but of "parents," and advocates (attorneys, the mothers themselves, and the judges) thus struggled to assign particular meanings to the generic "parent." The ways in which "mother" becomes obscured carry significant implications for the rhetorical goal of reconceptualizing the lesbian mother. Rendering the "mother" invisible in the rhetorics of lesbian dissolution and second-parent adoption cases (except to describe a biological connection between woman and child) hinders any effort to expropriate the "lesbian mother" in American rhetorical culture. Reliance on the rhetoric of "co-parenting" is potentially unsatisfactory to the extent that it encourages continued readings of "lesbian mother" as a contradiction in terms. It may be the case that "co-parent" draws attention to the labor enacted by both mothers and challenges the heteronormative ideal that two-parent families necessarily consist of one mother and one father. Nevertheless, my point is that choosing "co-parent" as a featured term in an affirmative rhetoric of lesbian motherhood may work against emancipatory redeployment of the oxymoron itself. Reinscribing the "lesbian mother" means, at the very least, that pro-lesbian advocates must not forsake those two words but must continue to use them next to each other.

Appeals to motherhood as a fundamental biological relationship between woman and child is significant for understanding the lesbian dissolution cases. The lesbian partner who carried and gave birth to the couple's child would employ this rhetorical strategy by claiming that the court had to grant a higher valence to her biological connection with the child, even though her partner also served an important maternal function. In each case where the birth mother played the biology trump card, she won primary custody of her child. The implications of employing such a strategy are two: it works to the advantages of lesbian mothers who can prove a "natural" (and thus "legitimate") connection to a child, but it works against the legitimation of functional approaches to motherhood. In effect, the biological mother says, "For the purposes of this case, I am going to buy into the hegemonic discourse of the family, which values biology." The practice divides and conquers in that it benefits individual lesbians but harms lesbians as a group.[3] Moreover, it encourages the biological mother to side with a culturally conservative argument in order to win custody.[4] The practice reifies biological motherhood at the expense of her partner's identity as a lesbian mother.

The naming practices employed by lesbian couples function as another rhetorical strategy used to legitimate lesbian families. In some cases the couple's child is given the last name of the non-birth mother. In other cases the couple bestow on the child a hybrid form of their last names, either by giving the child a hyphenated last name or by creating a single name. The former convention recognizes the significance of the non-birth mother; the latter ties the child's identity to both mothers. The significance of naming practices, at least within the context of lesbian dissolution cases and second-parent adoptions, however, is somewhat limited. Although the custom might craft some semblance of a legitimate family identity on an individual level, and perhaps within the lesbian community, it is all but ignored in public legal discourse. Judges might take note of such practices, but ascribe little significance to them: the child's surname, in other words, bears minor relevance to the outcome of custody cases.[5]

Appeals to extant legal concepts such as de facto parenthood and in loco parentis are also rhetorically ineffective for legitimating the non-birth mother's functional role. Constructions of lesbian maternal identity that rely on these two concepts limit the potential legitimacy of functional lesbian mothers. *Black's Law Dictionary* defines *de facto* as "characteriz[ing] an officer, a government, a past action, or a state of affairs which must be accepted for all practical purposes, but is illegal or illegitimate." The appropriation of "de facto" appears problematic because courts reject the claim that they "must accept" a lesbian who has functioned as a parent for "all practical purposes." The practice also grants the assumption that lesbian motherhood is "illegitimate." It would be more useful to employ a rhetorical practice that critiques the assumption rather than granting it. In loco parentis arguments serve a similar function. From a legal perspective, *in loco parentis* means "in the place of a parent; instead of a parent; charged, factitiously, with a parent's rights, duties, and responsibilities." This practice also works against the long-term goal of characterizing lesbian motherhood as a legitimate type of motherhood; and it works against the interests of individual lesbian mothers who have a functional rather than biological connection to their children. In the lesbian dissolution cases, judges feared that granting effect to functional definitions of parenthood would negate the rights of biological mothers. The use of an in loco parentis argument feeds such a fear with its language of replacement and substitution. To be "factitiously" charged with parental duties means that the performance of such duties lacks authenticity, that one's labor is a sham. The non-biological mother's role is thus circumscribed by the use of legal terms that deny validity to functional maternal practices.

Finally, pro-lesbian activists must move away from any characterizations of planned lesbian families as either "alternative" or "nontraditional." In its adjectival form, *alternative* bears at least two related meanings: "existing outside traditional or established institutions or systems," and "espousing or reflecting values that are different from those of the establishment." Marking "difference" is problematic to the extent that the embodied difference is automatically subject to domination. The meaning(s) attached to "alternative" and "nontraditional" tend to be used in heteronormative rhetorical contexts in which "alternative" is presumptively inferior. Unless and until pro-lesbian advocates can successfully contest and renegotiate the renderings of "alternative" and "nontraditional" to mean something other than "separate and unequal," then they should avoid representing lesbian families in this way. Advocates can instead describe lesbian-headed households as "families" with no modifier, thereby claiming the terrain of "family" and shifting the rhetorical burden to heteronormative advocates who wish to exclude lesbians from The Family. Instead of pro-lesbian advocates having to prove that lesbian families are indeed families, anti-lesbian advocates should bear the burden of proving (without relying on stereotypes) that they are not. Continued use of "alternative" and "nontraditional" embraces and affirms the power of an entity—the heterosexual married family—that retains hegemonic force as a cultural ideal. These terms imply value judgments about the relative rhetorical legitimacy of various family forms. A brief analogy to racialized discourses may be useful here. In their discussion of center/margin discourses and racial identities, Thomas Nakayama and Thomas Krizek note that "the experiences and communication patterns of whites are taken as the norm from which Others are marked. If we take a critical perspective to whiteness, however, we can begin the process of particularizing white experience. This move displaces whites from a universal stance which has tended to normalize and to naturalize their positionality to a more specific social location in which they confront the kinds of questions and challenges facing any particular social location."[6] In the interests of developing lesbian-affirmative rhetorics of motherhood, then, characterizing lesbian families as alternative fails to reject the hegemonic ideal and instead reaffirms, reinscribes, and reifies its power.

In sum, the rhetorical strategies employed by various legal and academic advocates to legitimate lesbian maternal identity are doomed to failure. Some unintentionally affirm the hegemonic status of the heterosexual nuclear family. Others may benefit individual lesbians but harm lesbians as a group. Mothers' legal representatives should stop relying on comparative psychological studies, since such studies replicate essentially anti-lesbian attitudes. If it is indeed the case that the rhetorical practices reviewed in this section ultimately fail to allow for a strategic expropriation of the lesbian mother oxymoron, what might be done to craft a rhetoric that legitimates lesbian maternal identity? I think that there are four central components to a lesbian-affirmative conception of motherhood.

First, I speak of "planned" lesbian families to draw attention to the complex process by which individual lesbians and lesbian couples create their kinship networks. There are few accidental pregnancies where lesbians (and, especially, lesbian couples) are concerned. Individual lesbians and lesbian couples have to *orchestrate* the creation of their families. The "planned" lesbian family is *chosen*. The concept of choice is central to a lesbian-positive crafting of maternal identity because it highlights the role of individual agency in the process of becoming a mother.

Second, a lesbian-positive rhetoric should not obscure the functional aspects of motherhood in lesbian motherhood. Such obfuscation occurs when the biological trump card is played in lesbian dissolution cases. The kinship rhetoric should instead privilege function over biology, and should affirm and celebrate functional approaches to motherhood. Indeed, I urge all Americans to adopt functional approaches to and definitions of "mother," "father," "parent," and "family." The innovative work of Nan Hunter, Nancy Polikoff, and Paula Ettelbrick could be followed and extended in this regard.

Third, a pastiche of strategies could be enacted in the legal sphere to affirm lesbian families. I believe that marriage should be abolished as the basis for family law and policy. The parent-child dyad should instead form the ground on which family law standards are developed. Martha Fineman's work in *The Neutered Mother* is exemplary here.[7] If the parent-child dyad (instead of the conjugal husband-wife dyad) were central, it would be much more difficult for judges to discriminate against lesbian couples in second-parent adoption cases—especially if the new dyadic focus were coupled with a functional approach to mothering. Other legal reforms could be pursued. Local, state, and federal officials need to educate themselves about the discrimination that lesbian mothers suffer. The struggle for gay/lesbian/bisexual/transgender rights is continuous, and I would suggest that more people contact their legislators to support gay-affirmative legislation such as the Employment Non-Discrimination Act (ENDA). Those legislators who oppose basic civil rights and protections for queer people often couch their opposition in the rhetoric of "special rights" and "traditional values." Pro-lesbian advocates must attack such constructions by asserting that basic civil protections are *not* "special rights" that violate "traditional values," and that proposed legislation such as ENDA does not confer "special" rights on queer citizens but instead extends equal protection. Pro–lesbian/gay civil rights activists must work harder to negate the false "special rights" rhetoric so popular among right-wing politicians.

Stigma-related claims should also be absolutely disallowed as grounds for denying custody. State legislatures should ban parental sexual orientation as a factor in determining a child's best interests. Given that legislative change can be painfully slow, pro-lesbian activists should in the meantime advance the "nexus" approach. Any anti-lesbian advocate who claims that lesbian mothers are "unfit" because of their sexual orientation should have the burden of proving, with clear and convincing evidence rather than stereotype, flawed presumptions, and anti-lesbian misrepresentations, that the mother in question is unfit. Moreover, judges should not be able to use "moral fitness" clauses in existing best interest statutes to deny lesbian mothers' custody and visitation claims. Taken together, this pastiche of strategies may help lesbian mothers escape the conditions of domination that threaten to tear apart their families. In a word, existing best interest statutes must be reformed to allow for legitimate lesbian motherhood. If "stigma" and "moral fitness" appeals were excluded, judges and anti-lesbian rhetors would need to find new ways to discriminate against lesbian families.

Finally, a lesbian-affirmative rhetoric must be constructed from a space of assumed rhetorical equality rather than a space of presumptive subordination. Psychological representations that reproduce stereotypes of lesbians as insufficiently feminine or as hypermasculine need continued contestation, if not rejection. Moreover, pro-lesbian activists ought to challenge the popular, legal, and psychological presumption that being gay or lesbian is "bad" or a "condition" to be avoided. Lesbian mothers will not enjoy justice and legitimacy if the rhetorical practices employed by their advocates unwittingly affirm the primacy of the heterosexual nuclear family.

Toward a Strategic Reinscription of "Lesbian Mother"

In a 1993 essay examining turn-of-the-century constitutions of American lesbian identity, Lisa Duggan concludes that "lesbians do not come from outside culture, outside history, or outside class, race, and gender to raise the flag for a self-evident version of freedom, justice, and equality. Rather, lesbian resistance consists of our determination to dissent—to retell our culture's dominant stories with an eye to reorganizing its distribution of cultural and material resources."[8] Given the sedimentation and, indeed, the reification of the criminal, proselytic, and pathologic characterizations of lesbianism, as well as the biologic representations of motherhood, to what extent is rhetorical resistance and reinscription possible? To this point I have tried to establish the critical framework from which to argue that to reconstruct lesbian maternal identity we must expropriate the three primary representations of "lesbian" and the biologic depictions that anchor the "mother." In this section I propose a "lesbian-as-agent/lesbian-as-function" and a "mother-as-function" reconstruction of the lesbian mother oxymoron.

I ground my proposal in a lesbian-feminist perspective that critiques heterosexuality as a systemic political regime. Based in radical feminist philosophy, my approach to lesbian feminism presumes that patriarchal definitions of gender, sex, reproduction, and sexuality are a key factor in lesbian oppression. Lesbian feminism asserts three major tenets relevant to my purpose: Lesbian identity is a political as well as a personal issue. Lesbian issues must not be absent, dismissed, or marginalized from feminist ideology and politics. Lesbian feminism as a political ideology is central to the liberation of women.[9]

It should be clear that in previous chapters I have drawn upon a lesbian-feminist perspective. I mentioned in the foreword, for instance, how this project was born of a personal interest both in issues that affect lesbian lives and in cultural forces such as media, religion, education, and government that tell women our primary contribution to culture is through breeding and raising children. Such pressures are never neutral (though they may masquerade as such) but instead replicate the asymmetrical social organization of gender and sexuality that privileges men over women and heterosexuals over lesbians. The political orientation offered by a lesbian-feminist perspective is consonant with critical rhetoric's emancipatory focus. Lesbian-feminist philosophy takes as a foundational assumption that ideologies of gender and sexuality cannot be treated separately, for they work together to create both possibilities and limits for women's lives. Females who do not follow the dictates of compulsory heterosexuality are punished through various rhetorical processes that judge them as sick, criminal, or sinful. Advocates opposed to legitimate lesbian maternal identity and agency often ask, in a supposedly innocent manner, questions such as "Yes, but what effect will a lesbian mother have on her children?" This question makes sense *if and only if* we grant legitimacy to stereotypical characterizations of lesbian identity. The ultimate goal of this project, following the philosophical orientation toward politics offered by lesbian feminism as well as the critical rhetorical orientation toward discourse, is to reveal such questions as nonsense. Before the question becomes moot, however, one must attend to the rhetorical reconfiguration of lesbian and maternal identities.

The ideographic renderings of lesbian identity that highlight characterizations of criminality and neurosis focus on the "what-ness" of lesbianism rather than the "who-ness." And, as Julia Penelope writes, defining lesbian identity is a "task of historical proportions. Unlike other sorts of identity, Lesbians possess no readily apparent identifying characteristics of space or time, nor can we look to origins or particular circumstances."[10] In addition, she contends, "If one wishes to understand the Lesbian experience, one must somehow imagine what it is like growing up into an identity that's unmentionable in any positive or helpful context. As the heterosexual agenda becomes clearer and clearer and its requirements and strictures become more and more insistently coercive, Lesbians have very few options, none of which are attractive."[11] The task of defining "lesbian" is at once seemingly futile yet necessary. I do not wish to advance a universal definition of the word; rather, I wish to tailor a non-criminal, non-proselytic, and non-neurotic definition so that "lesbian" reads more comfortably next to "mother" (since "mothers," in common usage, are typically conceived as law-abiding and healthy). A lesbian-as-function construction highlights the performative and nominalistic dimensions of identity formation whereby an individual is a "lesbian" if she names herself a "lesbian," and if she "functions" as a lesbian. But what does it mean to function as a lesbian?

Several recent works in lesbian-feminist theory contribute to my lesbian-as-function approach. Vera Whisman's commentary on the nature of contemporary lesbian identity politics posits that "in the end, a lesbian must simply be any woman who calls herself one, understanding that we place ourselves within that category, drawing and redrawing the boundaries in ever-shifting ways. For there is no essential and timeless lesbian, but instead lesbians who, by creating our lives day by day, widen the range of possibilities."[12] Penelope also asserts the existence of multiple and complex lesbian identities. "Lesbian identity cannot be based solely on one or more sexual acts," she writes, and "there is no one kind of Lesbian." Instead, there are "many paths" to a lesbian identity. . . . [A]n adequate definition must include our sexuality without making it the only deciding factor."[13]

In a similar vein, Ann Ferguson views "lesbian" as a "deconstructive category," whereby "'lesbian' is a sliding signifier with no fixed positive content: rather it is a deconstructive concept which can be applied to any woman who violates assumptions of gender dualism which are themselves historically specific."[14] Diana Fuss asserts that "lesbian" is a "historically contingent" category; moreover, in advancing emancipatory critical projects, we should retain a focus on the "realm of social and discursive formations" (the *produc-tion* of identity) rather than obsessing about "the realm of ontology" (what a lesbian *is*).[15] Lesbian identity is thus not reducible to a particular (or univer-sal, in the sense that lesbians "share" them) set of erotic or sexual practices. Nor is lesbian identity reducible to a set of commonly subscribed-to beliefs. But what American "lesbians" do have in common, I think, are two things: a shared history of oppression, and a shared desire to enact their most signifi-cant emotional, intellectual, erotic, and spiritual relationships with other les-bians. Lesbian identity can thus be constituted in various cultural contexts and across particular locales.

A reconstructed conception of lesbian motherhood must, at its founding moment, account for the multiple ways in which heterosexuality functions as a political institution in contemporary American culture.[16] As Monique Wittig writes, "The discourses which particularly oppress all of us, lesbians, women, and homosexual men, are those which take for granted that what founds soci-ety, any society, is heterosexuality. . . . These discourses of heterosexuality oppress us in the sense that they prevent us from speaking unless we speak in their terms."[17] According to Adrienne Rich, one crucial step in constructing *legitimate* lesbian maternal identity, then is, "to acknowledge that for women heterosexuality may not be a 'preference' at all but something that has to be imposed, managed, organized, propagandized, and maintained by force."[18]

The imposition of heterosexuality is subtle and is often taken for granted or naturalized. Many heterosexuals sometimes complain that they have no "problem" with gay men and lesbians, but simply wish that gay men and les-bians would "keep quiet" and not "advertise" their sexuality. In other cases, heterosexuals try to express a "liberal" attitude toward homosexuality by say-ing (usually in whispered tones) that "what people do in the privacy of their own homes is nobody's business." Or they claim that gay men and lesbians should "keep their private lives private," and then speak incessantly about their wives or husbands, boyfriends or girlfriends. Heterosexuality is propa-gandized in all such instances, taken for granted as the ultimate and only legitimate end of erotic, emotional, and spiritual fulfillment. The illegitimacy of lesbian and gay identity is maintained by force through gay-bashing, through rape, through sexual harassment and job discrimination, through various "Defense of Marriage" acts, and through the development of self-disclosure policies in a government that preaches "don't ask, don't tell." The struggle to conceptualize a rhetorically legitimate lesbian identity, then, necessitates the exposure of asymmetrical power relations along lines of gender and sexual orientation.

Pro-lesbian advocates could refuse to engage in debates about the "causes" of homosexuality. For instance, one might "naturalize" the lesbian by engaging in what Gayatri Spivak calls the "strategic use of essentialism."[19] Deploying this strategy would entail thinking and speaking of lesbian identity in ontological terms, whereby lesbianism is a natural state of being. Such deployments might serve the ultimate ideological interests of negating stereotypical definitions of lesbianism. Although strategic essentialism may serve a useful political function for the "lesbian" in the "lesbian mother" equation, it might not be applied so usefully to the "mother." As I mentioned earlier, the biological ideographic characterization of "mother" contributes to the oxymoronic status of lesbian motherhood. Particular "nurturing" practices can be highlighted to expand conceptions of motherhood. As the second-parent adoption cases demonstrate, such nurturing practices have been recognized and rewarded in the legal sphere. Pro-lesbian advocates must thus work on a variety of fronts—naturalizing the lesbian when necessary, and functionalizing the mother.

The employment of strategic essentialism, at least within the framework of crafting an authentic lesbian maternal identity, entails what I call a poststructural identity politics. Such a politics, grounded in both critical rhetoric and a lesbian-feminist political philosophy, recognizes the role of rhetoric and ideology in poststructural notions of identity *and* recognizes the political potential of engaging in identity politics. Traditional poststructuralist theory would typically eschew identity politics as somewhat regressive, but to my mind the two concepts are not mutually exclusive—especially if one's aims are emancipatory in nature. My goals are indeed emancipation-focused rather than equality-driven. A focus on gaining equality for lesbian mothers presumes a desire to remain within the bounds of heteronormative logic. It is eminently clear that lesbians and lesbian mothers live in conditions of domination and oppression. What would it mean for lesbian mothers to achieve "equality"? To whom would lesbian mothers be equal? Rather than "equality" as such, the long-term goal should be the total destruction of the reified binary systems of gender, sex, and sexuality that imprison all citizens in out-dated and oppressive modes of being. Epistemological and cultural revolu-tion, rather than reform, is the task. These binary systems enable and repro-duce the conditions of domination. Significant work is already under way in various queer and transgender movements to abolish the binary construc-tions of gender, sex, and sexuality. Pro–lesbian mother advocates could build coalitions with transgender activists, for instance, and work together to de-stroy the oppressive constructions of masculinity/femininity, male/female, and heterosexual/homosexual that constrain human agency in profoundly harmful ways. It appears pragmatic rhetorically to organize political efforts around the critique and destruction of those binaries, especially to the extent that hegemonic institutions and forces (and the voices, variously individu-ated and collectivized, which represent those institutions) wish to control the constitution of identities.

Implications for Contemporary Rhetorical Theory

Let us look briefly at the theoretical implications raised by my proposals.

The Rhetorical Problem of Identity: Re-asking the Question

I return to a question raised in the first chapter: What does this study teach us about the ways in which ideological discourses speak to the problem of iden-tity? In the first chapter I advanced a multilayered explanation for the ways in which human identities are crafted through rhetoric. Although human beings occupy individuated bodies, the identities we ascribe to ourselves and other people are necessarily influenced by the language we use—and the ways in which we use it—to describe them. As Althusser might say, rhetoric calls iden-tity categories into existence; these categories are then negotiated and regu-lated through sustained and complicated processes of public deliberation.

Individual rhetors, groups, and institutions engage in complicated rhetor-ical struggles to have "their" characterizations of identity function as the "real," the "only," or the "moral" constructions. Public argumentation could be characterized thus as a competition of sorts, with historical winners and losers, haves and have-nots, angels and demons, heroes and villains. Public deliberation regarding lesbian maternal identity has constituted lesbian mothers as some version of each of these typifications. But identities are not only constructed and represented. They are also performed or enacted, and the range of acceptable performance is regulated by how the identity has been formulated and negotiated through sustained public deliberation.

Of course, this project enters the fray of public argumentation as well, by advocating the eventual hegemony of a rhetorically legitimate identity for lesbian mothers (and one that is recognized legally as such). "Lesbians" will not be able to participate fully in the agency of motherhood until, for instance, the word "lesbian" is reconstituted as an affirmative identity. "Mothers" will be less able to participate in the range of agencies suggested by "lesbian" until the excessively biologic characterizations of "motherhood" are subdued and subverted. A rhetorically legitimate (and thereby culturally legitimate) lesbian motherhood has the potential to open a new realm of possibilities for lesbians (including lesbian non-mothers), mothers (including heterosexual mothers, married, single, partnered, or divorced), and lesbian mothers.

In addition to demonstrating the rhetorical nature and functions of identity and agency, this study contributes to our understanding of the complex relationships between rhetoric and law. Legal practitioners craft a vision of what it means to be a legitimate (and therefore "moral") mother by regulating and punishing specific performances of lesbian identity. The moral dimensions of motherhood and lesbianism thus became negotiated, for instance, through legal arguments about whether a specific lesbian mother should retain custody of her children given her romantic involvement with another lesbian. The chorus of voices who participated in public discussions about the "goodness" of lesbian motherhood thus participated actively in a broader cultural crafting of lesbian maternal morality.

This study illustrates that legal discourses, such as that involving the normative standards enacted through various legislative statutes and judicial opinions, provide fertile ground for critical intervention. To the extent that the law shapes and is shaped in turn by notions of the moral good, critics can sustain analyses of how legal discourses function to constitute and negotiate the legitimate bounds of identity performance. For example, scholars interested in feminist jurisprudence can critique how the law structures itself on gendered binaries to perpetuate the masculinist domination of women. Feminist jurisprudence can draw on the insights of the critical rhetorician to attend to the inherent rhetorical foundations of such constructions. I have argued, for instance, that the emancipation of maternal identity (writ large) cannot occur unless and until lesbian identity is also liberated from its criminal, proselytic, and pathologic characterizations, and until maternal identity is freed from the biologic metaphors that chain women to their procreative capacities. Freedom and justice for non-lesbian mothers, in other words, rest on our society's paying critical attention to lesbian oppression within the legal system. Feminist jurisprudence, such as the work of Mary Joe Frug, has taken the linguistic turn to attend to the "constructive function of legal language as a critical frontier for feminist reforms" and to the law "as a site of political struggle."[20] Feminist jurisprudence can benefit from this study by attending to the ways in which legal discourses constitute, negotiate, and regulate identity, and thereby proscribe human agency.

Reflexive Critique: A Sidebar on Limitations

Reflexive critique, a moment whereby the critic makes explicit her own motives and highlights the presences and absences of her own theory, is an integral aspect of critical rhetorical practice. Chapter 1 identified various personal motivations for undertaking this project. In my own experience, I have been and continue to be affected by the discourses of gender and sexuality that shape and limit my potentialities, though I neither necessarily identify as a lesbian nor inhabit or enact a maternal identity. The ideological pressures exerted on me as a woman to reproduce have come from a number of fronts, but one primary message is clear: women who choose not to reproduce and engage in maternal practices will be seen as selfish, flawed, or self-deluded. One acquaintance has maintained that I must have some secret wish for a child, and that enacting this study is "simply" an effort to craft a space for myself to enact a legitimate queer motherhood. But the specific character of motherhood is limited by narratives of sexuality (spoken by heterosexual and lesbian advocates) which maintain that only certain sorts of women become (or remain) mothers. The lesbian is thus, as we saw in chapter 3, sometimes placed in the awkward position of having to choose one identity over the other in order to obtain custody—and it is not the lesbian identity she can choose.

Again, I am not arguing that all lesbians who choose to become mothers should *necessarily* retain custody of their children. As I pointed out earlier, there are certainly some lesbians, as well as some heterosexual women, who fail to care for their children properly, and should be barred from any legitimate custodial claim. But lesbians should not be, as they have been to this point in American rhetorical history, categorized *outside* the realm of motherhood in a priori fashion. Nor is my critique of the institutions of motherhood and heterosexuality an attack on the choices that other women have made, and continue to make, to become mothers. Rather, my critique exposes how the rhetoric of motherhood alienates "women from our bodies by incarcerating us in them."[21]

Some might say that this is a conservative project insofar as it implicitly pushes for revalorization of the maternal preference presumption in custody disputes. Such an inference misinterprets my goals. I am arguing that we must reconstruct the asymmetrical relations of gender and sexuality that exclude lesbians from legitimate enactment of maternity and that also exclude mothers from nonprocreative sexuality. Furthermore, I do not argue for a monolithic approach to lesbian maternal identity through the critique of rhetorical ambivalence. I am trying to illustrate how hegemonic and oppositional discourses of gender and sexuality are dispersed through various rhetorical forums, which, taken together, contain spaces that both limit the enactment of a culturally legitimate lesbian maternal identity and provide opportunities for negotiation of rhetorically constituted identity categories.

The rhetorical silences on particular topics can be as significant as the speech about them. What, then, are the silences created through my own rhetorical constructions in this book? Some have been purposeful, while others have been created as a function of a particular orientation to discourse. Lesbian-feminist philosophy, for instance, tends to mute issues of race, class, and age, which are also constitutive features of identity and are therefore important to the maintenance and regulation of motherhood. Within the various forums of public argumentation examined here, issues of race and class were certainly subordinated (if covered at all) to place sexuality in high relief. One direction for future study, then, may be to reread the fragments of discourse to examine in much more detail the ways in which racial and ethnic identities, as well as socioeconomic class, play a part in the construction, negotiation, and regulation of lesbian maternal identity. Future studies might also attend to bisexual motherhood, since the present study did not address it. The exclusion of bisexuality from this project should be construed as a pragmatic choice rather than a malicious one. Some critics might argue that the women represented in divorce cases are not "really" lesbian but instead are more accurately described as "bisexual." Although that may indeed be a possibility, the judicial opinions that were subject to scrutiny in chapter 3 did not address bisexuality, nor did the journalistic articles or psychological studies. As bisexuality gains more visibility in American rhetorical culture, it will become possible to extend the findings of this study to bisexual motherhood. My silence regarding bisexuality replicates the silence of the rhetoric I studied.

The voices of children were also relatively silent within the original debates and as I have reconstituted them here. Given that I am arguing that people should have a voice in the construction of policies and rhetorics that affect the quality of their own lives, it is worth considering how pro–lesbian mother advocates might pay attention to children's voices. We should not, however, follow the lead of psychological professionals who do include children's voices. As chapter 4 illustrated, the questions that researchers and activists ask must be grounded in lesbian-affirmative terms rather than the essentially anti-lesbian ones currently in use.

Other silences have been purposeful, in the sense that I have limited my research to three forums, excluding other domains for purposes of manageability. To be sure, lesbian motherhood is constituted, contested, and represented in additional rhetorical spaces such as film and television, cyberspace, and contemporary Christian and other religious discourse. Future studies could include such forums to enrich the analysis provided here. The silences created and maintained by this project, however, do not undermine or negate its key conclusion that the emancipation of lesbians from profoundly oppressive narratives of gender and sexuality that limit their reproductive and erotic capacities can be central to a critical rhetorical project.

What, then, is to become of the "lesbian mother"? I have tried to show how hegemonic characterizations in journalistic, legal, and academic discourses of "lesbians" as neurotic, proselytic criminals, and of "mothers" as inherently tied through biology to their children, constitute three major strands in contemporary rhetorics of lesbian motherhood. "Debunking" (in

Kenneth Burke's sense) the oxymoron thus becomes a matter of expanding our notions of the performances that constitute it, and moving beyond strictly biological notions of legitimate motherhood.

A final caveat: rhetorical and cultural legitimacy will not occur overnight. As Lisa Duggan notes, identity construction is often a "historical process of contested narration."[22] To think otherwise would be to ignore the complex processes of negotiation that occur during extended periods of public deliberation. What I *have* tried to do is to reconstruct the "disparate scraps of discourse which, when constructed as an argument, serve to illuminate otherwise hidden or taken for granted social practices."[23] I have taken two crucial steps: I have identified the rhetorical fragments that ascribe to lesbian mothers an inherently negative oxymoronic identity, and I have also identified potential reconstructive moves. Lesbian maternal identity can achieve legitimacy only if pro-lesbian advocates reconceive motherhood as a function of nurturing practices rather than a strict biological relation, if we reconceive lesbians as agents who engage in a variety of practices, *and* if we found our reconceptualization on a critique of heterosexuality as a political regime bolstered by a debilitating rhetoric.

Notes

1. Lesbian Motherhood in American Culture

1. Adrienne Rich, *Of Woman Born*, 252.

2. Ibid., 250.

3. Phil Wander, "Marxism, Post-colonialism, and Rhetorical Contextualization," 420–21.

4. Audre Lorde, *Sister Outsider.*

5. Louis Althusser, "Ideology and Ideological State Apparatuses," in *Lenin and Philosophy and Other Essays*, 172–77.

6. See, for instance, Homi K. Bhabha, "The Other Question," and "Signs Taken for Wonders."

7. Bhabha, "Signs," 153.

8. Ibid., 158.

9. Ibid., 157.

10. Ibid., 162.

11. Victoria A. Brownworth, "Family in Crisis," 46: "Only three states allow single women (of any sexual orientation) to be inseminated by a sperm bank, the only source of anonymous donor sperm."

12. Michael Calvin McGee, "A Materialist's Conception of Rhetoric."

13. Althusser "Ideology," 171.

14. Ibid., 128.

15. Althusser is careful to note that the legal system also functions as an ideological state apparatus. Ibid., 143.

16. Ibid., 150.

17. Ibid., 152–57.

18. Lisa Duggan, "The Trials of Alice Mitchell," 793.

19. Kimberlé Williams Crenshaw, "Mapping the Margins," 375.

20. Judith Butler, *Gender Trouble*, 147.

21. Michael Calvin McGee, "The 'Ideograph.'"

22. Ibid., 15; cf. Celeste Michelle Condit and John Louis Lucaites, *Crafting Equality*.

23. McGee, "Ideograph," 6–7; Condit and Lucaites, *Crafting Equality*, xiii.

24. McGee, "Ideograph," 14; Condit and Lucaites, *Crafting Equality*, xiii.

25. M. M. Bakhtin, *The Dialogic Imagination*, 428.

26. Anthony Giddens, *Central Problems in Social Theory*, 188.

27. Georg Lukács, *History and Class Consciousness*, 95.

28. Judith Butler, "Critically Queer," 22.

29. Eve Kosofsky Sedgwick, *Epistemology of the Closet*, 58; see also Rodger Streitmatter, *Unspeakable*, 4.

30. Butler, "Critically Queer," 22.

31. Ibid., 18.

32. Judith Halberstam, *Female Masculinity*, 87.

33. Jonathan Ned Katz, *Gay American History*, 20. As Katz notes, the Massachusetts Colony did not adopt Cotton's proposals.

34. Ibid., 23. Such relations, one could argue, were considered unnatural because they were non-procreative and therefore violated the Christian God's edict to "go forth and multiply."

35. Ibid., 26.

36. Lillian Faderman, *Surpassing the Love of Men;* and Carroll Smith-Rosenberg, "The Female World of Love and Ritual."

37. Smith-Rosenberg, "Female World," 74.

38. The word "homosexual" apparently *predates* the word "heterosexual" in the modern English vocabulary. As Jonathan Ned Katz points out in his excellent rhetorical history *The Invention of Heterosexuality*, "heterosexuality" was constituted as homosexuality's other, and, in its initial formation, was also characterized as an abnormal psychopathology in the sense that "heterosexuals" were those individuals with excessive amounts of desire for persons of the opposite sex. It was not until after World War II that heterosexuality was considered "normal" in psychological terms.

39. Judy Grahn claims that "lesbian" originates in Western culture from Greek civilization, "from the island Lesbos that was made famous and infamous by the woman-loving poet/priestess Sappho," in *Another Mother Tongue*, 105.

40. Jeffrey Weeks, "Discourse, Desire, and Sexual Deviance," 82.

41. See chap. 2 of Lillian Faderman's *Odd Girls and Twilight Lovers* for an analysis of the early sexologists' influence on public conceptions of "lesbian" identity.

42. Richard von Krafft-Ebing, *Psychopathia Sexualis*, 295, 298.

43. Ibid., 298, 299.

44. Ibid., 295.

45. Ibid., 406.

46. Havelock Ellis, *Studies in the Psychology of Sex*, 2:190. Ellis elaborates the notion that biology and environment could both contribute to the development of homosexuality and lesbianism: "At the very least such congenital abnormality usually exists as a predisposition to inversion. It is probable that many persons go through the world with a congenital predisposition to inversion which always remains latent and unroused; in others the instinct is so strong that it forces its own way in spite of all obstacles; in others, again, the predisposition is weaker, and a powerful exciting cause plays the predominant part" (190).

47. Ibid., 121.

48. Ibid., 121, 132.

49. Ibid., 140.

50. Ibid., 182.

51. Ibid., 211.

52. August Forel, *The Sexual Question*, 244.

53. Ibid., 244.

54. Ibid., 4.

55. Ibid., 251.

56. Ibid., 273, 275.

57. Michel Foucault, *The History of Sexuality*, 1:36.

58. Ibid., 42–43.

59. See, for example, chap. 2 of Celia Kitzinger, *The Social Construction of Lesbianism*, 32–65; and Weeks, "Discourse," 76–111.

60. Wayne R. Dynes and Stephen Donaldson, *Lesbianism*, x.

61. Ibid.

62. Ellis *Psychology of Sex*, 147, 148.

63. See Katz, *Gay American History*, 170–73 and 201–7, for disturbing accounts of electroshock therapy, and 175–81 and 191–93 for equally chilling accounts of lobotomies. See also Louis Landerson, "Psychiatry and Homosexuality," 15 for an account of various aversion therapies for male homosexuals. One wonders when psychoanalysis will go the way of lobotomy.

64. See John D'Emilio, *Sexual Politics, Sexual Communities*, 49–53, 200–201; cf. Radicalesbian/A Flaming Faggot, "We're Not Gay, We're Angry."

65. D'Emilio, *Sexual Politics*, 184.

66. Ibid., 231.

67. Ibid., 231–32.

68. Ibid., 232.

69. Martin Duberman, *Stonewall*, xv; see also Duberman, *About Time*, xiii.

70. Barry D. Adam, *The Rise of the Gay and Lesbian Movement*, 82.

71. Streitmatter, *Unspeakable*, 117.

72. See, for instance, Robert E. Gould, "What We Don't Know about Homosexuality," 13.

73. Lois Timnick, "Homosexuals: Many Types, Many Causes."

74. For instance, according to Peter Steinfels, "Southern Baptists Condemn Homosexuality as 'Depraved,'" Baptists tie homosexuality to "a general problem of 'moral decline' in modern society," whereas other denominations support civil rights for gay men and lesbians. See "United Church Backs Homosexuals' Rights."

75. At this writing, nineteen states have criminalized homosexual and/or lesbian "sodomy": Alabama, Arizona, Arkansas, Florida, Idaho, Kansas, Louisiana, Maryland, Massachusetts, Michigan, Minnesota, Mississippi, Missouri, North Carolina, Oklahoma, South Carolina, Texas, Utah, and Virginia. For a state-by-state description of legislation affecting the lesbian and gay population in the United States, see www.actwin.com/eaton-hohio/gay.sodomy.html.

76. In the 1976 case, the Supreme Court affirmed the decision of the lower court but did not issue an opinion. See Morton Mintz, "The Supreme Court." The Court issued a written opinion in the 1986 Georgia case. See *Bowers v. Hardwick*.

77. Lawrence J. Hatterer, "What Makes a Homosexual?" 32. Hatterer uses masculine pronouns to refer to both men and women.

78. Lawrence J. Hatterer, "How to Spot Homosexuality in Children," 56. Note how gender-role expectations are enforced through homonegativity.

79. See, for example, Debra Rae Cohen, "Children of Homosexuals Seem Headed Straight," 44, citing a study which found that "children of gays and transsexuals are not likely to adopt their parents' sexual preference"; "Gays: A Family Phenomenon?" 66–67; "Study Hits Theories on Homosexuality"; Jean Seligmann, "Gays are Born, Not Made."

80. Steven Mintz and Susan Kellogg, *Domestic Revolutions*, xix.

81. Maxine L. Margolis, *Mothers and Such*, 12.

82. Mintz and Kellogg, *Domestic Revolutions*, 121, 122.

83. Ibid., 112–13.

84. Ibid., 128.

85. Ibid., xiii–xiv.

86. Ibid., 181.

87. Ibid., xvii.

88. Arlene Skolnick, *Embattled Paradise*, 224.

89. Since lesbian periodicals typically did not appear until after the advent of the contemporary gay rights movement in 1969, I selected 1970 as a starting point.

90. Roberta Achtenberg, *Preserving and Protecting the Families of Lesbians and Gay Men*, 2.

2. *"Real Lesbians and Sperm Don't Mix"*

1. Lindsy Van Gelder, "Mothers of Convention," 94–95.
2. Mark Draper, "Shall the Family Endure?" 140, 142.
3. D. Bruce Lockerbie, "The Drama of the American Family," 494.
4. Ibid.
5. Ibid., 497.
6. Jerrold K. Footlick, "What Happened to the Family?" 16, 17.
7. William Henry III, "The Lesbians Next Door," 78–79.
8. Ibid., 78.
9. Bettina Boxall, "Lesbians Work to Shed Label as 'Invisible Gays,'" A22.
10. Pat Wingert and Barbara Kantrowitz, "Two Kids and Two Moms."
11. See, for instance, "Gay America in Transition."
12. "Should Homosexuals Be Teachers?" 34.
13. Jonathan Ned Katz, *The Invention of Heterosexuality.*
14. Anonymous, Letter to the Editor, 18.
15. Melvin Anchell, "A Psychoanalytic Look at Homosexuality," 286, 287.
16. William F. Schulz, "Fostering Prejudice."
17. Quoted in Robert Joffee and John Mintz, "N.J. Officials Find Gay Foster Parents for Gay Teenagers," A4.
18. Enid Nemy, "The Movement Is Big Enough to Roll with the Punches," 46.
19. Katie Nix, "Homosexual Marriages," A15.
20. Betty Fairchild, "Homosexuality and Society," A23.
21. Judy Klemesrud, "For Homosexuals, It's Getting Less Difficult to Tell Parents," 32.
22. Tacie Dejanikus, "The Politics of Lesbians' Choosing Motherhood," 20.
23. Ibid.
24. George Dugan, "Archdiocese Asks City Council to Question Bill on Homosexuals," 41.
25. "Family Conference Rejects Antiabortion Amendment"; quotation from Donna Minkowitz, "Outlawing Gays," 420.
26. "Gay America in Transition."
27. Lesbian journalist Vicki Plotter commented on lesbian invisibility in her report of the 1980 Denver Gay Pride Festival. Speaking about identity issues, Plotter reported: "I asked another lesbian if she felt like she had a gay identity. She replied both yes and no—yes, she identifies as 'gay' when it comes to outsiders—people who have no understanding of her lesbianism or of her need to have her civil rights protected by law. 'I will identify with the gay movement when it is under attack by straight people,' she said, 'but, no, within the gay community, I do not feel 'gay.' 'Gay' to me means 'men.'" See Vicki Plotter, "Lesbians and the Gay Movement," 8.
28. Rodger Streitmatter, *Unspeakable,* ix.
29. Ibid., 7, 8.
30. "Raising Children in a Deviant Relationship," 9.

31. "The Politics of Choosing Children," 7.

32. Rebecca Dixon, "The Politics of Homophobia," 23.

33. Jeanne Cordova, "Cutting the Patriarchal Umbilical Cord," 3.

34. Jane Melnick, "Lesbian & Mother," 24.

35. "Support Lesbian Mothers," 14.

36. "The Case of the Seattle Lesbian Mothers"; Geraldine Cole and Karen Burr, "Lesbian Mothers Fighting Back," 7.

37. Barb Wire, "Pursuing the Goal of Parenting," 14.

38. Melvyn A. Berke and Joanne Grant, "Custody Odds against the Lesbian Mother," 7.

39. "Mothers' Day No Exception to Oppression of Lesbian Mothers," 3.

40. Tryna, "Mothers and the Law," 3.

41. A Redstocking Sister, "I AM 23, a Mother, and a Lesbian," 13.

42. Eleanor Cooper, "Lesbianism," 8.

43. Dixon, "Politics," 26.

44. Gia Berkman, "The Right to Be a Parent," 12.

45. Ruth Mahaney, "In the Best Interests of the Children," 6.

46. Jil Clark, "Defeat, Victory Mark Custody Fights," 1, 6; cf. another mother's decision to "downplay her lesbianism," "not publicize the case," and "petition for custody of the children with hopes of being granted visitation as a consolation prize," in "Mothers' Day No Exception," 3.

47. Robert W. Wood, "Homosexuality as an Answer to the Population Increase," 19.

48. "Homosexual Acts Morally Neutral, Priests Say," 4.

49. [News and Notes column], *Lesbian Connection*, 11.

50. "Dykes & Tykes," 7.

51. Ann Nemesis, "Holy Cow! The Dyke Is Having a Baby!" 7.

52. Sylvan Rainwater, "Mother-Bashing Is Not the Answer," 10.

53. Pam McAllister, "Mothers Speak Out on Child Custody," 5.

54. Dana Morrison, "Lesbian Mother," 16.

55. Noy Dublex, "Letter from a Mean Non Mom," 28.

56. "The Politics of Choosing Children," 7.

57. McAllister, "Mothers Speak Out," 5.

58. "Choosing to Have Children," 41.

59. Marcos Bisticas-Cocoves, "Town Meeting Focuses on Gay Parenting," 3.

60. Karen Burr, "Male Children—A Lesbian Mother Perspective," 8.

61. Nemesis, "Holy Cow!"

62. Rainwater, "Mother-Bashing," 10.

63. Pamela McDonald and Donna Cassyd, "Local Lesbian Fights Custody Battle," 3.

64. "New Hampshire: Law Passed," 16.

65. "Study Shows Child's Sexuality Not Affected by Parent's Sexuality," 3.

66. "UCLA Backs Lesbians as Mothers," 29.

67. "Lesbian Mothers' Custody News," 4.

68. Fran Boyce, "Toward a Better Understanding," 8.

69. "The Politics of Choosing Children," 7.

70. Lori, Letter to Editors, 9.

71. Neva, "Raising Children in the Lesbian Community," 7.

72. Lois Gilbert, "A 'Personal Is Political' Note on Lesbian Mothers," 7; cf. the claim by "Sarah" that "every lesbian has a responsibility to every other lesbian, if we want to get anywhere in the system. We just have to struggle against the social pressure," in "Lesbian Mothers' Custody Struggle," 13.

73. "Some Things We Can Do!"

74. Xenia Williams, "Bug Bug Speaking," 2.

75. Terri Poppe, "Lesbian Mothers Conference," 11.

76. Ellen Agger and Francie Wyland, "Lesbian Mothers Fight Back," 58.

77. Nan Hunter and Nancy Polikoff, "Lesbian Mothers Fight Back," 55.

78. Baba Copper, "Mothers and Daughters of Invention," 8.

79. Ibid., 14.

80. Judith Halberstam, *Female Masculinity*, 116.

81. "Lesbians Organize Rallies," 3.

82. Del Martin and Phyllis Lyon, "'The Law' and Lesbian Mothers," 19.

83. "Lesbian Mothers," 17.

84. Ginny Yaseen, "Thanks from Ginny," 27.

3. Neurotic, Criminal, and a Danger to Children

1. Zillah R. Eisenstein, *The Female Body and the Law*, 42.

2. Kenneth Burke, *Attitudes toward History*, 4, 5.

3. Ira Mark Ellman, Paul M. Kurtz, and Katharine T. Bartlett, *Family Law*, 491–92.

4. *Michigan Compiled Laws Annotated*, sec. 722.23. This treatment should not be construed as a comprehensive overview of the historical development of the best interest standard.

5. *S.N.E. v. R.L.B.*, 877.

6. Ibid., 877, 878.

7. Ibid., 879.

8. *Kallas v. Kallas*, 645.

9. *D.H. v. J.H.*, 290.

10. *Constant A. v. Paul C.A.*, 6, n. 6.

11. Ibid., 5.

12. *Dailey v. Dailey*, 394.

13. *S.E.G. v. R.A.G.*, 166.

14. *L. v. D.*, 243.

15. *M.P. v. S.P.*, 1270.

16. "Morals" clauses exist in several state statutes relative to child custody determinations. See, for example, *West's Annotated California Codes,* sec. 3040, n. 15; *Louisiana Civil Code,* art. 131.f.; *Oklahoma Statutes Annotated,* Title 10, sec. 21.1.5; *North Dakota Century Code,* sec. 14-09-06.2.f; and *McKinney's Consolidated Laws of New York,* bk. 14, sec. 220, art. 13.

17. *Constant A.,* 3.

18. *S.E.G. v. R.A.G.,* 167; *N.K.M. v. L.E.M.,* 186; *In re Mara,* 525.

19. *G.A. v. D.A.,* 728.

20. *Maradie v. Maradie,* 541.

21. Ibid., n. 4.

22. *Kallas,* 643.

23. *Thigpen v. Carpenter,* 514.

24. *DiStefano v. DiStefano,* 637.

25. *Constant A.,* 8.

26. *In re Jane B.,* 854.

27. *S. v. S.,* 66.

28. *Doe v. Doe* (Va.), 806.

29. *Ashling and Ashling,* 476.

30. To be fair, courts sometimes require this of unmarried cohabiting heterosexuals as well, or, if the couple wishes to continue cohabiting, the court might transfer custody to the other parent. See, for instance, *Jarrett v. Jarrett.*

31. *In re Breisch,* 819, 816.

32. *Dailey,* 396; *DiStefano,* 638; *S.E.G.,* 167; *Irish v. Irish,* 741; *L. v. D.,* 245; *M.P.,* 1259.

33. *Jacobson v. Jacobson,* 81.

34. Ibid.

35. *N.K.M. v. L.E.M.,* 183, 182.

36. Ibid., 186.

37. Ibid., n. 1.

38. *Stroman v. Williams,* 706.

39. *Doe v. Doe* (Mass.), 296.

40. Nancy D. Polikoff, "This Child Does Have Two Mothers," 471, 561.

41. Paula L. Ettelbrick, "Who Is a Parent?" 553.

42. Philip Kraft, "Lesbian Child Custody," 183–92; cf. Steve Susoeff, "Assessing Children's Best Interests," 876.

43. Nan D. Hunter and Nancy D. Polikoff, "Custody Rights of Lesbian Mothers," 714.

44. Susoeff, "Assessing Children's Best Interests," 869.

45. Ibid., 901.

46. David Dooley, "Immoral Because They're Bad," 417.

47. Polikoff, "This Child Does Have Two Mothers," 464.

48. Ibid., 533–34.

49. "Who Is a Parent?" 521.

50. Ibid., 548.

51. Polikoff, "This Child Does Have Two Mothers," 474.

52. Gena Corea, *The Mother Machine*, 35.

53. Ibid., 37–38.

54. Ibid., 40–42.

55. "Only about ten percent of treating physicians are willing to perform artificial insemination for unmarried women." E. Donald Shapiro and Lisa Schultz, "Single-Sex Families," 274–75.

56. In the seventh case the court ruled that the non-biological mother lacked standing to petition for custody, but also ruled that she might have standing to petition for visitation privileges. That portion of the case was remanded to a lower court. See *In re Custody of H.S.H.-K.*

57. *In re Custody of H.S.H.-K.*, 447.

58. *A.C. v. C.B.*, 662.

59. *Curiale v. Reagan*, 1600.

60. Ibid.

61. *Alison D. v. Virginia M.*, 322.

62. See *Black's Law Dictionary*, s.v. "in loco parentis."

63. *Nancy S. v. Michele G.*, 838.

64. *In re Interest of Z.J.H.*, 206.

65. Ibid., 206, n. 8.

66. Ibid., 207.

67. *Curiale*, 1599.

68. *Nancy S.*, 835.

69. *In re Interest of Z.J.H.*, 205.

70. Ibid., 208.

71. Ibid., 214.

72. Ibid., 215.

73. *Matter of Adoption of Evan*, 998.

74. Ibid., 998.

75. Ibid., 998, 1000.

76. *Matter of Adoption of Caitlin*, 839.

77. *Matter of S.M.Y.*, 902–3.

78. *Matter of Adoption of Evan*, 1000.

79. *Adoption of B.L.V.B.*, 1272.

80. *In the Matter of Dana*, 636.

81. Ibid.

82. *Matter of Adoption of Child by J.M.G.*, 551.

83. *Adoption of B.L.V.B.*, 1275, 1274, 1276; cf. *Adoption of Tammy*, 320.

84. *Matter of Adoption of Evan*, 998–99.

85. *Matter of Adoption of Child by J.M.G.*, 554–55.

86. *Matter of Adoption of Caitlin*, 841.

4. "Stop! You're Making Me Sick!"

1. Michel Foucault, "The Discourse on Language," 216.

2. Ibid., 220.

3. Ibid.

4. Ibid., 222.

5. Ibid., 224.

6. Ibid., 225–26.

7. Michel Foucault, "What Is an "Author?" 117.

8. Ibid., 118–19.

9. Ibid., 120.

10. Foucault, "Discourse," 234.

11. Robert Hariman, "The Rhetoric of Inquiry and the Professional Scholar," 213, 214.

12. Ibid., 218.

13. See www.apa.org/pi/bottoms.html.

14. Ronald Bayer, *Homosexuality and American Psychiatry*, 15–40; cf. Charles Silverstein, "Psychological and Medical Treatments of Homosexuality," 102.

15. Bayer, *Homosexuality*, 17–18.

16. Ibid., 17.

17. Ibid., 34.

18. Richard Green, "Homosexuality as a Mental Illness," 78.

19. Alan Bell, "Human Sexuality—A Response"; Judd Marmor, "Homosexuality—Mental Illness or Moral Dilemma?" 115; Martin Hoffman, "Philosophic, Empirical, and Ecologic Remarks," 106.

20. Charles Socarides, "Homosexuality—Basic Concepts and Psychodynamics," 120, 119.

21. Bayer, *Homosexuality*, 29–30.

22. Ibid., 39.

23. Ibid., 9.

24. Ibid., 72.

25. Ibid., 9–12.

26. Ibid., 82.

27. Ibid., 125. Bieber and Socarides continued to advocate the illness model well into the late 1980s. See Irving Bieber, *Homosexuality: A Psychoanalytic Study*, and Charles W. Socarides, *The Preoedipal Origin and Psychoanalytic Therapy of Sexual Perversions*.

28. Michèle Barrett, *Women's Oppression Today*, 226.

29. Patricia Hill Collins, "Shifting the Center," 57, n. 4. See also Deborah L. Rhode, *Justice and Gender*, 307; and Ann Ferguson, *Sexual Democracy*, 94, n. 10.

30. Nancy Chodorow, *The Reproduction of Mothering*, 199.

31. Ibid., 6, 8–9, 11.

32. Ibid., 11, 21–22, 17–30.

33. Ibid., 32, 34, 35–36, 38–39.

34. Ibid., 42, 39, 54, 78, 93.

35. Ibid., 156, 112, 113, 138.

36. Ibid., 193, 207, 208, 201.

37. Chodorow acknowledges this in one footnote. See ibid., 110n.

38. Ibid., 138, 168, 215, 217, 218–19.

39. Laura Benkov, *Reinventing the Family*, 9.

40. Sarah Lucia Hoagland, *Lesbian Ethics*, 57.

41. David Flaks et al., "Lesbians Choosing Motherhood," 105.

42. Beverly Hoeffer, "Children's Acquisition of Sex-Role Behavior in Lesbian Mother Families," 536–37.

43. Ibid., 536, 537–39.

44. Martha Kirkpatrick, Catherine Smith, and Ron Roy, "Lesbian Mothers and Their Children," 546, 547.

45. Ibid., 545, 546.

46. Ibid., 548.

47. Ibid., 550–51.

48. Richard Green et al., "Lesbian Mothers and Their Children," 168.

49. Ibid., 169–70, 179, 180.

50. Barbara McCandlish, "Against All Odds," 24, 26, 31, 27, 32.

51. Flaks et al., "Lesbians Choosing Motherhood," 107–8, 106, 109, 111.

52. Charlotte J. Patterson, "Lesbian Mothers and Their Children," 420, 424–25.

53. Ibid., 426, 427.

54. Hoeffer, "Children's Acquisition of Sex-Role Behavior," 537.

55. Flaks et al., "Lesbians Choosing Motherhood," 106, 112–13.

56. Patterson, "Lesbian Mothers and Their Children," 420, 428.

57. Hoeffer, "Children's Acquisition of Sex-Role Behavior," 538.

58. Ibid., 536.

59. Green et al., "Lesbian Mothers and Their Children," 170, 173.

60. Ibid., 181.

61. Ibid., 180, 181, 182.

62. Kirkpatrick et al., "Lesbian Mothers and Their Children," 550, 549.

63. Robert L. Scott, "Dialectical Tensions of Speaking and Silence," 15.

64. Ibid., 10.

65. Kirkpatrick et al., "Lesbian Mothers and Their Children," 551.

66. McCandlish, "Against All Odds," 33.

67. Hoagland, *Lesbian Ethics*, 5.

68. Flaks et al., "Lesbians Choosing Motherhood," 113.

69. Green et al., "Lesbian Mothers and Their Children," 90.

5. Toward the Legitimation of Lesbian Maternal Identity

1. Leslie Feinberg, *Transgender Warriors*, ix.

2. Maia Ettinger, "The Pocohontas Paradigm," 53.

3. The "biology" argument is not always effective, however, as we saw in chapter 3. The strategy thus might have limited applicability and effect.

4. This is conceptually similar to what Audre Lorde calls using "the master's tools." See "The Master's Tools Will Never Dismantle the Master's House," in *Sister Outsider* 110–13.

5. This is not to deny the individual symbolic significance of name choice, nor is the commentary to be taken as a directive to stop such naming practices. Rather, the point is to draw attention to the limitations of the practice as an efficacious route to social change.

6. Thomas K. Nakayama and Robert L. Krizek, "Whiteness," 293–94.

7. Martha Fineman, *The Neutered Mother*.

8. Lisa Duggan, "The Trials of Alice Mitchell," 811.

9. Charlotte Bunch, *Passionate Politics*, 197–99.

10. Julia Penelope, *Call Me Lesbian*, 22.

11. Ibid., 35.

12. Vera Whisman. "Identity Crises," 60.

13. Penelope, *Call Me Lesbian*, 33–34.

14. Ann Ferguson. "Is There a Lesbian Culture?" 73.

15. Diana Fuss, *Essentially Speaking*, 109.

16. Cf. Adrienne Rich, "Compulsory Heterosexuality and Lesbian Existence," 35.

17. Monique Wittig, "The Straight Mind," in *The Straight Mind and Other Essays*, 24, 25.

18. Rich, "Compulsory Heterosexuality," 50.

19. Gayatri Chakravorty Spivak, "Practical Politics of the Open End," dialogue with Sarah Harasym, in *The Post-colonial Critic*, 109.

20. Mary Joe Frug, *Postmodern Legal Feminism*, 126.

21. Adrienne Rich, *Of Woman Born*, 13.

22. Duggan, "The Trials of Alice Mitchell," 793.

23. Raymie E. McKerrow, "Critical Rhetoric," 101.

Bibliography

A.C. v. C.B. 829 P. 2d 660 (N.M. App. 1992).

Achtenberg, Roberta. *Preserving and Protecting the Families of Lesbians and Gay Men.* San Francisco: National Center for Lesbian Rights, 1990.

"ACLU Seeks to Lift Gay Marriage Bars." *Chicago Tribune* 29 Oct. 1986, 1–2.

Adam, Barry D. *The Rise of the Gay and Lesbian Movement.* Rev. ed. New York: Twayne Publishers, 1995.

Adoption of B.L.V.B. 628 A. 2d 1271 (Vt. 1993).

Adoption of Tammy. 619 N.E. 2d 315 (Mass. 1993).

Agger, Ellen, and Francie Wyland. "Lesbian Mothers Fight Back: Wages Due Lesbians." *Quest* 5 (Summer 1979): 57–62.

Alison D. v. Virginia M. 522 N.Y.S. 2d 321 (A.D. 2 Dept. 1990).

Allen, Jeffner. "Motherhood: The Annihilation of Women." In *Lesbian Philosophy: Explorations.* Palo Alto, Calif.: Institute of Lesbian Studies, 1986. 61–88.

Althusser, Louis. *Lenin and Philosophy and Other Essays.* New York: Monthly Review Press, 1971.

American Friends Service Committee. "Lesbian Loses Custody." *Big Mama Rag* (Apr. 1978): 3, 14.

Amish, M. "The Right to Be a Parent." *Gay Community News* 12 Apr. 1980, 12.

Anchell, Melvin. "A Psychoanalytic Look at Homosexuality: AIDS." *Vital Speeches of the Day* 15 Feb. 1986, 285–88.

"And Now, Gay Family Rights?" *Time* 13 Dec. 1982, 74.

Andrea. "Lesbian Mothers" [letter]. *Big Mama Rag* (May 1983): 18, 21.

Anonymous. Letter to the Editor. *New York Times* 4 June 1977, 18.

Anonymous. Letter to Editors. *Lesbian Connection* (Jan–Feb. 1987): 19–20.

Anonymous. Letter to the Editor. *New York Times* 4 June 1977, 18.

"Another Custody Battle in Buffalo." *Lavender Woman* (Feb. 1975): 12.

Arditti, Rita, Renate Duelli Klein, and Shelly Minden, eds. *Test-Tube Women: What Future for Motherhood?* 1984. London: Pandora, 1985.

Ashling and Ashling. 599 P. 2d 475 (Ore. App. 1979).

"AZ Women Win First Battle." *Lesbian Tide* (May–June 1980): 23.

Bailey, Michael, and Richard Pillard. "Are Some People Born Gay?" *New York Times* 17 Dec. 1991, A21.

Bakhtin, M. M. *The Dialogic Imagination.* Ed. Michael Holquist. Trans. Caryl Emerson and Michael Holquist. Austin: University of Texas Press, 1981.

Barbara and Judy. Letter to Editors. *Lesbian Connection* (May–June 1994): 5.

Barlow, Judy. "Denver Woman Faced with Custody Case." *Big Mama Rag* (June 1980): 1.

———. "Raising a Male Child in the Women's Community: A Mother's Struggle." *Big Mama Rag* (July 1979): 10.

———. "Raising a Revolutionary Child: A Mother's Struggle." *Big Mama Rag* (June 1980): 12.

Barrett, Michèle. *Women's Oppression Today: The Marxist/Feminist Encounter.* 1980. Rev. ed. London: Verso, 1988.

Barron-Levine, Dorie. "Hey Kid, Your Ma's a Dyke!" *Lavender Woman* (Jan. 1974): 4.

Bayer, Ronald. *Homosexuality and American Psychiatry: The Politics of Diagnosis.* 1981. Princeton: Princeton University Press, 1987.

Bell, Alan. "Human Sexuality–A Response." *International Journal of Psychiatry* 10 (Mar. 1972): 99–102.

Benkov, Laura. *Reinventing the Family: The Emerging Story of Lesbian and Gay Parents.* New York: Crown Publishers, 1994.

Berke, Melvyn A., and Joanne Grant. "Custody Odds against Lesbian Mother." *Gay Community News* 15 Dec. 1979, 7.

Berkman, Gia. "The Right to Be a Parent." *Gay Community News* 12 Apr. 1980, 12.

Bernstein, Robert A. "A 'Monster' Only Imagined, Not Real." *Chicago Tribune* 27 Oct. 1988, 1–23.

Beyer, Lauren A. "Meet My Family." *Lesbian Contradiction: A Journal of Irreverent Feminism* 20 (Fall 1987): 15.

———. "Step-Parenting." *Lesbian Contradiction: A Journal of Irreverent Feminism* 21 (Winter 1988): 11.

"Beyond Definitions of Woman: Lesbian Sexuality." *Other Woman* (Nov.–Dec. 1976): 3.

Bhabha, Homi K. "The Other Question." *Screen* 24 (1983): 18–36.

————. "Signs Taken for Wonders." *Critical Inquiry* 12 (1985): 144–65.

Bieber, Irving. *Homosexuality: A Psychoanalytic Study.* Northvale, N.J.: Jason Aronson, 1988.

Birns, Beverly, and Dale F. Hay, eds. *Different Faces of Motherhood.* New York: Plenum, 1988.

Bisticas-Cocoves, Marcos. "Town Meeting Focuses on Gay Parenting." *Gay Community News* 6 July 1985, 3.

Black, Edwin. *Rhetorical Questions.* Chicago: University of Chicago Press, 1992.

Bowers v. Hardwick. 478 U.S. 186 (1986).

Boxall, Bettina. "Lesbians Work to Shed Label as 'Invisible' Gays." *Los Angeles Times* 27 Dec. 1993, A1, A22, A23.

Boyce, Fran. "Toward a Better Understanding of Lesbian Mothers." *Gay Community News* 25 March 1978, 8–9.

"Breakthrough in Custody Law." *Lesbian Tide* (Mar.–Apr. 1977): 23.

Brown, Laura Sky. "A Local Lesbian Mother's Struggles for Custody." *Leaping Lesbian* (Aug. 1977): 12–14.

————. "Margareth Wins!" *Leaping Lesbian* (Winter 1978–79): 3–4.

Brownworth, Victoria A. "Family in Crisis: When AI Donors Claim Fatherhood." *Deneuve* (Mar.–Apr. 1994): 44–46.

————. "The Parent Trap." *Advocate* 24 Aug. 1993, 80.

Bunch, Charlotte. *Passionate Politics: Feminist Theory in Action.* New York: St. Martin's Press, 1987.

"Bunny Goes to Court." *Gay Community News* 10 May 1980, 2.

Burke, Kenneth. *Attitudes toward History.* 1937. 3d ed. Berkeley: University of California Press, 1959.

————. *A Grammar of Motives.* Berkeley: University of California Press, 1969.

————. *Permanence and Change: An Anatomy of Purpose.* 3d ed. Berkeley: University of California Press, 1954.

————. *The Philosophy of Literary Form,* 3d ed. Berkeley: University of California Press, 1973.

Burke, Phyllis. *Family Values: A Lesbian Mother's Fight for Her Son.* New York: Vintage Books, 1993.

Burr, Karen. "Male Children—A Lesbian Mother Perspective." *Lesbian Connection* (Feb. 1975): 8.

Butler, Judith. "Critically Queer." *GLQ: A Journal of Lesbian and Gay Studies* 1 (1994): 17–32.

————. *Gender Trouble: Feminism and the Subversion of Identity.* New York: Routledge, 1990.

"The Case of the Seattle Lesbian Mothers." *Focus: A Journal for Gay Women* (May 1973): 6.

Chandler, Russell. "Conference on Families Endorses ERA." *Los Angeles Times* 13 July 1980, 3, 25.

Chapman, Stephen. "Gay Moms and Gay Marriage: Can We Find a Better Way?" *Chicago Tribune* 1 Dec. 1994, 13.

Chesler, Phyllis. *Mothers on Trial: The Battle for Children and Custody.* 1986. Seattle: Seal Press, 1987.

Chicoine v. Chicoine. 479 NW 2d 891 (S.D. 1992).

"Child Custody Law." *Lesbian Tide* (Jan.–Feb. 1977): 26.

Chodorow, Nancy. *The Reproduction of Mothering: Psychoanalysis and the Sociology of Gender.* Berkeley: University of California Press, 1978.

"Choosing to Have Children: A Lesbian Perspective." *Women: A Journal of Liberation* 6, no. 2 (1979): 36–42.

"Church Affirms Homosexual Love." *New York Times* 3 June 1985, B3.

Clark, Jil. "Court Ruling Favors Lesbian in Custody Case." *Gay Community News* 19 Dec. 1981, 1, 7.

———. "Defeat, Victory Mark Custody Fights." *Gay Community News* 6 Mar. 1982, 1, 6.

———. "Lesbian Mother Charges Coercion in Custody Case." *Gay Community News* 11 July 1981, 1, 6, 7.

———. "Lesbian Mother Fights for Son." *Gay Community News* 9 Aug. 1980, 1, 7.

———. "Lesbian Mother Loses Appeal." *Gay Community News* 27 Feb. 1982, 3.

———. "Lesbian Mothers Lose Custody." *Gay Community News* 16 May 1981, 1, 6.

———. "Lesbian's Activism 'Confusing' to Children." *Gay Community News* 13 Aug. 1983, 3.

———. "Major Court Decision Allows Lesbian Mother to Retain Custody." *Gay Community News* 3 Feb. 1979, 1, 6.

———. "Michigan Lesbian Gets Another Day in Court." *Gay Community News* 26 Mar. 1983, 3.

———. "Tennessee Court Rules against Lesbian Mother." *Gay Community News* 19 Dec. 1981, 3.

———. "Top Court Won't Hear Ky. Lesbian Mother Case." *Gay Community News* 9 May 1981, 3.

Clark, Nancy. Letter to Editor. *New York Times* 11 Apr. 1971, 5.

Clifford, Robert. Letter to the Editor. *New York Times* 4 June 1977, 18.

Cohen, Debra Rae. "Children of Homosexuals Seem Headed Straight." *Psychology Today* (Nov. 1978): 44, 46.

Cohen, Richard. "The Puzzle of People Who Hate Homosexuals." *Washington Post* 8 June 1978, C1, C8.

Cole, Geraldine, and Karen Burr. "Lesbian Mothers Fighting Back." *Lesbian Tide* (Nov.– Dec. 1974): 7.

Collins, Patricia Hill, "Shifting the Center: Race, Class, and Feminist Theorizing about Motherhood." In *Representations of Motherhood,* ed. Donna Bassin, Margaret Honey, and Meryle Mahrer Kaplan. New Haven: Yale University Press, 1994. 56–74.

"Colorado Judge Rules Mother's Lesbianism Is Bar to Good Parenting." *Advocate* 12 June 1980, 12–13.

Condit, Celeste Michelle, and John Louis Lucaites. *Crafting Equality: America's Anglo-African Word.* Chicago: University of Chicago Press, 1993.

Constant A. v. Paul C.A. 496 A. 2d 1 (Pa. Super. 1985).

Cooper, Eleanor. "Lesbianism: The Experience of Being against the Law." *Majority Report* 12 June 1976, 8.

Copper, Baba. "Mothers and Daughters of Invention." *TRIVIA: A Journal of Ideas* 11 (Fall 1987): 8–20.

Cordova, Jeanne. "Cutting the Patriarchal Umbilical Cord." *Lesbian Tide* (Jan.–Feb. 1977): 3, 15.

Corea, Gena. *The Mother Machine: Reproductive Technologies from Artificial Insemination to Artificial Wombs.* London: The Women's Press, 1985.

Cotter, Kitty. "Mary Jo: What Next?" *The Lesbian Feminist* (February 1977): 3.

"Court" [news clip]. *The Advocate* 24 Mar. 1976, 9.

Crenshaw, Kimberlé Williams. "Mapping the Margins: Intersectionality, Identity Politics, and Violence against Women of Color." In *Critical Race Theory,* ed. Kimberlé Crenshaw et al. New York: New Press, 1995. 357–83.

Curiale v. Reagan. 222 Calif. App. 3d 1597 (1990).

"Custody Appeal Lost." *Off Our Backs* (Dec. 1987): 7.

"Custody Battles." *Lavender Woman* (June 1975): 13.

"Custody Battles: Carter Hurts Case." *Lesbian Tide* (Mar.–Apr. 1978): 29.

"Custody Case." *Focus: A Journal for Gay Women* (Feb. 1974): 7.

"Custody Victory." *Lesbian Tide* (Nov.–Dec. 1976): 25.

Dailey v. Dailey. 635 S.W. 391 (Tenn. App. 1981).

D.A.R. "News: Lesbian Custody." *Off Our Backs* (Aug.–Sept. 1987): 16.

Davenport, Katherine. "Lesbian Mother Fights Conservative Courts." *Big Mama Rag* (May 1976): 8–9.

Dejanikus, Tacie. "The Politics of Lesbians' Choosing Motherhood." *Off Our Backs* (Dec. 1984): 20–25.

D'Emilio, John. *Sexual Politics, Sexual Communities: The Making of a Homosexual Minority in the United States, 1940–1970.* Chicago: University of Chicago Press, 1983.

D.H. v. J.H. 418 N.E. 2d 268 (Ind. App. 1981).

Diamond, Irene, ed. *Families, Politics, and Public Policy: A Feminist Dialogue on Women and the State.* New York: Longman, 1983.

"A Display of Homophobia in Appeals Court." *Advocate* 12 Mar. 1975, 6.

DiStefano v. DiStefano. 401 N.Y.S. 2d 636 (1978).

Dixon, Rebecca. "The Politics of Homophobia." *Harvest Quarterly* 7 (Fall 1977): 22–27.

Doe v. Doe. 284 S.E. 2d 799 (Va. 1981).

Doe v. Doe. 452 N.E. 2d 293 (Mass. App. 1983).

"A Dollar a Day Keeps the Husbands Away." *Lesbian Tide* (July–Aug. 1977): 27.

Dooley, David. "Immoral Because They're Bad, Bad Because They're Wrong: Sexual Orientation and Presumptions of Parental Unfitness in Custody Disputes" [note]. *California Western Law Review* 26 (1990): 395–424.

Draper, Mark. "Shall the Family Endure? The Presence of Love." *Vital Speeches of the Day* 15 Dec. 1994, 140–44.

Duberman, Martin. *About Time: Exploring the Gay Past.* 1986. Rev. ed. New York: Penguin, 1991.

———. *Stonewall.* New York: Dutton, 1993.

Dublex, Noy. "Letter from a Mean Non Mom." *Dyke: A Quarterly* 3 (Fall 1976): 28–29.

Dugan, George. "Archdiocese Asks City Council to Question Bill on Homosexuals." *New York Times* 28 Apr. 1974, 41.

Duggan, Lisa. "The Trials of Alice Mitchell: Sensationalism, Sexology, and the Lesbian Subject in Turn-of-the-Century America." *Signs* 18 (1993): 791–814.

"Dykes & Tykes." *Lesbian Connection* (July 1976): 7.

Dynes, Wayne R., and Stephen Donaldson. *Lesbianism.* New York: Garland, 1992.

Eisenstein, Zillah R. *The Female Body and the Law.* Berkeley: University of California Press, 1988.

Elliott, Beth. "Lesbian Mother Victory." *Lesbian Tide* (Sept. 1972): 13.

Ellis, Havelock. *Studies in the Psychology of Sex.* Vol. 2. *Sexual Inversion.* 1901. 2d ed. Philadelphia: F. A. Davis, 1902.

Ellman, Ira Mark, Paul M. Kurtz, and Katharine T. Bartlett. *Family Law: Cases, Texts, Problems.* 2d ed. Charlottesville, Va.: The Michie Company, 1991.

Ettelbrick, Paula L. "Who Is a Parent? The Need to Develop a Lesbian Conscious Family Law." *New York Law School Journal of Human Rights* 10 (1993): 513–53.

Ettinger, Maia. "The Pocohontas Paradigm, or Will the Subaltern Please Shut Up?" In *Tilting the Tower*, ed. Linda Garber. New York: Routledge, 1994. 51–55.

Ex parte J.M.F. 730 So. 2d 1190 (Ala. 1998).

Faderman, Lillian. *Odd Girls and Twilight Lovers: A History of Lesbian Life in Twentieth-Century America.* New York: Columbia University Press, 1991.

———. *Surpassing the Love of Men: Romantic Friendships and Love between Women from the Renaissance to the Present.* New York: William Morrow, 1981.

Fairchild, Betty. "Homosexuality and Society" [letter to the editor]. *Washington Post* 28 July 1975, A23.

"Family Conference Rejects Antiabortion Amendment." *New York Times* 22 June 1980, 24.

Feinberg, Leslie. *Transgender Warriors.* Boston: Beacon Press, 1996.

Ferguson, Ann. *Blood at the Root: Motherhood, Sexuality, and Male Dominance.* London: Pandora, 1989.

———. "Is There a Lesbian Culture?" In *Lesbian Philosophies and Cultures*, ed. Jeffner Allen. Albany: SUNY Press, 1990. 63–88.

—————. *Sexual Democracy: Women, Oppression, and Revolution.* Boulder: Westview Press, 1991.

Fineman, Martha Albertson. *The Neutered Mother, the Sexual Family, and Other Twentieth-Century Tragedies.* New York: Routledge, 1995.

Fineman, Martha Albertson, and Isabel Karpin, eds. *Mothers in Law: Feminism and the Legal Regulation of Motherhood.* New York: Columbia University Press, 1995.

Flaks, David, et al. "Lesbians Choosing Motherhood: A Comparative Study of Lesbian and Heterosexual Parents and Their Children." *Developmental Psychology* 31 (1995): 105–14.

"Florida Adoption Ban Violates Constitution, State Court Determines." *Advocate* 23 Apr. 1991, 33.

Footlick, Jerrold K. "What Happened to the Family?" *Newsweek* (Winter–Spring 1990) [Special Issue: *The 21st-Century Family*]: 14–18, 20.

Forel, August. *The Sexual Question: A Scientific, Psychological, Hygienic, and Sociological Study.* New York: Medical Art Agency, 1914.

Foucault, Michel. "The Discourse on Language." In *The Archaeology of Knowledge and The Discourse on Language.* Trans. A. M. Sheridan Smith. New York: Pantheon, 1972. 215–37.

—————. *The History of Sexuality.* Vol. 1. New York: Pantheon, 1980.

—————. *Power/Knowledge.* Trans. Colin Gordon et al. Ed. Colin Gordon. New York: Pantheon, 1980.

—————. "What Is an Author?" In *The Foucault Reader.* Trans. Josué V. Harari. Ed. Paul Rabinow. New York: Pantheon, 1984. 101–20.

Fox v. Fox. 904 P. 2d 66 (Okla. 1995).

Freedman, Mark. "Homosexuals May Be Healthier Than Straights." *Psychology Today* (Mar. 1975): 28, 30–32.

Frug, Mary Joe. *Postmodern Legal Feminism.* New York: Routledge, 1992.

Fuss, Diana. *Essentially Speaking: Feminism, Nature, and Difference.* New York: Routledge, 1989.

G.A. v. D.A. 745 S.W. 2d 726 (Mo. App. 1987).

"Gaining Ground in the Battle." *Advocate* 25 Jan. 1994, 78.

Gallagher, John. "Parenthood Denied." *Advocate* 22 Feb. 1994, 27–28.

Gallup, George. "Americans Are Convinced Homosexuality on the Rise." *Washington Post* 18 July 1977, A3.

"Gay America in Transition." *Newsweek* 8 Aug. 1983, 30–36, 39–40.

"Gay Men in Twin Study." *New York Times* 17 Dec. 1991, C5.

"Gays: A Family Phenomenon?" *Psychology Today* (Apr. 1987): 66–67.

Giddens, Anthony. *Central Problems in Social Theory.* Berkeley: University of California Press, 1979.

Gilbert, Lois. "A 'Personal Is Political' Note on Lesbian Mothers." *Leaping Lesbian* (July 1977): 7.

Gina. Letter to Editors. *Lesbian Connection* (Sept.–Oct. 1993): 10.

Goding, Susan. "Denver Lesbian Mom Wins Custody, Needs Money." *Big Mama Rag* (July 1980): 1.

Goldberger, Rita A. "Lesbian Mother Appeal Denied." *Lesbian Tide* (Apr. 1974): 15.

Gould, Robert E. "What We Don't Know about Homosexuality." *New York Times Magazine* 24 Feb. 1974, 12–13, 51,54, 56, 58, 60, 62–63.

Grahn, Judy. *Another Mother Tongue: Gay Words, Gay Worlds.* 1984. Rev. ed. Boston: Beacon Press, 1990.

Green, Richard. "Homosexuality as a Mental Illness." *International Journal of Psychiatry* 10 (Mar. 1972): 77–98.

Green, Richard, et al. "Lesbian Mothers and Their Children: A Comparison with Solo Parent Heterosexual Mothers and Their Children." *Archives of Sexual Behavior* 15 (1986): 167–84.

Gregory, Sasha. "Gay Mother Wins Children's Custody." *Advocate* 19 July 1972, 6, 12.

Greif, Geoffrey L., and Mary S. Pabst. *Mothers without Custody.* Lexington, Mass.: D. C. Heath, 1988.

Gutis, Philip S. "Family Redefines Itself, and Now the Law Follows." *New York Times* 28 May 1989, sec. 4, 6.

Halberstam, Judith. *Female Masculinity.* Durham: Duke University Press, 1998.

Hariman, Robert. "The Rhetoric of Inquiry and the Professional Scholar." In *Rhetoric in the Human Sciences,* ed. Herbert W. Simons. London: Sage, 1989. 211–32.

Hatfield, Sarah. "'Why Is Grandma Different?'" *Ladies' Home Journal* (Jan. 1985): 18, 20, 140.

Hatterer, Lawrence J. "How to Spot Homosexuality in Children." *Harper's Bazaar* (July 1975): 56–57.

———. "What Makes a Homosexual?" *McCall's* (July 1971): 32, 34–35, 37.

Henry, William, III. "The Lesbians Next Door: Though They May Be as Numerous as Gay Men, They Remain America's Invisible Women." *Time* (Fall 1990) [Special Issue: *Women: The Road Ahead*]: 78–79.

"Her Two Moms." *Advocate* 21 Sept. 1993, 16.

"Heterosexism." *Other Woman* (July–Aug. 1976): 4.

Hiltner, Seward. "The Neglected Phenomenon of Female Homosexuality." *Christian Century* 29 May 1974, 591–93.

Hoagland, Sarah Lucia. *Lesbian Ethics.* Palo Alto: Institute of Lesbian Studies, 1988.

Hoeffer, Beverly. "Children's Acquisition of Sex-Role Behavior in Lesbian Mother Families." *American Journal of Orthopsychiatry* 51 (1991): 536–44.

Hoffman, Martin. "Philosophic, Empirical, and Ecologic Remarks." *International Journal of Psychiatry* 10 (Mar. 1972): 105–7.

"Homosexual Acts Morally Neutral, Priests Say." *Advocate* (Feb. 1968): 4.

Humm, Andrew, and Betty Santoro. "'If We Gay Men and Lesbians' Stand Up." *New York Times* 1 Nov. 1980, 25.

Hunter, Nan, and Nancy Polikoff. "Lesbian Mothers Fight Back: Political and Legal Strategies." *Quest* 5 (Summer 1979): 55–57.

Hunter, Nan D., and Nancy D. Polikoff. "Custody Rights of Lesbian Mothers: Legal Theory and Litigation Strategy." *Buffalo Law Review* 25 (1976): 691–733.

"Illinois Women Lose Adoptions." *Deneuve* (Mar.–Apr. 1995): 12.

In the Matter of Dana (Anonymous). 624 N.Y.S. 2d 634 (A.D. 2 Dept. 1995).

In re Breisch. 434 A. 2d 815 (Pa. Super. 1981).

In re Custody of H.S.H.-K. 533 N.W. 2d 419 (Wisc. 1995).

In re Interest of Z.J.H. 471 N.W. 2d 202 (Wisc. 1991).

In re Jane B. 380 N.Y.S. 2d 848 (Supreme Ct., Onondaga County, 1976).

In re Mara. 150 N.Y.S. 2d 524 (N.Y. 1956).

In re Marriage of McKay. 1996 W.L. 12658 (Minn. App.).

Irish v. Irish. 300 N.W. 2d 739 (Mich. App. 1980).

"Is Lesbianism a Matter of Genetics?" *Newsweek* 22 Mar. 1993, 53.

Jacobson v. Jacobson. 314 N.W. 2d 78 (N.D. Sup. 1981).

Jacque. Letter to Editors. *Momazons* (Apr.–May 1993): 5.

Jarrett v. Jarrett. 400 N.E. 2d 421 (Ill. 1979).

Joffee, Robert, and John Mintz. "N.J. Officials Find Gay Foster Parents for Gay Teenagers." *Washington Post* 26 Nov. 1979, A4.

"Judge Rules against Lesbian Mother." *Gay Community News* 3 Nov. 1979, 6.

"Jury Trial." *Advocate* 28 Jan. 1976, 9–10.

Kallas v. Kallas. 614 P. 2d 641 (Ut. Sup. Ct. 1980).

Kath. Letter to Editors. *Lesbian Connection* (Sept.–Oct. 1993): 10.

Katz, Jonathan Ned. *Gay American History: Lesbians and Gay Men in the U.S.A.* 1976. Rev. ed. New York: Meridian, 1992.

———. *The Invention of Heterosexuality.* New York: Dutton, 1995.

Kaye, Harvey E. Letter to Editor. *New York Times* 11 Apr. 1971, 55.

Kelly, Janis. "Lesbian Challenging Loss of Parental Rights." *Off Our Backs* (April 1980): 14.

Kirkpatrick, Martha, Catherine Smith, and Ron Roy. "Lesbian Mothers and Their Children: A Comparative Survey." *American Journal of Orthopsychiatry* 51 (1981): 545–51.

Kitzinger, Celia. *The Social Construction of Lesbianism.* London: Sage, 1987.

Klemesrud, Judy. "The Disciples of Sappho, Updated." *New York Times Magazine* 28 Mar. 1971, 38–39, 41–42, 44, 46, 48, 50, 52.

———. "For Homosexuals, It's Getting Less Difficult to Tell Parents." *New York Times* 1 Sept. 1972, 32.

Konner, Melvin. "Homosexuality: Who and Why?" *New York Times Magazine* 2 Apr. 1989, 60–61.

Krafft-Ebing, Richard von. *Psychopathia Sexualis.* 1st English ed. Trans. Daniel Blain. New York: Stein and Day, 1965.

Kraft, Philip. "Lesbian Child Custody" [note]. *Harvard Women's Law Journal* 6 (1983): 183–92.

L. v. D. 630 S.W. 2d 240 (Mo. App. 1982).

Landerson, Louis. "Psychiatry and Homosexuality: New 'Cures.'" *Radical Therapist* (July 1972): 15.

"Lesbian Declared 'Unfit Mother.'" *Lesbian Tide* (July–Aug. 1975): 18.

"Lesbian Denied Custody." *Lesbian Tide* (May–June 1980): 22.

"The Lesbian Difference." *Big Mama Rag* (Apr. 1980): 4.

"Lesbian Gets Children, Keeps Lover." *Lesbian Tide* (Oct. 1974): 21.

"Lesbian Gets Custody of Daughter." *Advocate* 8 Mar. 1979, 8–9.

"Lesbian Gets Visitation Rights." *Gay Community News* 27 Oct. 1979, 2.

"Lesbianism 'Harmful.'" *Lesbian Tide* (Nov.–Dec. 1976): 25.

"Lesbian Loses Custody." *Big Mama Rag* (Apr. 1978): 3, 14.

"Lesbian Mother Custody News." *Out and About* (Mar. 1979): 20.

"Lesbian Mother Fights for Her Children." *Majority Report* (June 1976): 8.

"Lesbian Mother Loses." *Leaping Lesbian* (Spring 1979): 43.

"Lesbian Mother Seeks Custody." *Focus: A Journal for Gay Women* (Nov. 1974): 6.

"Lesbian Mother Wins Custody." *Big Mama Rag* (Feb. 1979): 6.

"Lesbian Mothers." *Lesbian Tide* (May–June 1975): 17.

"Lesbian Mother's Custody Case." *Out and About* (Apr. 1982): 14.

"Lesbian Mothers' Custody News." *Leaping Lesbian* (Feb. 1977): 4–5.

"Lesbian Mothers' Custody Struggle." *Leaping Lesbian* (May 1977): 11–14.

"Lesbian Mothers Keep Custody." *Advocate* 29 Nov. 1978, 8.

"Lesbian Mothers Union: Women Unite at LA Conference." *Mother* (Aug. 1971): 1, 5.

"Lesbians, Children Win." *Gay Liberator* (Dec. 1974): 5.

"Lesbian's Daughters Awarded to Father." *Advocate* 12 July 1979, 7–8.

"Lesbian in Virginia Fights to Keep Son." *Advocate* 6 Sept. 1979, 11–12.

"Lesbians Organize Rallies, Plan Mother's Day Weekend Demonstrations." *Gay Community News* 13 May 1978, 3.

"Lesbians Win Hard-Fought Battle." *Northwest Passage* 9 Sept. 1980, 9.

"Lesbians Win 2 Key Rulings." *Advocate* 10 Aug. 1977, 10, 41.

Lewin, Ellen. *Lesbian Mothers: Accounts of Gender in American Culture.* Ithaca: Cornell University Press, 1991.

Lillian. Letter to Editors. *Lesbian Connection* (Sept.–Oct. 1994): 10.

Lockerbie, D. Bruce. "The Drama of the American Family: Merely Players." *Vital Speeches of the Day* 1 June 1993, 494–501.

London, Sharon. Letter to Editor. *New York Times* 9 May 1971, sec. 6, 79.

Lorde, Audre. *Sister Outsider.* Freedom, Calif.: Crossing Press, 1984.

Lori. Letter to Editors. *Momazons* (Apr.–May 1993): 9.

Louisiana Civil Code, Articles 1–177. Vol. 1. St. Paul: West, 1993.

Lukács, Georg. *History and Class Consciousness: Studies in Marxist Dialectics.* Trans. Rodney Livingstone. Cambridge, Mass.: MIT Press, 1971.

Luker, Kristin. *Abortion and the Politics of Motherhood.* Berkeley: University of California Press, 1984.

Mahaney, Ruth. "In the Best Interests of the Children: Lesbian Mothers Speak Out." *Jump Cut* 19 (Dec. 1978): 6.

Maradie v. Maradie. 680 So. 2d 538 (Fla. App. 1 Dist. 1996).

"Margareth Denied Custody, Again!!" *Leaping Lesbian* (Mar.–Apr. 1978): 31.

Margolis, Maxine L. *Mothers and Such: Views of American Women and Why They Changed.* Berkeley: University of California Press, 1984.

Marmor, Judd. "Homosexuality—Mental Illness or Moral Dilemma?" *International Journal of Psychiatry* 10 (Mar. 1972): 114–17.

Martin, Del, and Phyllis Lyon. "'The Law' and Lesbian Mothers." *Lesbian Tide* (Jan. 1975): 19.

Martin, Emily. *The Woman in the Body: A Cultural Analysis of Reproduction.* Boston: Beacon Press, 1987.

Matter of Adoption of Caitlin. 622 N.Y.S. 2d 835 (Fam. Ct. 1994).

Matter of Adoption of Child by J.M.G. 632 A. 2d 550 (N.J. Super. 1993).

Matter of Adoption of Evan. 583 N.Y.S. 2d 997 (Surr. 1992).

Matter of Dana (Anonymous). 624 N.Y.S. 2d 634 (A.D. 2 Dept. 1995).

Matter of S.M.Y. 620 N.Y.S. 2d 897 (Fam. Ct. 1994).

McAllister, Pam. "Mothers Speak Out on Child Custody." *Off Our Backs* (June 1986): 4–6, 23.

McCandlish, Barbara. "Against All Odds: Lesbian Mother Family Dynamics." In *Gay and Lesbian Parents,* ed. Frederick W. Bozett. New York: Praeger, 1987. 23–36.

McDonald, Pamela, and Donna Cassyd. "Local Lesbian Fights Custody Battle." *Sister* (Feb. 1978): 3.

McDonald, Sharon. "Lesbian Mothers: In Court." *Lesbian Tide* (July–Aug. 1976): 23.

McGee, Michael Calvin. "A Materialist's Conception of Rhetoric." In *Explorations in Rhetoric: Studies in Honor of Douglas Ehninger,* ed. Ray E. McKerrow. Glenview, Ill.: Scott, Foresman, 1982. 23–48.

———. "The 'Ideograph': A Link between Rhetoric and Ideology." *Quarterly Journal of Speech* 66 (1980): 1–16.

McKerrow, Raymie E. "Critical Rhetoric: Theory and Praxis." *Communication Monographs* 56 (1989): 91–111.

McKinney's Consolidated Laws of New York, Annotated. St. Paul: West, 1986.

McKnight, Jennie. "Judge Upholds Lesbian Custody Case." *Gay Community News* 6 Aug. 1989, 3.

Melnick, Jane. "Lesbian & Mother." *In These Times* 8–14 Mar. 1978, 24, 19, 21.

Michigan Compiled Laws Annotated, Sections 701.1–749. St. Paul: West, 1993.

Minkowitz, Donna. "Outlawing Gays." *The Nation* 19 Oct. 1992, 420–21.

Mintz, Morton. "The Supreme Court: Remaining Silent on Homosexual Rights." *Washington Post* 11 Dec. 1979, A3.

Mintz, Steven, and Susan Kellogg. *Domestic Revolutions: A Social History of American Family Life*. New York: Free Press, 1988.

"Mississippi Mother Loses." *Out and About* (Feb. 1978): 25.

M.J.P. v. J.G.P. 640 P. 2d 966 (Okla. 1982).

Mohrman v. Mohrman. 565 N.E. 2d 1283 (Ohio App. 1989).

Morrison, Dana. "Lesbian Mother." *Cowrie: Lesbian/Feminist* (Feb. 1974): 16–18.

"Mother Wins in Court, Loses to Poverty." *Lesbian Tide* (Nov.–Dec. 1976): 24–25.

"Mothers and Daughters" [special issue]. *Frontiers* 3 (Summer 1978).

"Mothers: A Win . . . and a Loss." *Lesbian Tide* (July–Aug. 1979): 18.

"Mothers' Day No Exception to Oppression of Lesbian Mothers." *Out and About* (June 1978): 3.

M.P. v. S.P. 404 A. 2d 1256 (N.J. Super. 1979).

Muriel. "Sisters Speakout" [letter to editor]. *Lavender Woman* (Mar. 1974): 2.

Nakayama, Thomas K., and Robert L. Krizek. "Whiteness: A Strategic Rhetoric." *Quarterly Journal of Speech* 81 (1995): 291–309.

Nancy S. v. Michele G. 228 Cal. App. 831 (1 Dist., Div. 1, 1991).

Nealon, Chris. "Lesbian Seeks Visitation Rights in Custody Battle." *Gay Community News* 25 Nov. 1990, 1, 6.

Nemesis, Ann [pseud.]. "Holy Cow! The Dyke Is Having a Baby!" *Lesbian Contradiction* (Summer 1989): 7–8.

Nemy, Enid. "The Movement Is Big Enough to Roll with the Punches." *New York Times* 2 Oct. 1972, 46.

Neva. "Raising Children in the Lesbian Community." *Big Mama Rag* (Feb. 1981): 7.

"New Hampshire: Law Passed." *Off Our Backs* (Aug.–Sept. 1987): 16.

News and Notes Column. *Lesbian Connection* (Aug. 1976): 11.

News Clipping. *Lesbian Connection* (May–June 1990): 4.

News Clipping. *Lesbian Connection* (July–Aug. 1990): 5.

News Clipping. *Lesbian Connection* (Jan.–Feb. 1992): 2.

News Clipping. *Lesbian Connection* (July–Aug. 1992): 2.

News Clipping. *Lesbian Connection* (Sept.–Oct. 1992): 2.

News Clipping. *Lesbian Connection* (Jan.–Feb. 1993): 3.

News Clipping. *Lesbian Connection* (Sept.–Oct. 1993): 1.

News Update. *Deneuve* (July–Aug. 1995): 14.

News Updates. *Advocate* 11 Dec. 1980, 13.

News Updates. *Advocate* 15 Apr. 1982, 4.

Nix, Katie. "Homosexual Marriages" [letter to editor]. *Washington Post* 19 July 1975, A15.

N.K.M. v. L.E.M. 606 S.W. 2d 179 (Mo. App. 1980).

Nobile, Philip. "The Meaning of Gay: An Interview with Dr. C. A. Tripp." *New York* 25 June 1979, 36–38, 40–41.

North Dakota Century Code, 1991 Replacement. Charlottesville, Va.: Michie, 1991.

O'Brien, Mary. *The Politics of Reproduction*. Boston: Routledge and Kegan Paul, 1981.

Okin, Susan Moller. *Justice, Gender, and the Family*. New York: Basic Books, 1989.

Oklahoma Statutes Annotated. St. Paul: West, 1987.

"Oregon Lesbians Win Custody Case." *Out and About* (Oct. 1980): 20.

Overton, Bridget, ed. "Mothers: Custody Updates—Custody Battles Keep Women in Line." *Lesbian Tide* (July–August 1978): 30.

Palmer, Julie. "Hundreds Attend Lesbian Mothers [sic] Day Rally." *Gay Community News* 27 May 1978, 1, 5.

Patterson, Charlotte J. "Lesbian Mothers and Their Children: Findings from the Bay Area Families Study." In *Lesbians and Gays in Couples and Families: A Handbook for Therapists*, ed. Joan Laird and Robert-Jay Green. San Francisco: Jossey-Bass, 1996. 420–37.

Penelope, Julia. *Call Me Lesbian: Lesbian Lives, Lesbian Theory*. Freedom, CA: Crossing Press, 1992.

Peterson, Robert W. "Lesbian Custody Fight Intensifies: Dispute Can Go To Trial, Judge Rules." *Advocate* 14 Mar. 1989: 12, 14.

Pleasant v. Pleasant. 628 N.E. 2d 633 (Ill. App. 1 Dist. 1993).

Plotter, Vicki. "Lesbians and the Gay Movement: Are Lesbians Glad to Be 'Gay'?" *Big Mama Rag* (July 1980): 8–9, 17.

Polikoff, Nancy D. "This Child Does Have Two Mothers: Redefining Parenthood to Meet the Needs of Children in Lesbian-Mother and Other Nontraditional Families." *Georgetown Law Review* 78 (1990): 459–575.

"The Politics of Choosing Children. Or, Real Lesbians and Sperm Don't Mix?" *Momazons* August/September 1993: 7.

"Poor Lesbian Mother Ripped Off Again." *Off Our Backs* Feb. 1982: 11.

Poppe, Terri. "Lesbian Mothers Conference." *Off Our Backs* (Oct. 1978): 11, 22.

Proudfoot, Philippa, and Maria Scipione. "Reflections on a Victory." *New Women's Times* (Dec. 1982): 4–6.

Quindlen, Anna. "Women's Conference Approves Planks on Abortion and Rights for Homosexuals." *New York Times* 21 Nov. 1977, 44.

Radicalesbian/A Flaming Faggot. "We're Not Gay, We're Angry." *[Libe]RAT[ion]* 25 (Sept. 1970): 3, 27.

Radway, Janice. "Reception Study: Ethnography and the Problem of Dispersed Audiences and Nomadic Subjects." *Cultural Studies* 2 (1988): 359–76.

Rainwater, Sylvan. "Mother-Bashing Is Not the Answer." *Lesbian Contradiction* (Fall 1989): 10.

"Raising Children in a Deviant Relationship." *The Ladder* 1 (Oct. 1956): 9.

Raymond, Janice G. *Women as Wombs: Reproductive Technologies and the Battle over Women's Freedom*. San Francisco: Harper, 1993.

Redstockings Sister, A. "I Am 23, a Mother, and a Lesbian." *[Libe]RAT[ion]* 23 Aug. 1970, 13, 24.

Rhode, Deborah L. *Justice and Gender*. Cambridge, Mass.: Harvard University Press, 1989.

Rich, Adrienne. "Compulsory Heterosexuality and Lesbian Existence." In *Blood, Bread, and Poetry: Selected Prose, 1979–1985*. New York: W.W. Norton, 1986. 23–75.

———. "It Is the Lesbian in Us . . ." In *On Lies, Secrets, and Silence: Selected Prose, 1966–1978*. New York: W.W. Norton, 1979. 199–202.

———. *Of Woman Born: Motherhood as Experience and Institution*. 1976. New York: W.W. Norton, 1986.

Richman, Vicki. "Can a Mother Love Another Woman?" *Majority Report: The Women's Newspaper* 29 Oct. 1977, 1.

Ricketson, James W. Letter to the Editor. *New York Times* 4 June 1977, 18.

"Rights Update." *Off Our Backs* (Apr. 1995): 3.

Riley, Kathy. "Custody Battle Won by Lesbian." *Big Mama Rag* (July 1977): 5, 14.

Rist, Darrell Yates. "Are Homosexuals Born That Way?" *The Nation* 19 Oct. 1992, 424–29.

Rothman, Barbara Katz. *In Labor: Women and Power in the Birthplace* 1982. New York: W.W. Norton, 1991.

———. *Recreating Motherhood: Ideology and Technology in a Patriarchal Society*. New York: W.W. Norton, 1989.

Rubenstein, William B. "We Are Family: A Reflection on the Search for Legal Recognition of Lesbian and Gay Relationships." *Journal of Law and Politics* 8 (1991): 89–105.

Ruddick, Sara. *Maternal Thinking: Towards a Politics of Peace*. New York: Ballantine, 1989.

S. v. S. 608 S.W. 2d 64 (Ky. App. 1980).

Sanchez, Rene, and Richard Morin. "Straight Talk about Being Gay." *Washington Post* 19 Apr. 1993, A1, A6.

Schulz, William F. "Fostering Prejudice." *Progressive* (Jan. 1987): 15.

Scipione, Maria. "Lesbian Custody: Another Battleground." *New Women's Times* (Dec. 1982): 7–8.

Scott, Robert L. "Dialectical Tensions of Speaking and Silence." *Quarterly Journal of Speech* 79 (1993): 1–18.

Scott v. Scott. 665 So. 2d 760 (La. App. 1 Cir. 1995).

Sedgwick, Eve Kosofsky. *Epistemology of the Closet*. Berkeley: University of California Press, 1990.

S.E.G. v. R.A.G. 735 S.W. 2d 164 (Mo. App. 1987).

Seligmann, Jean, with Mariana Gosnell. "Gays are Born, Not Made." *Newsweek* 7 Sept. 1981, 42.

Shapiro, E. Donald, and Lisa Schultz. "Single-Sex Families: The Impact of Birth Innovations upon Traditional Family Notions." *Journal of Family Law* 24 (1986): 271–81.

"Should Homosexuals Be Teachers?" [editorial]. *New York Times* 24 May 1977, 34.

Silverstein, Charles. "Psychological and Medical Treatments of Homosexuality." In *Homosexuality: Research Implications for Public Policy*, ed. John C. Gonsiorek and James D. Weinrich. Newbury Park, Calif.: Sage, 1991. 101–14.

"Sisters Seek Support." *Sisters* (Oct. 1973): 24–26.

Skolnick, Arlene. *Embattled Paradise: The American Family in an Age of Uncertainty.* New York: Basic Books, 1991.

Smith-Rosenberg, Carroll. "The Female World of Love and Ritual: Relations between Women in Nineteenth-Century America." In *Disorderly Conduct: Visions of Gender in Victorian America.* New York: Oxford University Press, 1985. 53–76.

S.N.E. v. R.L.B. 699 P. 2d 875 (Alaska 1985).

"So Much for Family Values" [News and Notes column]. *Deneuve* (June 1994): 14.

Socarides, Charles. "Homosexuality—Basic Concepts and Psychodynamics." *International Journal of Psychiatry* 10 (Mar. 1972): 118–25.

———. *The Preoedipal Origin and Psychoanalytic Therapy of Sexual Perversions.* Madison, Conn.: International Universities Press, 1988.

"Some Things We Can Do!" *Leaping Lesbian* (July 1977): 6–7.

Spivak, Gayatri Chakravorty. *The Post-colonial Critic Interviews, Strategies, Dialogues.* London: Routledge, 1990.

Stanworth, Michelle, ed. *Reproductive Technologies: Gender, Motherhood and Medicine.* Minneapolis: University of Minnesota Press, 1987.

Steinfels, Peter. "Southern Baptists Condemn Homosexuality as 'Depraved.'" *New York Times* 17 June 1988, B6.

Streitmatter, Rodger. *Unspeakable: The Rise of the Gay and Lesbian Press in America.* Boston: Faber and Faber, 1995.

Stroman v. Williams. 353 S.E. 2d 704 (SC App. 1987).

"Study Hits Theories on Homosexuality." *Chicago Tribune* 24 Aug. 1981, sec. 1, 2.

"Study Shows Child's Sexuality Not Affected by Parent's Sexuality." *Gay Community News* 29 July 1978, 3.

"Support Lesbian Mothers." *Northwest Passage* 17 June 1980, 14.

"Supreme Court Balks at Custody Ruling." *Advocate* 11 June 1981, 9.

Susoeff, Steve. "Assessing Children's Best Interests when a Parent Is Gay or Lesbian: Toward a Rational Custody Standard" [comment]. *UCLA Law Review* 21 (1985): 852–903.

Swisher, Kara. "We Love Lesbians! Or Do We?" *Washington Post* 18 July 1993, C1, C2.

Thigpen v. Carpenter. 730 S.W. 2d 510 (Ark. App. 1987).

Timnick, Lois. "Homosexuals: Many Types, Many Causes." *Los Angeles Times* 1 Nov. 1978, 1, 30, 31, 32.

"Toward a Feminist Theory of Motherhood" [special issue]. *Feminist Studies* 4 (June 1978).

Tracy, Anne. "Another Lesbian Mother Goes to Court." *Lesbian Connection* (Sept. 1975): 21–22.

Tryna. "Mothers and the Law." *Lavender Woman* (Jan. 1974): 3.

Tucker v. Tucker. 910 P 2d 1209 (Utah 1996).

"UCLA Backs Lesbians as Mothers." *Lesbian Tide* (Nov.–Dec. 1976): 29.

"United Church Backs Homosexuals' Rights." *Washington Post* 4 July 1975, D16.

United States Bureau of the Census. *Census of the Population: 1970.* Vol. 1. Washington, D.C.: Government Printing Office, 1973.

United States Bureau of the Census. *1990 Census of the Population.* Vol. 1. Washington, D.C.: Government Printing Office, 1992.

"Updates on Custody." *Lesbian Tide* (Nov.–Dec. 1974): 24.

Van Driel v. Van Driel. 525 N.W. 2d 37 (S.D. 1994).

Van Gelder, Lindsy. "Mothers of Convention." *Ms.* (July/Aug. 1992): 94–95.

Wander, Philip. "Marxism, Post-colonialism, and Rhetorical Contextualization." *Quarterly Journal of Speech* 82 (1996): 402–26.

Ward v. Ward 742 So. 2d 250 (Fla. App. 1 Dist. 1996).

Wechsler, Nancy. "Lesbian Appeals Custody Ruling." *Gay Community News* 8 Aug. 1981, 1, 3.

————. "Lesbian Mothers Plan National Mother's Day Celebrations." *Gay Community News* 8 Apr. 1978, 3.

Weeks, Jeffrey. "Discourse, Desire, and Sexual Deviance: Some Problems in the History of Homosexuality." In *The Making of the Modern Homosexual,* ed. Kenneth Plummer. Totowa, N.J.: Barnes and Noble, 1981. 76–111.

Weston, Kath. *Families We Choose: Lesbians, Gays, Kinship.* New York: Columbia University Press, 1991.

West's Annotated California Codes: Family Code, Sections 2500–6199. St. Paul: West, 1994.

"When Women Love Other Women: A Frank Discussion of Female Homosexuality." *Redbook* (Nov. 1971): 84–85, 186, 188, 190–92, 194–95.

Whisman, Vera. "Identity Crises: Who Is a Lesbian, Anyway?" In *Sisters, Sexperts, Queers: Beyond the Lesbian Nation,* ed. Arlene Stein. New York: Plume, 1993. 47–60.

Williams, Xenia. "Bug Bug Speaking: One Lesbian's 'Family.'" *Lesbian Contradiction: A Journal of Irreverent Feminism* 18 (Spring 1987): 1–2.

Wingert, Pat, and Barbara Kantrowitz. "Two Kids and Two Moms." *Newsweek* 20 Mar. 2000, 50–53.

Wire, Barb [pseud.]. "Pursuing the Goal of Parenting." *Lesbian Contradiction: A Journal of Irreverent Feminism* 20 (Fall 1987): 14–15.

Wittig, Monique. *The Straight Mind and Other Essays.* Boston: Beacon Press, 1992.

"A [Woman] Has the Right to Be a Lesbian, but a Lesbian Does Not Have the Right to Be a Mother." *Lesbian Feminist* (June 1976): 7.

Wood, Robert W. "Homosexuality as an Answer to the Population Increase." *The Ladder* (Sept. 1963): 7–23.

www.actwin.com/eatonohio/gay.sodomy.html.

www.apa.org/pi/bottoms.html.

www.dictionary.com.

Yang, Jacob Smith. "Sperm Donor Entitled to Limited Parental Rights." *Gay Community News* 18 Aug. 1991, 2.

Yaseen, Ginny. "Thanks from Ginny." *Lesbian Tide* (July–Aug. 1977): 27.

Yukins, Elizabeth. "Chicago Court to Rule on Gay/Les[bian] Parents." *Gay Community News* 2 Apr. 1991, 1, 3.

Zambo, Deborah E. "Pregnant Lesbians?" *Sister* (June 1978): 5.

Index

binary oppositions, 8, 9, 10, 53–54, 119–20, 134

biological arguments: Chodorow on, 95; and custody cases, 69, 71–72, 75–76, 77, 83; and lesbian mother legitimization, 124–25, 127–28, 152*n*4; limitations of, 152*n*3

bisexuality, 138

Black, Edwin, 1

Bottoms, Sharon, 42

Boyce, Fran, 50

Burke, Kenneth, 57, 85, 139

Burr, Karen, 48

Butler, Judith, 13, 16, 17

Catholic News, 38–39

ceremonial oratory, 36

children of lesbian parents: feminist socialization of, 52; and gender roles, 26, 104–5, 106, 107–9; lesbian press on, 49; male children, 47–48, 51; stigma, 38, 48, 66–68, 71, 128–29; voices of, 138. *See also* lesbians as proselytizers; psychological studies; sexual orientation formation

Children of the Rainbow curriculum, 32–33

Chodorow, Nancy, 87, 93–99, 115–16, 120

Christianity. *See* religious rhetoric

civil rights legislation, 34, 128

class, 137–38

Collins, Patricia Hill, 94

constitution of identity, 13–15

Cooper, Eleanor, 44

co-parenting rhetoric, 77–78, 79, 81, 124

Copper, Baba, 51–52

Cordova, Jeanne, 41

Corea, Gena, 73–74

Cotton, John, 19

court system. *See* judicial rhetoric

Crenshaw, Kimberlé, 13

Curiale v. Reagan, 75, 76–77

custody cases: 56–84; best interest standard, 57–59, 71, 129; and biological arguments, 69, 71–72, 75–76, 77, 83; and denial of lesbian identity, 43–44, 45, 146*n*46; and functional approaches, 71–73, 78; and heteronormativity, 60–61; and lesbian motherhood as oxymoron, 83, 84; lesbian press on, 41–44, 52; between lesbians, 69–71, 74–78, 149*n*56; and lesbians as criminal, 62–63; and lesbians as essentially sexual, 59; and lesbians as proselytizers, 63–66, 67; moral deficiency arguments, 61–62, 129, 148*n*16; nexus approach, 59–60, 70; per se approach, 59, 60, 61; and psychological studies, 89–90, 102; and relationship intervention, 64–66, 148*n*30; and reproductive technology, 73–74; and rhetorical ambivalence, 82–83, 121; and second-parent adoption, 79–82; and stigma, 66–68, 71, 128–29. *See also* lesbian motherhood, legitimization of

Daughters of Bilitis, 24, 92

de facto parenthood, 125–26

Dejanikus, Tacie, 38

D.H. v. J.H., 60

Diagnostic and Statistical Manual (DSM). *See* APA decision (1973)

Dickenson, Vicky, 42

"The Discourse on Language" (Foucault), 85–86

DiStefano, Maureen, 63

Dixon, Rebecca, 41, 45

Donaldson, Stephen, 22

Dooley, David, 71

doxastic claims, 16, 110–11

Draper, Mark, 32

DSM. See Diagnostic and Statistical Manual

Duberman, Martin, 24

Dublex, Noy, 47

Duck, Linda, 45

moral deficiency arguments, 61–62, 129, 148*n*16

Morrison, Dana, 47

motherhood: Chodorow on, 93–99; as compulsory, 3–4, 38, 136; effects on all women, 1–5; functional approaches, 71–73, 78, 127–28, 129–34; nineteenth-century, 26–27; rejection of, 2, 3–4, 136; and sexuality, 6. *See also* lesbian motherhood

Moynihan, Daniel Patrick, 102

Nakayama, Thomas, 127

naming practices, 125, 152*n*5

Nancy S. v. Michele G., 76, 77

negotiation of identity, 15

Newsweek, 33

nexus approach, 59–60, 70

N.K.M. V. L.E.M, 67

"nontraditional" families. *See* "alternative/nontraditional" families

nuclear family. *See* family

object relations theory, 96–97

Out and About, 43

Palmore v. Sidoti, 71

Patterson, Charlotte, 104–5, 107

Penelope, Julia, 130–31

performance of identity, 17

per se approach, 59, 60, 61

Plotter, Vicki, 145*n*27

Polikoff, Nancy, 38, 51, 70–71, 72, 73, 128

Poppe, Terri, 51

postcolonial theory, 9–10

poststructural theory, 5, 133–34

press. *See* journalistic rhetoric; lesbian press; straight press

psychoanalytic theory: 91–92, 96–97, 150*n*27. *See also* Chodorow, Nancy

psychological studies: 99–115; and custody cases, 89–90, 102; descriptions of, 101–5; doxastic claims, 110–12; historical context, 88–93; on masculinity, 112–14; motivations of, 88–89; and sexual orientation formation, 105–11, 116–17

Psychopathia Sexualis (Krafft-Ebing), 20

public forums: 7–8, 11–12, 25–26, 118–19, 138; as ideological state apparatuses, 8–9, 12, 87, 142*n*15. *See also* academic rhetoric; journalistic rhetoric; judicial rhetoric

Puritanism, 19, 142*nn*33, 34

Quayle, Dan, 102

race, 137–38

Rado, Sandor, 92

Rainwater, Sylvan, 47, 48

Reagan/Bush administrations, 2

recruitment. *See* lesbians as proselytizers

reflexive critique, 136–38

regulation: and academic rhetoric, 85–86; of identity, 16; and journalistic rhetoric, 54–55; negative effects of, 10–11

reification of identity, 9, 15–16

religious rhetoric: and lesbians as essentially sexual, 30–31; and lesbians as immoral, 26, 144*n*74; and lesbians as proselytizers, 38–39; and lesbians as sick, 91

repressive state apparatuses (RSAs), 12

The Reproduction of Mothering (Chodorow), 87, 93–99, 115–16, 120

reproductive technology, 73–74

resistance, 23–26

rhetorical ambivalence: and academic rhetoric, 121–22; authorizing function of, 8–9; and binary oppositions, 8, 9, 10, 53–54, 119–20, 134; and custody cases,

82–83, 121; earliest formation of, 28; and journalistic rhetoric, 9, 53–55, 57, 120–21; and postcolonial theory, 9–10. *See also* lesbian motherhood as oxymoron

rhetorical constructions of identity: 12–17, 134–36; constitution, 13–15; and ideological state apparatuses, 11–12; negotiation, 15; performance, 17; regulation, 16; reification, 9, 15–16; and social functions of rhetoric, 11

Rice, Louise, 48

Rich, Adrienne, 1, 2, 132

Roy, Ron, 102, 110

RSAs. *See* repressive state apparatuses

Rubenstein, William, 72

Sappho, 20, 142*n*39

Scott, Robert L., 111

Scott v. Scott, 56, 65

second-parent adoption, 70, 79–82

Sedgwick, Eve, 16

sexologists, 20–23, 90, 143*n*46

sex roles. *See* gender roles

sexual orientation formation: 26, 144*n*79; Chodorow on, 97–98; and custody cases, 67, 69; lesbian press on, 49; psychological studies on, 105–11, 116–17; sexologists on, 21, 90, 143*n*46; straight press on, 35–36, 37. *See also* lesbians as proselytizers

Sister, 48

Skolnick, Arlene, 27, 28

Smith, Catherine, 102, 110

Smith-Rosenberg, Carroll, 20

S.N.E., 59–60

Socarides, Charles, 91, 92, 150*n*27

social learning theory, 106

sodomy laws, 7, 26, 63, 144*nn*75, 76

Spivak, Gayatri, 133

Sporleder, Wendy L., 76, 77

Steinfels, Peter, 144*n*74

stigma: 38; and custody cases, 66–68, 71, 128–29; lesbian press on, 48

St. Mery, Moreau, 19

Stonewall Riots, 24

straight press: 31–39; on custody cases, 42; on family, 31–33, 53–54; lesbian invisibility in, 33–35, 57; lesbians as intrinsically non-procreative in, 37–39, 53–54; lesbians as proselytizers in, 35–37, 38–39, 53–54; and rhetorical ambivalence, 9

Streitmatter, Rodger, 25, 39–40

Stroman, 68–69

Susoeff, Steve, 71

Szasz, Thomas, 93

Thigpen v. Carpenter, 63

Time magazine, 33

Townend, Larraine, 42

Uniform Marriage and Divorce Act, 58

Van Gelder, Lindsy, 30, 31

Vice Versa, 40

Wander, Phil, 5

Weeks, Jeffrey, 20

Whisman, Vera, 131

White House Conference on Families (1980), 39

Williams, Xenia, 51

Wilson, Nancy, 63

Wingert, Pat, 34

Wittig, Monique, 118, 132

Wood, Robert W., 46

Wyland, Francie, 51

Z.J.H., 76, 77, 78